The Arhoolie Foundation's Strachwitz Frontera Collection of Mexican and Mexican American Recordings

THE CHICANO ARCHIVES

This series brings together resources related to major Chicano special collections. The goal is to facilitate access to these collections and thereby stimulate new critical and historical research based on archival sources. Each book includes original scholarship, one or more finding aids, reproductions of key documents and images, and a selected bibliography. The series draws primarily on collections in the UCLA Chicano Studies Research Center Library. Because preserving Chicano history requires efforts and coordination across multiple institutions, the series includes projects undertaken in collaboration with other Chicano archives.

Series Editors

Chon A. Noriega

Lizette Guerra

www.chicano.ucla.edu

The Arhoolie Foundation's Strachwitz Frontera Collection of Mexican and Mexican American Recordings
Agustín Gurza, with Jonathan Clark and Chris Strachwitz (2012)

The Oscar Castillo Papers and Photograph Collection
Edited by Colin Gunckel

The Latino Theatre Initiative/Center Theatre Group Papers, 1980–2005
Essay by Chantal Rodríguez (2011)

The Mexican Museum of San Francisco Papers, 1971–2006
Essay by Karen Mary Davalos (2010)

The Fire of Life: The Robert Legorreta–Cyclona Collection
Essay by Robb Hernandez (2009)

Self Help Graphics & Art: Art in the Heart of East Los Angeles
Essay by Kristen Guzmán (2005)

The Chicano Archives, Volume 6

The Arhoolie Foundation's Strachwitz Frontera Collection of Mexican and Mexican American Recordings

Agustín Gurza
with Jonathan Clark and Chris Strachwitz

UCLA Chicano Studies Research Center
Los Angeles
2012

CSRC Director: Chon A. Noriega
Senior Editor: Rebecca Frazier
Copyeditor: Catherine A. Sunshine
Production: William Morosi

UCLA Chicano Studies Research Center
193 Haines Hall
Los Angeles, California 90095-1544 USA
www.chicano.ucla.edu

Distributed by the University of Washington Press
PO Box 50096
Seattle, Washington 98145-5096
www.washington.edu/uwpress

Front cover (*clockwise from top*): Florencio and Frumencio Estrada; Mariachi Coculense de Cirilo Marmolejo; Las Norteñitas; Lydia Mendoza; Narciso Martínez; Little Joe. Photographs courtesy of the Arhoolie Foundation.

Back cover: Juanita and María Mendoza. Photograph courtesy of the Arhoolie Foundation.

Library of Congress Cataloging-in-Publication Data

Gurza, Agustín.
 The Arhoolie Foundation's Strachwitz Frontera Collection of Mexican and Mexican American recordings / Agustín Gurza with Jonathan Clark and Chris Strachwitz.
   p. cm. -- (The Chicano archives ; v. 6)
 Includes bibliographical references.
 ISBN 978-0-89551-148-5 (pbk. : alk. paper)
1. Arhoolie Foundation. Strachwitz Frontera Collection. 2. Strachwitz, Chris. 3. Sound recordings--Collectors and collecting. 4. Popular music--Mexico--Discography. 5. Popular music--Mexican-American Border Region--Discography. 6. Popular music--Mexico--History and criticism. I. Clark, Jonathan (Jonathan D.) II. Strachwitz, Chris. III. Title.
 ML138.A76G87 2012
 781.640972'0266--dc23
                    2012009932

To find out more about the CSRC Library, contact:
Lizette Guerra, Librarian
310-206-6052 (phone)
310-206-1784 (fax)
librarian@chicano.ucla.edu
UCLA Chicano Studies Research Center Library
144 Haines Hall
Los Angeles, CA 90095-1544
www.chicano.ucla.edu/library/

Contents

Illustrations

This book is made possible in part by the Los Tigres del Norte Fund at UCLA

The Los Tigres del Norte Fund at UCLA
promotes the research and preservation of Spanish-language
musical folk traditions. It also seeks to educate and enlighten the public
about these traditions and to support and reinforce traditional community values.

The fund was established in 2000 through a
generous gift to the Chicano Studies Research Center
from the Los Tigres del Norte Foundation.

Acknowledgments

First and foremost, I owe an enormous debt of gratitude to Chon A. Noriega, editor of the Chicano Archives Series and director of the UCLA Chicano Studies Research Center, for offering me this unique assignment at a time of sudden crisis in my career. Like many fellow journalists in the depressed newspaper business, I found myself abruptly out of work in December 2008, in the wake of the global financial collapse. As a writer for the *Los Angeles Times* in better days, I had often had occasion to consult Chon as an informed and articulate source on issues related to Latino art and culture. After I was laid off, he was one of the first to call to offer sympathy, support and, most important, an opportunity. The chance to write this book came as a lifeline, emotionally and financially. There is no better antidote for the doldrums of unemployment than diving right back into work, especially on a job that turned out to be so rewarding in so many ways. Thanks for having faith in me in hard times, when others tend to turn their backs.

I am also enormously indebted to Chris Strachwitz, whose nonpareil record collection is in itself a work of art. Chris is one of the most knowledgeable people I have ever met in the field of Mexican and Mexican American music and recordings, and he shared that knowledge generously as I struggled to grasp the scope of his massive cultural archive. Throughout the process, Chris was accessible and accommodating, both during frequent pestering phone calls and on occasional visits to his Arhoolie Foundation headquarters in El Cerrito, California, where he welcomed me with a down-home hospitality. I cannot stress enough the value of Chris's contribution when it came time to review the manuscript. He made critical clarifications and corrections with a keen perspective that only he could bring to this project. After all, he personally knew and interacted with many of the artists the rest of us can only read about or listen to.

In addition, Chris encouraged the cooperation of his small but devoted staff, who became important resources in their own right. Tom Diamant, project manager, was especially helpful in offering background on the digitization process. Tom and Adam Machado were also instrumental in making Arhoolie's extensive photo catalog available, providing the historic and often striking images that grace the book and its cover. Last but not at all least, digital archivist Antonio Cuéllar shared his truly singular insights on the collection as the only person in the world who has listened to virtually every recording. His own recorded voice—dutifully reciting the title, artist, label and matrix number at the start of all those old 78-rpm discs—made me feel like I had a musical buddy during my lonely, late-night listening sessions.

My colleague Jonathan Clark, who authored the informative chapter on mariachi music, performed above and beyond his assignment by reviewing the entire manuscript. His conscientious attention to minute detail helped make the text a smooth, clean, and consistent read. He undertook the task with the rigors of an academic researcher and the passion of a mariachi musician, which he is. Very few people have done so much independent and unpaid research on the mariachi and its history, purely out of love for the genre. He has scoured the dusty vaults of record labels in Mexico City and tracked down a dying generation of fellow musicians in Mexico to document their untold stories before they disappear. Jonny, who plays with a mariachi in San Jose, where I grew up, understands like few other Americans the urgency of preserving the history of this important art form. I can't thank him enough for his selfless contributions to this book.

Throughout the course of this project, from research to production, I received absolutely vital assistance from key people at UCLA. This book would never have seen the light of day without the steady hand and disciplined direction of Rebecca Frazier, senior editor with the Chicano Studies Research Center Press. She steered the editing process with persistence and patience, then shepherded the production with an enviable equanimity, considering all the print projects she must oversee, and the occasionally competing personalities she must referee. Thank you for keeping the project, and its absent-minded author, on track, always with good cheer and a tempered tone. Thanks as well to Cathy Sunshine, whose meticulous copyediting greatly improved the manuscript. Invaluable guidance in navigating the Frontera online archive was provided by Stephen Davison, head librarian with the UCLA Digital Library Program, as well as Henry Chiong, digital library architect. Their efforts eventually made the collection seem like a readily accessible extension of my home computer. Any time I needed to work on campus, Lizette Guerra, librarian and archivist with the Chicano Studies Research Center, always made me feel at home.

Finally, I want to thank my mother and father, Dr. Agustín Gurza Villareal and María Esther Sanchesviesca, for instilling in me a love for Mexican music. They imparted their appreciation in the most natural way for music lovers—showing how much they enjoyed it and how deeply it touched them.

Agustín Gurza, April 2012

Series Editor's Note

The Strachwitz Frontera Collection is the largest repository of Mexican and Mexican American vernacular recordings in existence. The collection represents the passion and dedication of Chris Strachwitz, founder of Arhoolie Records and president of the Arhoolie Foundation. As a young man, newly immigrated from Germany, Strachwitz discovered New Orleans jazz and what is today termed "roots music"—traditional and regional vernacular music—of the American south and southwest: down home blues, zydeco, bluegrass, gospel, and border music. He began collecting this music on 78s, 45s, LPs, and cassette tapes, and in 1995 he founded the Arhoolie Foundation to preserve his vast collection.

Guillermo Hernández, former director of the UCLA Chicano Studies Research Center (CSRC) and an expert on corridos, was instrumental in the development of the project to digitize and provide online access to the Frontera Collection through UCLA. Hernández, who died in 2006, knew that the historical value of Strachwitz's collection was unparalleled. In the 1990s he began laying the groundwork for the digitization project by securing the participation of Los Tigres del Norte, the legendary norteño group based in San Jose, California, and popular throughout the Americas. Through their Los Tigres del Norte Foundation, the group established the Los Tigres del Norte Fund at UCLA, administered by the CSRC, for the study and preservation of Spanish-language music. The Los Tigres del Norte Fund provided much of the funding for digitizing the Frontera Collection's 78-rpm records.

The project represented a unique collaboration between the CSRC and other organizations deeply committed to the preservation of the Spanish-language recording heritage of the United States (and of the Americas), including the Arhoolie Foundation, Arhoolie Records, the Los Tigres del Norte Foundation, the Fund for Folk Culture, the UCLA Music Library, and the UCLA Digital Library Program. As the project has developed, additional funding has been provided by Arhoolie Records, the UCLA Library, the National Endowment for the Humanities, the National Endowment for the Arts, the Grammy Foundation, the Lucasfilm Foundation, and others.

To date, nearly all of the 78s and about one-third of the 45s have been digitized and uploaded to the Frontera Collection database at UCLA. Each record has two entries, one for each side; each entry offers information about the performers, the composers, and the label. In addition, the database can be searched by keywords and subject areas in both English and Spanish. Each entry includes a digital image of the record.

Music from the US-Mexico border region is the heart of the Frontera Collection. The recordings in the database include song forms like corridos and boleros, as well as instrumentals such as norteño, tejano, and conjunto music. Yet the collection is wide ranging, embracing the music of other regions in Mexico and Latin America, with mambo from Cuba, tango from Argentina, plena from Puerto Rico, and sones from Veracruz, among other regional forms and styles. Some recordings are the earliest recorded examples of the genre, and some of the records are one of a kind—they exist nowhere but in the Frontera Collection. These recordings were produced not only by large US companies like

RCA Victor and Columbia but also by much smaller companies that recorded Mexican and Mexican American artists exclusively. Nearly 1,000 labels are represented in the collection.

Author Agustín Gurza's love of this music is evident. He explores the recordings from different viewpoints, discussing genres, themes, and some of the thousands of composers and performers whose work is contained in the collection. Chapters by Jonathan Clark, who surveys the mariachi recordings, and Chris Strachwitz, who writes about the development of the collection, round out the volume.

Instead of the finding aid that is typical for the volumes in The Chicano Archives series, this book includes guidelines for using the online database. These instructions are enhanced by eleven detailed lists that are presented as appendixes. These lists provide a tool for searching the collection. They include, for example, the most frequently recorded songs and the most prolific songwriters and performers, as well as the personal favorites of Gurza, Clark, Strachwitz, and the Arhoolie Foundation's archivist, Antonio Cuéllar.

The UCLA Chicano Studies Research Center is honored to have played a role in the preservation of and access to this important collection and to have worked closely over the last decade with such committed partners. By making these rare and fragile recordings easily accessible, the Frontera Collection not only enables wide-ranging research in Mexican and Mexican American culture but also provides a hemispheric context for the Spanish-language musical heritage of Mexico and the United States.

Chon A. Noriega, Director
UCLA Chicano Studies Research Center

A Cultural Treasure for the Ages

I have been listening to Latin music since I was a child in the 1950s (fig. 1). My father was an obsessive record collector who scooped up every Mexican LP he could find at his favorite discount department stores, Gemco and White Front, precursors of Walmart.[1] Most Mexican American kids growing up in the first decade of rock 'n' roll considered the music of their parents and home country to be corny, but I didn't. I was the only one in a family of eight children who really embraced the rancheras, boleros, and ballads of our parents' pre-rock generation. My brothers and sisters used to make fun of me, so I would hide behind my father's big Curtis Mathes console while I played his records by Miguel Aceves Mejía, Pedro

Figure 1. In this family photograph, the author (*left*) wears the iconic charro outfit of the Mexican cowboy. He is shown with his older siblings, María Esther and Eduardo. The photograph was taken in Tacoma, Washington, in 1950, the year the family emigrated from northern Mexico. Immigrants to the United States sometimes dress their children in folkloric costumes to preserve homeland traditions. Photograph courtesy of Agustín Gurza Villarreal.

Vargas, and Trío Los Panchos. My conversational Spanish was so pocho (Anglicized) that I'd run to the kitchen and ask my mother for the meaning of words used in the poetic lyrics of boleros, such as *sendero* (path) or *púrpura encendida* (flaming purple).

When I was a painfully shy boy on the verge of adolescence, these records taught me the meaning of romance. More important, they taught me what it means to be Mexican, an identity that was purged from our generation in those days through peer pressure and monocultural indoctrination. I was raised on the Eastside of San Jose, California, where the Mexican community was segregated as an ethnic subculture. My family arrived fifteen years ahead of Los Tigres del Norte, the great norteño band that settled there in the late 1960s, when I turned twenty. It was only then that the Chicano civil rights movement started opening mainstream paths for Latinos in politics, higher education, the professions, and the arts.

Those forces that championed cultural pride and awareness helped bring us to where we are today: publishing a book that celebrates a digital library collection that was created entirely by the labor of immigrants. Chris Strachwitz, the collector, hails from Germany. Guillermo Hernández, the professor who brought the collection to the University of California, Los Angeles (UCLA), has roots in Mexico. So do Los Tigres, who made a major contribution to finance the digitization of the music, and Antonio Cuéllar, the young musician hired to complete the painstaking digital transfers.

Now, I have the honor of writing the first in-depth exploration of the Frontera Collection and its contents.

This book is not meant to be an exhaustive or comprehensive study, but rather a map or guide to future investigation. It contains profiles of those who devoted their careers to

elevating this music to its rightful place as a cultural treasure, especially Los Tigres, Chris Strachwitz, and Hernández, who died in 2006. Without their efforts, it is likely that much of this material would be lost to the world. By preserving these records, particularly the neglected folk music of Mexico's working class, they have preserved the popular history of an entire people whose voices would have been forever silenced (fig. 2).

The topical chapters reveal the richness of the collection as a source for cultural studies. Two chapters focus on key genres. "A Century of Corridos" takes a close look at the archetypically Mexican narrative ballad that is a major focus of the Frontera Collection. A chapter on mariachi music, written by guest author and musician Jonathan Clark, provides a window on the roots of this iconic genre—a rich cultural tradition that has come to symbolize Mexico itself.

Other chapters address themes that cut across genres. "Transcending Machismo" is devoted to the category that encompasses the vast majority of songs, namely love in all its blissful and woeful variants. Song by song, the chapter traces a wide range of attitudes toward love and marriage, romance and rejection, as reflected in Mexican popular music. By allowing access to so many love songs in one place, the Frontera Collection helps shatter the stereotypes of both idealized love and macho dominance in Mexican culture, revealing a far more thoughtful and nuanced sensibility in dealing with everything from infatuation to true love, heartbreak to revenge, self-pity to self-sacrifice.

The chapter on intercultural conflict helps us appreciate the value of recordings as contemporaneous expressions of people's shifting attitudes and values. It highlights songs that reveal the angry, bitter, but also often humorous relationship between Mexicans and the dominant Anglo

Figure 2. Miguél Aceves Mejía and Lola Beltrán, shown here in the 1957 musical *Guitarras de Media Noche*, represented a golden era in Mexican pop culture. Their recordings held special appeal for U.S. immigrants who sought to retain their cultural identity. Photograph courtesy of Agrasánchez Film Archive.

society, as well as Mexican racism toward other ethnic groups, especially the Chinese. Of particular interest to Mexican Americans are songs, such as "El Charro y la Pocha," that explore the still-heated friction between Mexican nationals and their more assimilated immigrant counterparts in the United States.

Love and conflict are, of course, just two of the most prominent themes represented in the collection. Systematically browsing the database, I started noticing trends. There are songs about food, always a Latino obsession. Songs about drinking, a cultural curse. And songs that start with *Soy* (I Am), suggesting that many artists use music as an expression of

personal identity. There are songs about wars, immigration, and natural disasters, as well as vaudeville-style comedy skits and dramatic re-enactments of political events. I found songs about mothers and songs that told morals (with many tracks featuring both). There are songs composed for *serenata* (serenading), songs with *mambo* in the title, and songs that start with the word *Ay*, a quintessentially Mexican expression of surprise, excitement, or lament.

Many of these themes are among the more than 300 formal subject areas that can be browsed and searched in the online Frontera archive.[2] They include topics such as "undocumented immigration," "marriage proposal," "jealousy," and "praise of country." Among the larger subject categories in the database, with almost 1,000 songs each, are "pride," "murder," "advice," and "looking for love." Each song can be categorized under multiple subjects; for example, the deadly combination of "drinking" and "murder" yields 101 results, using Frontera's advanced search function.

In the appendixes to the book, song titles are sorted and compiled in lists that suggest even more topics for further study. "The Frontera 400" (appendix A) is a compilation of songs that are today considered Latin American standards, from "Bésame Mucho" to "La Malagueña," "Guadalajara," and "Mambo No. 5." In general these are not the songs that Strachwitz set out to collect, as he was more interested in the earthy roots music of the border region. Yet the collection has grown to contain a representative sample of the best and most beloved songs produced on the Latin American continent during the first century of recorded music. "Top Ten Songs" (appendix B) compiles the most recorded compositions in the collection, yielding a list of songs such as "La Bamba" that attained global popularity and became culturally emblematic. Antonio Cuéllar, digital archivist for the Frontera Collection, has a unique perspective: he is the only person alive who has listened to every recording. His favorite recordings in the historic 78-rpm format are presented in "The Archivist's List: Seventy-eight Favorite 78s" (appendix C).

Across different genres and song styles, the collection helps us see the hidden antecedents of today's popular music, from the rousing breakup songs (*canciones de despecho*) of Juan Gabriel to the narcocorridos of Los Tigres del Norte and even the authentic rhythmic roots of a modern-day Cuban contrivance called the Buena Vista Social Club. As a fan of salsa music, I was amazed to find old songs from the

1920s and '30s that continue to inspire contemporary performers who echo the lyrical refrains or melodic phrases of their predecessors. Fans of Panamanian salsa star Rubén Blades will be delighted to find three excellent 78-rpm versions of César Miró's "Todos Vuelven," the Peruvian waltz that Blades popularized half a century later.

The Frontera Collection, in other words, takes us to the source of Latin American musical traditions. Despite more than thirty years' experience as a writer specializing in Latin music, I found it humbling to delve into this amazing archive and realize how much music it contains that I had never heard before. It's hard not to be awed by the sheer scope of the collection, representing a depth and breadth of musical styles far beyond what its official title suggests.

With my headphones on, exploring the archives late into the night, I sometimes couldn't stop listening. The task of reviewing the almost 35,000 titles uploaded to the UCLA database so far was made much more time consuming by the pleasure of listening to songs for my own enjoyment. The song titles alone were often too compelling to pass up. How can you resist a song called "¿Quién Mató a Consuelo?" (Who Killed Consuelo?) or "Vendo una Cama de Agua" (I'm Selling My Water Bed)? Not to mention the many classics I remembered from my childhood, such as "Un Rayito de Sol," by Guty Cárdenas, "Una Copa Más," by Trío Los Panchos, "Serenata Huasteca," by Miguel Aceves Mejía, or "Noche de Ronda," by my *tocayo*, Agustín Lara.

Surprisingly, however, some of the most intriguing and insinuating titles were instrumental polkas that give no verbal clue as to what inspired them. They have provocative titles such as "¿Voy Bien o Me Devuelvo?" (Am I Going the Right Way or Shall I Turn Around?), "El Travieso Don Rafael" (The Mischievous

Don Rafael), or "Una Tarde en el Alamo" (An Afternoon at the Alamo). One of these polkas, "Una Noche en Piedras Negras" (A Night in Piedras Negras), piqued my interest because that Mexican border town, across from Eagle Pass, Texas, is where Strachwitz recorded his very first Mexican record, "Corridos de la Frontera" by Los Pingüinos del Norte, taped in a cantina in 1970. The only clue as to what the town might have been like is the song's formal but happy melody.

Through these lovingly preserved recordings, performers who might otherwise have vanished into anonymity can share the personal, human motivations that inspired them to compose and sing—their deep feelings, disappointments, aspirations, tragedies, political commentary, social insights, and folk wisdom, not to mention their way with words. Browsing the archive feels like a journey, like dropping in on some tango bar in Buenos Aires, a mambo club in New York or Havana, and, of course, a cantina in San Antonio or El Paso for a night of rousing polkas and corridos.

More than that, the Frontera Collection transports us to an early era in the recording industry, before globalized corporations and mass marketing forced the homogenization of music styles. Today, major US record labels have their own Latin music divisions, yet commercially available Latin music is becoming less and less distinctive. There is a universal tendency for artists to incorporate nonnative elements—be it rap, rock, soul, or electronica—in order to sound cool or simply to sell. Latin artists seem to be conforming to some sort of international standard, so they all start sounding the same no matter what country they come from.

By contrast, in the 78-rpm era represented so well in this collection, major US record companies made it their practice to go where the artists were. Their goal was to capture the music on its own terms, and on its own turf. Strachwitz suspects that often these roaming record executives didn't even know the meaning of songs they were recording, whether in Los Angeles or Mexico City. A clue to their cluelessness can be found in the English translations added in parentheses under Spanish titles on some record labels. RCA Victor, for example, offered two entirely different—and entirely wrong—translations for the song "Voy de Gallo," a Mexican vernacular expression that means "I'm going to deliver a midnight serenade." (The word *gallo*, or rooster, is also used in the Spanish term for midnight mass, *misa de gallo*.) On the version by mariachi singer Miguel Aceves Mejía (RCA 23-6895), the English title is given as "I'll Rule the Roost." And on the one by Trío Calaveras (RCA 23-6522), it's "On a Spree." In both cases the label, based in Camden, New Jersey, missed both the literal and the essential meaning of the song. Written by Ramiro Hernández, it is a sad lament by a heartbroken man who still serenades a woman a year after she dumped him. This confusion gives new meaning to RCA's iconic logo of the dog listening to an old phonograph player with a cocked head and a quizzical look. On these records, "his master's voice" was in a language the curious canine couldn't understand.

Consciously or not, the American record companies managed to capture a small slice of culture with every one of their recordings, many of them made in cities of the Southwest with portable equipment set up in hotels, radio stations, and other temporary venues. During World War II, the shortage of raw material forced the big labels to cut back on the production of shellac discs. Taking up the slack were a host of smaller, independent record labels devoted exclusively to recording Mexican and Mexican American artists on both sides of the border. Many of these, such as Azteca,

Imperial, and Latin America, were based in Los Angeles, which until recently was an important recording center for Latin music. One 78-rpm record carried a sticker from a record dealer, Repertorio Musical Mexicano, located at 408 North Main Street, that proclaimed its slogan proudly: "La Única Casa Mexicana de Música Mexicana Para Los Mexicanos" (The Only Mexican House of Mexican Music for Mexicans). The store's sales pitch played on the powerful link between culture, commerce, and community: "Be Patriotic. Protect Businesses Owned by Your Paisanos" (fig. 3).

The fact that many of these records never achieved significant national distribution was both a curse and a blessing. On the one hand, the lack of distribution was one factor in the lack of acceptance of this music as a valuable art form, argues Tom Diamant, project manager for the Frontera Collection. But by staying local and not assimilating into the mainstream, artists were able to maintain distinctive regional styles, such as Tejano and Chicano music, with unique Mexican American themes.[3]

As a result, the music captured on these records has an air of authenticity that is lacking in pop culture today. Though the sound may be thin, tinny, and scratchy on some of the older recordings, the artistry comes through loud and clear. Taken together, these records add up to a vast cultural mural that will require decades to study, analyze, and appreciate, as it took decades to assemble. The hope is that this book will provide a first step toward that serious study by musicians and academics, as well as more casual exploration by everyday music lovers.

There is much to learn, and much to enjoy, in this priceless archive.

Figure 3. This Columbia 78-rpm record label still has a sticker with a patriotic message from a downtown Los Angeles retailer. The Columbia recording, an instrumental march titled "Compañeros Antiguos" (Old Companions), by the obscure Banda Ellery, cites patents dating to 1902. Photograph courtesy of the Arhoolie Foundation.

About the Frontera Collection

The Strachwitz Frontera Collection of Mexican and Mexican American Recordings is the largest and most comprehensive music archive of its kind in the world. The collection consists of an indexed and searchable database of commercially recorded, Spanish-language music and spoken-word performances spanning the history of recorded sound, starting with some of the first records ever made at the beginning of the twentieth century. Although digitizing the massive collection is still underway, plans call for the Frontera Collection at UCLA ultimately to contain reproductions of the entire physical collection of Latin music and memorabilia compiled over more than half a century by renowned collector Chris Strachwitz, founder of Arhoolie Records, a roots music label in El Cerrito, California. Now owned by the Arhoolie Foundation, the complete archive consists of over 147,000 individual recordings, primarily of Mexican and Mexican American music, as well as over 1,500 photographs of musicians, posters, songbooks, and extremely hard-to-find record company catalogs.

The music and related data are made available in digital format through a dedicated, user-friendly website created by the UCLA Library (http://frontera.library.ucla.edu/index.html). This unique archive contains many rare recordings, including acetates and test pressings. In many cases, the Frontera Collection holds what are believed to be the only surviving copies of recordings for which no master is known to exist, since many of the original metal parts used as masters were melted down during World War II for the war effort. Unlike blues and country records from the 78-rpm era, very little of this historic Mexican music has been reissued on LP or CD, and much of what does exist was released as reissues by Arhoolie Records itself. As Tom Diamant, the Arhoolie Foundation's director of digital archiving, has stated, "Since the beginning of the recording era, commercial companies have been making Mexican recordings and selling them to audiences in both the United States and Mexico, but even though Mexican Americans now comprise the largest minority group in the United States, their recorded cultural heritage has been all but ignored by modern society" (fig. 4).[1]

Now, for the first time, this vast and invaluable cultural archive is becoming available for review by researchers and historians, as well as for the enjoyment of music lovers everywhere. Until recently, this musical treasury was accessible only to a small and privileged group of people who could visit the storage site at Arhoolie's El Cerrito headquarters and play the fragile physical discs, one at a time. Now, anyone can search through a century of recordings and sort the results by artist, song title, genre, record label, and the like. Making the collection available on the Internet opens a new world of possibilities for research and study, not only of the music itself but of the cultural, social, and political history documented over decades by the thousands of artists represented on these records.

As Diamant puts it, "The Frontera Collection offers a valuable window into the development of this culture as it has blended elements uniquely Mexican with styles, lyrics, vocabulary, social attitudes, forms, struggles, and politics that are clearly the result of the American experience. . . . The entire collection represents a window into the changes in American and Mexican American culture during the last one hundred years."[2]

The Collection

Although the Frontera Collection consists mainly of Mexican and Mexican American music, it also includes samples of other popular Latin music styles from countries throughout the Spanish-speaking world. For example, there are recordings of flamenco from Spain, sones and mambo from Cuba, tango from Argentina, and plena from Puerto Rico, and even an Inca-style fox-trot from Peru ("Baile Incaico," Brunswick 41223). The Frontera database lists hundreds of separate genres and subgenres, from the familiar to the exotic. As of late 2011, the database had identified 2,600 separate styles of music by more than 12,000 performers on almost 1,000 record labels. Appendix D, "Top Fifty Songwriters," and appendix E, "Top Fifty Performers," list the artists with the

Figure 4. Tom Diamant, manager of Arhoolie Records, at the organization's headquarters in El Cerrito, California, in 2012. Tom oversees the digital transfer of recordings for the Frontera Collection. Photograph courtesy of Haley Ausserer.

largest numbers of recordings in the database. Appendix F lists the top twenty genres.

Despite the global origins of the music, most of the recordings in the Frontera Collection were made in the United States on domestic record labels, large and small. And while the Mexican recordings concentrate on what is known as regional border music, including some of the earliest norteño and conjunto recordings, folk styles from other parts of Mexico are also amply represented. There are rancheras from Jalisco, sones from Veracruz, and romantic songs from Yucatán, as well as many types of instrumental music. "This early work is the foundation for Latino music today, since the singers and musicians who made these records helped popularize and propagate a number of traditions, including regional Mexican, Tejano, Chicano, and Mexican American music," states the Frontera Collection website.[3]

One of the main goals of this ongoing digital project, now entering its tenth year, is to preserve for posterity the fragile and irreplaceable record collection held by Chris Strachwitz. Over the past six decades, Strachwitz, a respected roots music expert, has amassed the world's premier private collection of Spanish-language discs, consisting of more than 147,000 individual recordings on multiple media—78-rpm and 45-rpm singles, as well as 33⅓-rpm long-play (LP) albums and cassette tapes. Eventually, if resources permit, the Frontera Collection will contain digital copies of all the music from the Strachwitz collection in every format, along with digital images of related documents such as photos, posters, catalogs, and broadsides.

The Strachwitz Frontera Collection can be divided into three sections spanning two distinct eras in Mexican and Mexican American recording history. The first section represents the first half of the twentieth century,

comprising 33,472 individual performances on 78-rpm discs, including the first corridos ever recorded. The second section includes 25,090 45-rpm records representing some 50,000 performances from the mid-1950s to the 1990s, including many tracks by contemporary Tex-Mex stars such as Flaco Jiménez, Freddy Fender, and Little Joe. Many of the 45s were produced by small regional record labels that served the burgeoning immigrant community along the border. The last section contains approximately 4,000 albums (33⅓-rpm long-play recordings) and 650 cassette tapes from around 1955 to 1990.

Strachwitz, a German-born businessman, stored the vast inventory in a special climate-controlled building on the site of his business headquarters in Northern California. The location on a busy thoroughfare in El Cerrito, north of Berkeley, is also home to Arhoolie Records, the independent label Strachwitz launched in 1960 to record American roots music, particularly blues, country, gospel, zydeco, and Cajun. By 1970 he had expanded into collecting and producing Mexican and Mexican American border music, representing every major style within the regional music umbrella, including norteño, conjunto, Tex-Mex, banda, and bolero.[4] Strachwitz doggedly sought out and acquired major collections from record retailers, secondhand stores, and flea markets, as well as Spanish-language radio stations, jukebox operators, record labels and distributors, and private collectors from Louisiana to Los Angeles. The collection grew to include 16,736 two-sided 78-rpm disks featuring Mexican American and other Latin music, plus many spoken performances, such as patriotic speeches and satirical, vaudeville-style comedy skits spoofing the issues and mores of the day.

These rare and fragile shellac platters are kept in protective sleeves and stored on custom-built shelves, protected from falling and shattering by small chains strung across each separate storage space. For many years, Strachwitz and his staff worried that the priceless collection would be vulnerable to destruction from a fire or severe earthquake, particularly since the Arhoolie complex sits in between two fault lines in the quake-prone San Francisco Bay Area. In addition, Strachwitz, who turned eighty in 2011, was concerned about what would happen to his cherished collection should he pass away. In 1996, as a first step toward protecting the collection, he transferred ownership of all his Mexican, Mexican American, and other Latin music recordings to the Arhoolie Foundation, the nonprofit arm of his enterprise. In deciding how to preserve this musical legacy for future generations, Strachwitz insisted on avoiding the fate of other record collections, which are often forgotten after being bequeathed to institutions where they're stored in dark, inaccessible vaults, never to be heard again. Digitizing the recordings was a high-tech way to keep the music alive by making it available online.

Digitization

Before digitizing could begin, an inventory had to be taken of all the items contained in the physical Strachwitz collection. That initial phase of cataloguing all the recordings was funded by the National Academy of Recording Arts and Sciences (NARAS), the National Endowment for the Arts (NEA), and Arhoolie Productions. The work, carried out under the direction of Strachwitz and Diamant, resulted in the creation of the Arhoolie Encyclopedia, a searchable catalog of the music listed by artist, label, and song. This constitutes the master database of all items in the collection. Since the UCLA digital project is a work in progress,

the university's database currently contains only a portion of what exists in the overall Arhoolie archives.

Once the collection was cataloged, the transfer process could begin. This enormous undertaking was launched on October 15, 2001, under the auspices of the Arhoolie Foundation in collaboration with New Mexico's Fund for Folk Culture. The project was made possible through the efforts of the late Guillermo Hernández, former director of the UCLA Chicano Studies Research Center, who helped pull all the participants and resources together. Hernández, a corrido expert who first met Strachwitz in the mid-1970s, enlisted the support of Los Tigres del Norte, the premier exponents of Mexican regional music, based in San Jose, California. The band members, who shared the desire to preserve this important part of Mexican culture, got the project off the ground with an initial commitment of $500,000, believed to be the largest grant ever received by a university from a community group for the study of cultural traditions. The money was donated by the band's nonprofit arm, Los Tigres del Norte Foundation, and channeled to the university through a new campus agency, the Los Tigres del Norte Fund at UCLA, created April 19, 2000. With about half of the funds earmarked for the Frontera Collection, work began on the first phase of the project, digitizing the numerous 78-rpm recordings made between 1908 and 1958.

The work is carried out at Arhoolie headquarters in El Cerrito, where a small digitizing studio was created on the upper floor of the building that houses the record collection. Top-quality equipment was assembled especially for the transfer project. At the heart of the system is the analog-to-digital converter, which transforms analog sound waves into a digital signal that can be stored on a computer hard drive. Since there was no studio standard for mastering 78s, a special preamplifier is used to re-create a variety of equalization curves selected for the technical characteristics of each recording era.

Before playback begins, each disc is carefully cleaned using a custom record-washing machine. In the case of very dirty discs with grime in the grooves, they are washed by hand using a soft brush and dish soap, then rinsed with very warm water under the faucet. To complete the preparation for computer capture, the correct stylus, or playback needle, must be selected for each recording, using a trial-and-error method. The project's digital archivist, Antonio Cuéllar, listens to many sample records with styluses of different diameters to find the one that extracts the best original sound without extraneous noise. Using the wrong needle, or choosing the wrong equalization setting, can lead to tinny or muddy sound. The recordings are digitized in high-resolution 24-bit/96kHz format and saved as uncompressed Broadcast WAV files, which allow for the storage of metadata along with the musical track. The higher sampling rate ensures more complete and thus better-quality sound capture, especially as the songs are reproduced. The music files captured on the hard drive are finally burned to DVD-R discs, which are then sent to UCLA for uploading into the mainframe computer of the university's Digital Library.

In 2006, the second phase of the digitizing process received initial funding through a grant from the National Endowment for the Humanities. Work then began on the task of digitizing the collection's 45-rpm phonograph recordings, representing music from the second half of the twentieth century.

The Future: A Digital Encyclopedia

As of the fall of 2010, the entire collection of 78s and about half of the 45s had been digitized and entered into the UCLA database. The goal is to continue the digitizing process until every item in the Strachwitz inventory is placed online. That includes the remainder of the musical recordings, specifically the LPs and cassette tapes (which, along with CDs, constitute the most recent material). Depending on future funding, the archive will also eventually feature a trove of related items that Strachwitz has assembled over the years. These include concert posters, videos, historical photographs of musicians, artist bios, rare record company catalogs, studio session logs, song lyrics, and even broadsides, the printed pages of lyrics that predated or coincided with the mass distribution of recorded music.

In the vision of the Arhoolie Foundation and its leaders, the Frontera Collection will gradually evolve into a comprehensive digital encyclopedia of Mexican and Mexican American music and culture. In prepared presentations to colleges and libraries across the country, Diamant eloquently captures that vision of Frontera's future:

> We are working on digitizing all this information and linking it together so that as you listen to a recording, you can view photos of the artist, read a biography of the artist, a history of the record label, view a poster of a concert, look up the recording log and see how much the musicians were paid for the recording session, read the lyrics, and even view a video or listen to an interview of the recording artist, getting an entire view of the music and where it came from. This way of examining an archive gives the end user as complete an educational and emotional experience as a computerized experience can be. It may not be the same as holding the actual artifact in your hand and listening to it on a turntable, but in some ways it can be much richer.[5]

Chris Strachwitz
The Making of a Music Man in America

One day during lunch at a Mexican restaurant near Berkeley, California, in the early 1970s, a man approached the table of a tall, lanky German immigrant who had moved to the United States two years after the end of World War II. The stranger claimed to recognize the surprised diner from what by then must have seemed like another life.

"Aren't you Mr. Strachwitz?" asked the man, with a vaguely accusatory tone. "I took German from you at Los Gatos High School, and let me tell you, you were a *terrible* teacher. But we had the most fantastic time listening to jazz and blues and all kinds of amazing music we had never heard before. I just wanted to say thanks for a great experience."[1]

The former teacher was Chris Strachwitz, who had abandoned his brief classroom career a decade earlier to devote himself full time to Arhoolie Records, the independent label he had started as a sideline while he was still teaching (fig. 5). Blues, jazz, cajun, and hillbilly—the music that had once distracted his high school classes—had become his life's passion. Any teacher would be thrilled to learn that he had left a vivid, lifelong impression on even one pupil. In fact, the former student who interrupted lunch that day was wrong. Strachwitz had not been a terrible teacher. He was just teaching the wrong subject.

It might have seemed natural for a German immigrant to teach German, but he lasted just three years in the classroom, from 1959 to 1962. At the time, it was obvious to both teacher and students that his heart and mind were not entirely committed to the subject, or the job. On the other hand, Strachwitz could talk enthusiastically for hours about the earthy,

Figure 5. Chris Strachwitz, president of the Arhoolie Foundation, with his priceless collection of Mexican and Mexican American records, which is the basis of the Frontera Collection. Photograph courtesy of the Arhoolie Foundation.

down-home music he discovered after coming to this country as a teenage refugee.

"I had always enjoyed history in school, but it was usually [taught] from the perspective of the ruling classes and their culture," wrote Strachwitz in the liner notes for *The Journey of Chris Strachwitz*, an Arhoolie box set released in 2000 to celebrate his label's fortieth anniversary.

> Suddenly, [as a record producer] I found myself face to face with other social strata, whose culture, music and history no one seemed to have charted. . . . I got high from listening to these incredible sounds and felt I should share them with others around the world, especially Europeans, who were not as fortunate as I and could not make this journey themselves.[2]

After quitting the classroom, Strachwitz went on to earn renown and respect as a folklorist, not in academia but in the rough-and-tumble arena of the music business. He has emerged as one of the country's premier producers and collectors of American roots music, a passionate preservationist of musical styles that were largely marginalized before he started collecting them for posterity. Like some Indiana Jones of pop culture, Strachwitz made daring journeys to seek out the best artists the public had never heard of, becoming part detective and part anthropologist. He tracked down the blues along the back roads of Texas, sought out zesty zydeco in the Louisiana countryside, and unearthed exuberant polkas and dramatic corridos by criss-crossing the US-Mexico border.

In order to share his passion for music that he considered undervalued and underappreciated, Strachwitz started the Arhoolie label in 1960. Over the years, he has released hundreds of records in a variety of roots styles, from guitar-based blues to accordion-spiced norteño music. Many are recordings he made himself, live in the bars and cantinas where he found musicians playing. Others are compilations of music taken from the collection of rare 78 recordings he has amassed over half a century.

Now, fifty years after leaving his comfortable classroom job for the uncertain adventures of musical exploration, Strachwitz has managed to merge his love of music with an educational mission by creating the Strachwitz Frontera Collection of Mexican and Mexican American Music at UCLA. His principal partner in the digital project, the late Guillermo Hernández, had been a friend and collaborator since the early 1970s, when the former Spanish professor was a graduate student at UC Berkeley. In fact, Hernández was there during that lunchtime encounter when Strachwitz was recognized by his former high school pupil, a story the professor was fond of telling over the long years of their mutual friendship, always with a smile.

Behind Strachwitz's academic accomplishment there lies the personal story of how a tall, blue-eyed descendant of European nobility came to be the champion of a humble strain of Mexican music ignored by most Americans and disdained by many upper-crust and middle-class Mexicans. It's the story of an immigrant teenager who came to this country on the eve of the birth of rock 'n' roll and resisted the pull of peer pressure and commercialized pop culture in order to follow the sound of music that spoke to his own heart.

The Strachwitz saga is one of fearless immersion in a gritty folk culture that was as foreign to his own upbringing as the Sonoran desert is to the Swiss Alps. He may have nearly flunked out of college and fallen short as a teacher, but his life work in documenting the history of Mexican American music marks one of the great social and artistic contributions to US pop culture of the twentieth century.

His full name is a mouthful: Christian Alexander Maria, Graf Strachwitz von Gross-Zauche und Camminetz. The German word

"Graf" before his surname means "Count," representing a noble pedigree that dates back more than seven centuries, complete with family castle.

In the United States, people just call him Chris.

Strachwitz was born July 1, 1931, in the former Prussian province of Lower Silesia, which had long been a part of Germany and now belongs to Poland. His father was a farmer and a German army officer, part of a long line of military ancestors active as far back as the Mongol invasion of Poland in the Middle Ages. Another relative was a decorated German officer who led a Nazi panzer division in World War II.

Strachwitz also has a strong and distinguished American lineage. His mother was born in Berlin but has roots in Nevada, where the young Strachwitz first settled after coming to the United States. His maternal great-grandfather was former US Senator Francis Newlands of Nevada, a prominent lawyer and developer whose landholdings included Chevy Chase, Maryland, now a suburb of Washington, DC.[3]

Strachwitz got his first taste of American pop music while still in war-torn Europe. He was delighted with the new 78-rpm recordings his mother brought back from her visits to the States. "We had a wind-up Victrola and I played those records to death," he told musician and author Elijah Wald in an interview for the liner notes to the fortieth anniversary compilation.[4] "I remember one of them was Al Jolson singing 'Sonny Boy,' and another was called 'Oh I Hate to Be Alone with Mary Brown.' I never found out who the hell recorded that, but I wore that sucker out."

Strachwitz is certain he would have died— or been exiled to Siberia as a capitalist—if his family in the United States had not helped him escape the vengeful aftermath of the German defeat, when occupying Soviet forces massacred civilians and confiscated property, including his family's landholdings. Two great-aunts on his mother's side were so concerned that they fought to bring the family to the United Sates. Strachwitz, along with his mother and five siblings, fled first to West Germany, then to Sweden on their way to a new home and a new life.

The young man entered the country in 1947 and moved in with a great-aunt in Reno, Nevada. Almost from the moment of his arrival, he embarked on an exploration of American roots music that would last his entire adulthood and span the last half of the twentieth century.

Nothing in his upbringing, however, had prepared him for the kinds of music that would become his lifelong obsession. What he heard here were lively, rhythmic, and spontaneous sounds that set his foot tapping and his heart pounding, and always brought a broad smile to his face. The styles were all new to him, but they made the music of his childhood sound empty—and oddly foreign.

"I was raised in the countryside, but our country folks never had any music," says Strachwitz. "They listened to Nazi music, war marches, and pop music which was horribly schmaltzy. In most of Europe, opera and classical music was so embedded in the popular culture and they had no local dance music like people have here."[5]

The situation did not improve after the war, when his homeland became part of Poland. Nazi music was replaced by politically driven socialist music, devoid of heart and soul. "There was sort of an attempt to pick up folkloric elements as long as there was socialism involved, but it was always artificial," recalls Strachwitz. "They would put on their nice little costumes and dance around the maypole in these fertility rites, or whatever. And that was it."[6]

By contrast, Strachwitz marshals a host of colorful expressions to convey his enthusiasm for the music he discovered in the United States. It "blew my mind" and "knocked me down" (or "out"), he exclaims frequently. He likes to say that he "wigged out" and was "totally hooked" upon hearing certain styles for the first time.

It wasn't just the sounds that stirred his soul. Strachwitz was also drawn to this music—and the people who make it—for deeper, personal reasons. Marginalized, ridiculed, and rejected, these musicians were struggling to find acceptance and respect in American society without compromising who they were. Strachwitz yearned for that connection too. As a teenager, he was so tall and skinny that kids in high school called him "Pencil." He spoke broken English and felt insecure. Like all adolescents, he longed to fit in, but his musical tastes served only to isolate him further. "Sometimes, in fact, it seemed like his real love was for the raw, rural, working class cultures that produced the sounds as much as for the music itself," writes Wald in his liner notes. "It was outsiders' music, and he had felt very much like an outsider" after coming to this country.

Being an outsider eventually became an advantage. In exploring commercially uncharted musical territory, Strachwitz often found himself on the cutting edge of popular tastes. He may have felt isolated in his love of offbeat sounds, but his interest often anticipated future commercial trends, as wider audiences later "discovered" the styles he had once explored alone.

"They thought I was absolutely nuts"

The newly arrived teenager undertook his search for music in a world that was unfamiliar even to most Americans at the time. In the late 1940s, the blues and R&B (rhythm and blues), which would later become the foundations for rock 'n' roll, were still categorized as "race music" or "sepia music" and were largely ignored by mainstream radio and record labels. Throughout his life, Strachwitz relied on cultural informants (to extend the anthropological metaphor) who would tell him where to find the best artists wherever he went. His first such guide was the black gardener hired by his great-aunt, who pointed him to a beer joint known as the Harlem Club, located near the Reno railroad station. It was there that he heard his first live bluesman, "a really good, lowdown, blues piano player" whose music "just grabbed me."[7] Strachwitz didn't yet have the nerve to approach the musician and ask his name, much less discuss the music. That skill would develop later as he went on the road and started recruiting some of these anonymous musicians to record for him.

His continuing education in US roots music came mostly at night, in the quiet of his own room. There he stayed tuned to a radio signal that offered an alternative to the musical mainstream he found so insipid and uninspiring. The station, with the call letters XERB, was a so-called "border blaster" that pumped 50,000 watts up the Wesdt Coast from a base in Rosarito Beach, Mexico, south of Tijuana. (The station later gained fame as the home of Wolfman Jack, the growling late-night deejay who specialized in R&B and early rock 'n' roll.) The teenage Strachwitz was entranced by the hillbilly music coming across those airwaves.

"Actually I could hear it loud and clear even in Reno at night," he recalls of the station. "It just blasted up the West Coast, playing nothing but hillbilly music at that time. In those days, Mexican music was not a viable, saleable product to anybody because the poor Mexicanos couldn't afford anything. . . . So the station was totally beamed and geared to the Arkies and Okie population that was booming in the Los Angeles area in those days."[8]

The artists he heard all had names as colorful as their song titles. There was singer T. Texas Tyler with "Remember Me." The hillbilly family band known as the Maddox Brothers and Rose doing "You Got to Live and Love Always." And the country duo of Floyd and Lloyd, the Armstrong Twins, playing "The Mandolin Boogie" or "Three Miles South of Cash in Arkansas." Strachwitz never dreamed that soon he'd be reissuing the works of some of these artists on his own label.

It was still 1947, the same year he arrived in the States, when Strachwitz was sent to school in Southern California, ostensibly to continue his formal education. His great-aunt had sent him to a private high school in Santa Barbara, but he was far more interested in hillbilly music and the blues than history and biology. One day that year, the teen went to the movies with a friend to see a new film titled *New Orleans*, featuring jazz greats Louis Armstrong and Billie Holiday, along with pianist Meade Lux Lewis and trombonist Edward "Kid" Ory and others. The sound was so new to him he didn't know what to call it. But he could feel the soulfulness deep down to his toes.

"I was totally hooked on New Orleans jazz when I saw that movie," says Strachwitz, with an enthusiasm that lingers in his voice more than half a century later. "I couldn't get over it."[9]

It was a pivotal moment, putting him on the path to serious record collecting. He left the theater with a hunger for black New Orleans jazz and boogie-woogie, the piano-based blues with roots in southern honky-tonks. The very first record he bought was "Bully Wully Boogie," by Hadda Brooks, released in 1948. He paid 79 cents, a few pennies more than his weekly allowance at the time. And he learned an important first lesson of his collecting career: the records he loved would be hard to find. "My father was an avid hunter of wild game but I seem to have transposed his passion into a hunt for music, both live and on records, which I call gathering without having to kill any living creatures," he was quoted as saying in the box set liner notes.[10]

His passion for music also led him to another youthful pastime: playing hooky. When he heard that Kid Ory would be playing in nearby Montecito, Strachwitz felt he had no choice but to skip theater practice. He didn't get into the club, so he stood outside and listened. Like a true fan, he remembers it as if he had a front-row seat.

After graduating from high school in 1951, Strachwitz attended Pomona College in Claremont, east of Los Angeles, where he continued his afternoon cultural education on the radio. This time, he tuned into pioneering LA deejay Hunter Hancock, the first radio host on the West Coast to play R&B. Hancock, nicknamed "Ol' H.H.," hosted an afternoon show called *Harlem Matinee*, blasting blues legends like Lightnin' Hopkins and Howlin' Wolf that would become so influential in shaping Strachwitz's musical tastes. The desire to record Hopkins, in fact, would soon become the inspiration for Strachwitz to get into the record business. The great Texas bluesman had not yet been discovered by the hip listeners of the 1960s, those future readers of *Rolling Stone*, the rock magazine that would name Hopkins one of the top one hundred guitarists of all time. It was the raw, improvisational energy of Hopkins in these early years that attracted Strachwitz. "That voice just absolutely floored me, and he became my favorite of all blues singers," he told Wald.[11]

As a student, however, Strachwitz still had better attendance at concerts than at college lectures. He frequently trekked to Los Angeles to catch his favorite acts, making the five-hour round-trip by car in the pre-freeway 1950s. He was among the few whites in the mostly Mexican American crowds attending blues shows emceed by Ol' H.H. at the Olympic Auditorium, where he also got his first whiff of marijuana. He made it to the Beverly Cavern thanks to his friend Frank Demond, now a trombonist with the Preservation Hall Jazz Band. Demond was equally enthralled by the New Orleans clarinetist George Lewis, plus he had a car. For a change of pace on Sunday nights, the pair made the pilgrimage to St. Paul's Baptist Church in downtown LA to hear the gospel choir under the direction of J. Earl Hines. "I heard gospel music on Sunday night and R&B, all these totally bizarre vernacular things I had never encountered, even in my dreams," he recalls. "I was really blown away by all of it."[12]

While he was obsessed with hillbilly music and traditional jazz, his classmates were tuned to the Top 40, listening to the likes of the Four Freshmen, Doris Day, and Frank Sinatra. He found their music "wimpy" and empty, especially by comparison with the energy and emotion he found in the blues and country, sounds still totally unfamiliar to his friends and classmates. "They thought I was absolutely nuts," he says.[13]

In 1952 Strachwitz transferred to the University of California, Berkeley, where he would finally find a home. He dabbled in engineering, chemistry, and physics, but his real "major" was still music. "I'd never been a big football fan but I found out that if I became a member of Berkeley's Big Game Committee, I could help pick and choose which artists would entertain for homecoming and the such," he told Larry

Benicewicz in a biography published by the Austrian online magazine *BluesART Journal*.[14] "Naturally, I would recommend George Lewis and even earned a reputation for picking crowd-pleasing performers."

Before completing college, Strachwitz was drafted, and in 1954 he returned to his homeland during peacetime as a soldier in the US army, stationed in Austria and Germany. Two years later, he was back at Berkeley on the GI Bill, earning his bachelor's degree in political science in 1958 and a teaching credential two years later. He was still teaching German in 1960 when he established Arhoolie with a Los Gatos, California, post office box. After his short teaching stint, he moved back to Berkeley to dedicate himself full time to his music business.

As Wald explained in his liner notes, Strachwitz did not share the contempt of many fellow folklorists for the record business. Over the next four decades he would engage in almost every aspect of the industry, in addition to being a producer and label executive. Early on, he launched the International Blues Record Club, a mail-order business to sell records by subscription. He later became a wholesale distributor for other labels and also produced live concerts, including the first Berkeley Blues Festival in 1966. He served as booking agent for some of the acts he had brought out of obscurity, including Lightnin' Hopkins. He opened his own record store, Down Home Music, which is still operating at the front of his small company complex on San Pablo Avenue in El Cerrito, north of Berkeley. He even hosted his own Sunday afternoon radio show for thirty years, from 1965 through 1995, on public radio station KPFA-FM, the Pacifica station in Berkeley.

In the early years, Strachwitz was barely making ends meet. He survived by auctioning off his old 78s or by selling his artists' records at their concerts. At first he ran his business out of his Berkeley apartment, using a post office box and leasing storage space for $15 a month across the bay in San Francisco. While on the road, he stayed at $3-per-night motel rooms. It took almost a decade for him to start making money, and then it came not from records or concerts but from music publishing. Wisely, he had purchased the rights to songs that eventually paid off. In publishing, it only takes one big hit to keep a company afloat. For Strachwitz, that hit would be the satirical antiwar song "I Feel Like I'm Fixin' to Die Rag," by Country Joe and the Fish, a 1960s counterculture band he recorded in his Berkeley living room. He also fought for royalties for the tune "You Gotta Move" by Mississippi Fred McDowell, a blues singer and slide guitar player whom Strachwitz had tracked down and recorded earlier in the 1960s. The song was used by the Rolling Stones on their 1971 hit album *Sticky Fingers*, but it took perseverance and legal action for Strachwitz to collect the money due the songwriter. McDowell died the following year, July 3, 1972, but not before getting paid for the Stones' use of his song. It was a proud accomplishment for Strachwitz, who travelled to the bluesman's hometown of Como, Mississippi, and delivered "the biggest check he had ever seen in his life."[15]

In an industry known for exploiting and defrauding its artists, Strachwitz gained a reputation for playing fair. He did more than due diligence to locate performers and composers, or their heirs, a task complicated by the quasi-underworld they often inhabited. "We tried to pay wherever I could find them," he says.[16] His straight dealing in money matters helped nurture trust among some ethnic artists who were understandably skeptical of a white businessman asking them to sign on the

dotted line. But artists also instinctively had faith in his intentions, because he communicated such genuine enthusiasm and respect for their marginalized music.

"I guess I got their trust by being such a fanatic," Strachwitz was quoted as saying in an article published by the now-defunct music magazine *Dirty Linen*. "I think that's how I must have won the trust of a lot of Mexican musicians later on, I was such a fanatic [about their music]. . . . I feel at home in almost every funky culture that I come across."[17]

Over the years, Strachwitz kept expanding the scope of the ethnic music styles he recorded or collected, including Greek, Polish, and Ukrainian. But next to country and blues, nothing compares to the work he did in the world of Mexican American music. He recorded his first norteño album in 1970, a performance by Los Pingüinos del Norte in a cantina in the out-of-the-way border town of Piedras Negras, across the Rio Bravo from Eagle Pass, Texas. Since then, Strachwitz has done more to research, collect, produce, and protect Mexico's working-class country music than any other individual, company, or organization in the United States or Mexico. That's quite an accomplishment for someone who, to this day, doesn't know a lick of Spanish.

"I somehow fell in love with what most people call low-class or cantina music, especially the norteño music the way I heard it in Piedras Negras or San Antonio and all these places," he says.

> The music didn't sound to me all that different. It had all the soulfulness that American music had, but in a different way. And it also had more European elements, with all those polkas and waltzes, you see, and somehow that must have appealed to me. . . . There's a certain aura, or feeling that I can't describe, in all those musical genres. I mean, I heard it in blues. I heard it in hillbilly duet singing. And I heard that same

kind of soulfulness in these [Mexican] *duetos*. . . . I never thought if it was artistic or not, I just loved it. God, it had this sound, and the way these two voices blend together. To me, that's the most soulful stuff I've heard. It's sort of a common rural quality that I felt. And I just loved it.[18]

In all genres, Strachwitz has helped break down social barriers for roots music. He has introduced popular ethnic artists to wider audiences outside their own communities and has discovered others who would never have been noticed. He has used every medium available to showcase his artists, including two groundbreaking musical documentaries. In 1976, he conceived and produced *Chulas Fronteras*, a film about Texas-Mexico border music directed by Les Blank. Thirteen years later, again working with Blank, he co-directed *J'ai Eté au Bal*, a film about Cajun and zydeco music featuring Arhoolie artist Clifton Chenier.

Recently, the spotlight has turned on Strachwitz himself. He is the subject of a documentary being produced by two longtime associates, folklorist Chris Simon and film editor Maureen Gosling, who worked on both previous films. "One of the things that's most important about what Chris has accomplished in his life is he's given voice to people who would not have been heard at all except in their own communities," said co-director and cinematographer Simon in a 2009 article in the San Francisco Film Society's online magazine.[19] In recognition of those lifelong accomplishments, the National Endowment for the Arts bestowed on Strachwitz its first "keeper of tradition" award as part of its 2000 National Heritage Fellowships.

There's a black and white photo that's now part of Arhoolie lore, capturing what can be considered the birth of the label on November 3, 1960. Strachwitz, along with his friend and graphic designer Wayne Pope, is seen sitting at a kitchen table pasting together the covers for the label's first release by an unknown blues singer he had recorded on the road the previous summer (fig. 6). The inaugural run was just 250 copies of Arhoolie LP 1001, *Mance Lipscomb: Texas Sharecropper and Songster*. It was truly a down-home production. But Strachwitz, the budding music executive, turns at that moment to look straight at the camera with a beaming smile, proud as any new father.

He could scarcely have imagined then that he and Arhoolie would be featured in the *New York Times* fifty years later, in an article marking the golden anniversary of his humble, homespun business. Famed musicologist and archivist Richard K. Spottswood told the newspaper,

> He is probably more American than many of us, but he experienced this music not as something he was born into and took for granted like the air we breathe, but as something rare and delightful, not available to the rest of the world. Coming from another language and culture, he perhaps saw the artistry in this music a little sooner, a little earlier than the rest of us, and his vision of a kaleidoscopic American musical culture, from Tejano to country and Southwestern blues, has helped thwart the single standard the music industry has tried to impose on us over the years.[20]

For his part, Strachwitz sums it up in a simple, folksy way. "I've been lucky all along to do what I love to do and make a living at it," he says. "You can't beat that."[21]

Figure 6. Chris Strachwitz and designer Wayne Pope paste slicks to the initial run of 250 covers for the LP that launched the Arhoolie label in 1960, *Mance Lipscomb: Texas Sharecropper and Songster.* Photograph courtesy of the Arhoolie Foundation.

The Story of the Frontera Collection
The Mission to Collect, Catalog, and Conserve a Neglected Culture

The origins of the Frontera Collection can be traced to the meeting of two men, Guillermo Hernández and Chris Strachwitz, who came from vastly different backgrounds but shared a common vision (fig. 7). Hernández, a professor of Spanish literature at UCLA, had immigrant roots in Mexico and an early academic interest in medieval history. Strachwitz, the music

Figure 7. The creators of the Frontera Collection (*from left*): Guillermo Hernández and collector Chris Strachwitz, with key ally James Nicolopulos, professor of Latin American studies at the University of Texas at Austin. The photograph was taken during a 1995 corrido conference at UC Berkeley's International House, held as part of the thirty-fifth anniversary of Arhoolie Records. Photograph courtesy of the Arhoolie Foundation.

collector and record producer, was an immigrant from Germany with little knowledge of Spanish and a decidedly anti-academic bent.

The story of their unlikely collaboration starts almost four decades ago, in the early 1970s, as they were building their separate careers in and around Berkeley, California, then a lively center of emerging multicultural arts. As a result of a chance meeting, the two men discovered they shared a passion—bordering on obsession—for the music of the US-Mexico frontier. The lasting ties that the music created would eventually yield one of the most extensive public archives of Mexican and Mexican American recordings available anywhere in the world.

"Really, what Chris has is an archaeological site," Hernández says in a promotional video produced by the Arhoolie Foundation. "You open it, and thousands of musicians come out. It's one of the treasures, not only of Mexico, but of the United Sates and of the world."[1]

Strachwitz had spent the 1960s building his grassroots independent label, Arhoolie Records, which had quickly earned a national reputation for its catalog of American roots music: blues, hillbilly, bluegrass, Cajun, and zydeco. By 1970 he had begun expanding Arhoolie's repertoire with several new series, one of which was devoted exclusively to ethnic music, especially the accordion-based sounds of norteño and conjunto music, the folk styles popular throughout northern Mexico and the southwestern United States. Though he didn't speak or understand Spanish, Strachwitz became enthralled by this working-class genre, which he compared to the blues for its soulfulness and its marginalized social status. He decided to share the thrill of his discovery by producing an English-language documentary that would explore the roots of the music and the story of the people who make it, immigrant

laborers shunned by society on both sides of the border. He hired respected cinematographer Les Blank to steer the landmark film, romantically titled *Chulas Fronteras*, a name taken from a norteño song that means lovely or beloved borderlands (fig. 8). The Frontera Collection contains two versions of the song by Lalo González "El Piporro," a 78 on Mexico's Musart label and a very personalized version, a yet-to-be digitized 45-rpm on the Oro label operated by the singer's friend Willie López, who had a radio show also called *Chulas Fronteras*.

With a rough-cut of the film in the can, Strachwitz organized a screening for students at the University of California, Berkeley, where Hernández was working toward his doctorate in comparative literature. The filmmakers were seeking feedback for their project, setting up what today might be called a focus group. Though music was far from his field of interest, Hernández was curious about the project. Like many young Mexican Americans coming of age on the cusp of the Chicano Movement, Hernández was drawn to explore his own cultural roots, a search for identity that was a hallmark of that age of ethnic awakening. The ethos of the movement was to raise awareness and appreciation of the cultural contributions of Mexican Americans—in music, the arts, literature, and film. It was an attempt to find value in what had previously been considered inferior fare in popular culture and unworthy of study in academia. The very title *Chulas Fronteras*—christening as lovely what some considered ugly—seemed consistent with that search for value in Chicano culture. So Hernández, unaware that his life and career were about to change dramatically, showed up for the screening at Arhoolie headquarters on San Pablo Avenue in the suburb of El Cerrito, a short drive north of Berkeley but a far cry from the Ivory Tower.

Hernández was impressed by the film because, as he would later explain, "I had never seen Mexican reality the way he had captured it."[2] But the discovery was just the beginning. Hernández became equally intrigued with the vast music collection Strachwitz had amassed over the years, an archive of Mexican and Mexican American music on fragile 78-rpm records dating from the beginning of the twentieth century. Hernández asked Strachwitz for permission to come back and listen to some of the stored shellac recordings. But what started as a casual listening session on a Friday afternoon would became a daily ritual for Hernández, who became like the proverbial kid in a candy shop. Totally hooked on what he was hearing, the young student returned religiously every day, from 4 p.m. until closing time at 9, trying to absorb decades of musical history in just a few weeks.

"The music to me was just amazing," Hernández says in the Arhoolie video titled *El Mundo del Corrido de Guillermo Hernández* (The Corrido World of Guillermo Hernández).[3] "It really made me aware there was a tradition that was unknown. . . . Even the musicians [in Mexico] didn't know about the history."

Hernández was so inspired by the music that he switched his academic focus to Chicano studies and emerged as a leading force in the formal study of border music. Two decades later, he broke ground by organizing a series of international conferences on the corrido, the traditional Mexican narrative ballad. More important, the partnership between Hernández and Strachwitz would ultimately lead to the creation of the digital collection now known as the Strachwitz Frontera Collection of Mexican and Mexican American Recordings at UCLA.

Figure 8. Chris Strachwitz (*right*) and cinematographer Les Blank in 1976, during the filming of the documentary *Chulas Fronteras*. Photograph courtesy of the Arhoolie Foundation.

Technically, the title of the collection is a misnomer. The musical holdings go far beyond the genres and styles of the US-Mexico border region. There are many other slices of Mexican culture here, and not all are musical (fig. 9). Notably, the collection contains many historic comedic skits, often stinging social satires that targeted Anglo Americans and Europeans with racially based ridicule, providing a creative outlet for the frustration and anger caused by political domination and social discrimination. But there are also many refined and sophisticated instrumentals by large orchestras, which were popular in Mexico and the Southwest in the first half of the twentieth century. Somewhat surprisingly, the archives also include some classic Cuban music tracks, such

Figure 9. The Frontera Collection contains many recordings featuring dramatic reenacts of historic events, in quasi-documentary style. This rare 78-rpm release by RCA Victor, "Última Proclama del Libertador Simón Bolívar," is a dramatization of the final speech by the South American liberator, just before his death on December 17, 1830. It is performed by José Antonio Lugo, accompanied by the Orquesta Venezuela. The special label features a patriotic portrait of Bolívar where the label logo would normally go. Photograph courtesy of the Arhoolie Foundation.

as danzones, sones, cha cha chás, and rumbas, the antecedents of what is now popularly known as salsa. Researchers of Afro-Cuban music, often drawn to more specialized collections on the East Coast, can find many fine examples of the genre in the UCLA archive. Also in the mix are examples of Mexican folk or country music from other parts of Mexico, far south of the border, such as mariachi music from the central Mexican state of Jalisco, featuring singers such as Miguel Aceves Mejía and Lola Beltrán, who were considered glamorous celebrities in their day. Although popular in the border region, this type of Mexican music is not native to that area, and thus it is not central to the mission of the Frontera Collection.

The vast array of styles is a result of the shopping-spree strategy used by Strachwitz to acquire the collection. Like a fisherman casting a wide net, he scooped up an assortment of other Latin music styles in his acquisitions. Many times it was a matter of buying the entire stock of a radio station, private collector, or jukebox operator, taking whatever it contained. And since many of the major US labels that recorded Mexican music in the period before World War II also recorded other forms of Latin music, all styles were bound to wind up in the mix.

Still, the collection's focus on Mexican and Mexican American music reflects Strachwitz's main interest: compiling, promoting, and preserving for posterity the music that others considered cheap cantina or bar music. No doubt, without the effort of Strachwitz to protect this popular folk music heritage, much of it would have been lost forever.

Sometimes even Strachwitz himself was not aware of the value of what he had picked up and preserved. Since he didn't understand Spanish, you might say he collected by ear. He felt the vitality, energy, and passion of the music through the piercing *gritos*, the cries of the singers and musicians, a passion that reminded him of the earthy feeling of the blues. Beyond listening to his gut, Strachwitz, the musical explorer, relied on interpreters like Hernández, who served as informants do for anthropologists.

One day, after one of his long listening sessions at Arhoolie, Hernández excitedly told Strachwitz about one particularly worn and scratchy record he had found. It was an obscure two-part corrido titled "Ramón Delgado," recorded by Pedro Rocha and Lupe Martínez for the Vocalion label (fig. 10). Even the label itself had been worn down from use, with spiral grooves etched into the paper from the many times the heavy arm of a record player or juke box had latched onto the disc to play it. Strachwitz at first didn't understand why this particular record appealed so much to Hernández. It was only in the collection because it was a rare two-part corrido, or

Figure 10. Spiral grooves from heavy use are etched into the label of the two-part corrido "Ramón Delgado" by Pedro Rocha and Lupe Martínez. The two were leading exponents of the genre in San Antonio during the 78-rpm era. Photograph courtesy of the Arhoolie Foundation.

extended narrative ballad, the type that started on one side of the old 78-rpm discs and finished on the other. Naturally, the historic format would be of particular interest to collectors like Strachwitz, who bought every two-part recording he could find. But this one was in such bad shape, he told Hernández, "I almost didn't pick that damn record up at a person's house in San Antonio." So he was curious as to why Hernández would be so interested in the worn-down platter.

"He said, 'Chris, I was interested because it was so beat up,'" Strachwitz recalled.[4] "Obviously this record meant a lot to the people because they played it to death. The ones that are really worn are the ones that people love."

Hernández also deemed the song one of the most interesting and important corridos he had unearthed. He was intrigued by its lyrics, discussing the death of a worker, the Ramón Delgado of the title, whose demise was blamed on the inhumane treatment of Mexicans at the hands of whites. "It goes on about how the Germans hate the Mexicans," explains Strachwitz. "Oh, my God, it was really a heavy song."[5]

Strachwitz also noticed the wear and tear on records in jukeboxes, one of his primary early sources for used 78-rpm records that were popular before the long-play album was introduced in the 1950s. He noticed that one side was always played and the other remained like new. The more popular the record was in its day, the harder it was for collectors to find later. Not surprisingly, the titles that didn't sell well were more likely to be left in the stock of old record distributors, another key source for his collection. Plus, the popular songs were the ones people wanted to keep. That is just one reason why private sales were not as fruitful as the large hauls from distributors and jukebox operators. Strachwitz was often led to homes in cities such as San Antonio, Texas, a recording center for the genre, where private parties sought to sell their personal record stashes. But the quality and selection offered by these private dealers was often disappointing.

Over the years, Strachwitz developed a reputation as a collector and people started alerting him to important opportunities for large purchases, at radio stations, warehouses, and even in the vaults of the record labels themselves. It wasn't all luck that put him in the right place at the right time. When it came to collecting Mexican folk records, he had the field to himself, because, as he once told the *San Francisco Chronicle*, "nobody in the gringo world ever paid attention to this music."[6]

In an interview, Strachwitz later elaborated: "Since I was the only one, apparently, in the whole wide world collecting this sort of stuff, the word got out: 'Oh yeah, you can call Chris. He'll take that whole stash.'"[7]

Right Place, Right Time

Strachwitz entered the US music scene at the perfect time for a record collector. He arrived in this country in 1947, the very year the long-play record was invented. At the same time, the 45-rpm single record was introduced as a way to promote sales of individual tracks from multitrack albums, replacing the old 78s used in jukeboxes and by radio deejays. It didn't take long for the outdated shellac discs to be removed and discarded as obsolete, creating a gold mine for collectors through private dealers, as well as estate sales, swap meets, yard sales, secondhand stores, and so on.

Strachwitz began, both as a collector and as a music producer, with the blues, hillbilly, and Cajun music. His search for obscure blues singers, country fiddlers, and Cajun accordion aces took him through much of Texas,

where he became increasingly exposed to the border music that would later become his obsession. As in any good hunt, one thing always led to another. Strachwitz first became aware of Mexican American music as he scoured the back roads and beer joints of Texas looking for the blues.

During the 1960s, long before he met Hernández in Berkeley, his lack of Spanish was one of the obstacles to collecting Mexican music. In his search for African American blues artists in the South, he could simply stop people on the street and ask if they knew any good guitar pickers 'round these parts, so to speak. It wasn't so easy finding his way around in a foreign language:

> I had no way of getting in touch with people.... You see, with blacks, at least they spoke English. But with this Mexican music, first of all, I didn't know where to find it. And secondly, I didn't know how to approach them. I didn't realize most of them also spoke English. Thirdly, and perhaps most important thing, I didn't think I could sell it.[8]

Eventually, Strachwitz found sources to serve as guides through this underground subculture. As he did with other forms of American roots music, Strachwitz helped bring a wider—and whiter—audience to once-obscure Mexican American artists. One of the first 78-rpm recordings he acquired was "Viva Seguín," a lively polka instrumental by "Old Man"—as he refers to him affectionately—Santiago Jiménez Sr. (fig. 11). One of the versions in the Frontera Collection, on the Imperial label, features Jiménez pumping out the bright melody while his Valedores backup duo playfully weave intricate guitar and bass lines through the tune. "I love that polka rhythm," Strachwitz tells a visitor with enthusiasm. "Oh yeah, you've got to hear that!"[9]

That enthusiasm helped draw attention to a style of music many people otherwise

Figure 11. Don Santiago Jiménez Sr., one of the most important accordion players to come out of San Antonio, is seen here with bassist Ismael González and guitarist Lorenzo Caballero. His recording of the polka "Viva Seguín" was one of the first 78s acquired by Chris Strachwitz for the Frontera Collection. Photograph courtesy of the Arhoolie Foundation.

might never have noticed. And it helped bring international acclaim to at least one Texas performer, Grammy-winning accordion ace Flaco Jiménez (fig. 12), the son of Santiago Sr. After playing in his hometown of San Antonio for years, the younger Jiménez went on to work with Buck Owens and Bob Dylan and record with the Rolling Stones ("Voodoo Lounge") and Ry Cooder ("Chicken Skin Music"), with whom he toured Europe. Yet Strachwitz did not share in the commercial success of the Tex-Mex artists he helped popularize, any more than he did with the bluesmen who

went on to enjoy broader popularity in sixties rock circles.

"While largely ignoring commercial trends, normal business sense, or much of anything but his own personal taste, Chris has made Arhoolie into one of the most respected labels in the world," writes Elijah Wald in his liner notes to Arhoolie's fortieth anniversary compilation.

Who knows whether Cajun and zydeco music would be drawing dancers all over the United States and Europe were it not for Arhoolie's recordings of Clifton Chenier, BeauSoleil and dozens of other Louisiana players? How many

Figure 12. A young Flaco Jiménez, holding an accordion, is shown with a conjunto performing at a wedding in the early 1950s. Part of a San Antonio family of musicians led by Santiago Jiménez Sr., Flaco helped bring international attention to Mexican American conjunto music through his collaborations with Buck Owens, Bob Dylan, the Rolling Stones, and others. Photograph courtesy of the Arhoolie Foundation.

people outside south Texas were aware of Flaco Jimenez and the wailing, pumping accordion sound of the Tex-Mex cantinas before Chris started recording it? And that is not to mention all the blues singers whose music might be forgotten, or might never have been heard, had they not happened to catch Chris's ear.[10]

The Birth of Arhoolie Records

In 1959, twelve years after coming to this country, Chris Strachwitz embarked on a trip to Houston, Texas, that would start him on an endless road of musical exploration. That summer, the twenty-eight-year-old set off by car and bus in search of his favorite blues musician, Lightnin' Hopkins. He had received a tip from his friend Sam Charters, who was writing a book about the blues and had located Hopkins playing beer joints with names like Pop's Place and the Sputnik Club. Charters sent a postcard alerting Strachwitz to his hero's whereabouts. The nascent music producer then undertook the trip with a zeal that far outstripped his budget. "That was like the holy grail to me, so I took a pilgrimage, literally," says Strachwitz.

When I heard him in these beer joints, he was like an African griot. . . . I don't know if you've ever been to a Texas beer joint. They're tiny little joints sometimes in the middle of a block, a house almost. And here he was in front of a few people, who were jiving and dancing, with his drummer pounding away and him playing his electric guitar, and hollering [at the audience] and they would yell back at him.[11]

Strachwitz was amazed by the spontaneous, interactive quality of the performance. Hopkins would shout out lines about his arthritis, the bad weather, the bumpy car ride on the way to the club, or the sexy woman he spotted in the crowd—all in improvised rhyme. He even came up with a verse for Strachwitz when he saw his new number one fan walk into the club. "Oh my God," thought Strachwitz, "I've got to capture this guy in one of these beer joints!"[12]

To his everlasting regret, Strachwitz never did successfully capture Lightnin' live in one of these raw, rustic settings. However, the experience was enough to inspire Strachwitz to start his record label, a move that would define his career and occupy the rest of his adult life.

Strachwitz had already dabbled in recording as an amateur. He started as a teenager, recording his Latin teacher on a crude turntable that cut small acetates. "I bought my first tape recorder while at Pomona College in the early 1950s, but it was a piece of junk!" recalls Strachwitz in a label history posted on Arhoolie's website.

> I taped radio programs and the jazz band led by school mate Frank Demond, who is now the trombonist with the Preservation Hall Jazz Band. When I moved north to attend UC Berkeley in 1952, I soon began to visit Oakland record producer Bob Geddins on many occasions and he, more than anyone else, showed me how to make recordings.[13]

The owner of another small label, Jaxyson Records, taught Strachwitz a lesson that would

help him survive on a shoestring as an independent record producer.[14] Jesse Jaxyson (pronounced "Jackson," as his record label indicated) made recordings in the back of a small electrical repair shop in Oakland during the 1940s. "He showed me how primitively you could make a record," recalled Strachwitz in the liner notes to Arhoolie's fortieth anniversary box set.[15] "Just stick a microphone in front of somebody and turn on the damn cutter." While at Berkeley, Strachwitz used those practical lessons to record a street-corner musician named Jesse "Lone Cat" Fuller, who operated a shoeshine stand while performing as a one-man blues band. His early venture into professional recording ended in disappointment, however, when a cheap Japanese tape recorder he had acquired overmodulated the sound and ruined many of the tapes he made for his fledgling label during his second trip to Texas.

Strachwitz returned to Houston in the summer of 1960 with a renewed desire to capture the live music he had found so stirring, toting the recorder that had worked fine the first year. His dream, of course, was to finally record his blues hero. But to his dismay, Strachwitz arrived just as Hopkins was leaving for a concert date, ironically at a folk festival back in Berkeley. But as the old saying goes when someone makes the best of bad luck, the budding record man used the rest of that summer to turn lemons into lemonade. Along with his newfound guide, musicologist Robert "Mack" McCormick, he set out to track down blues musicians and record them in their natural environment, to share their music with the world. Later, in a 2000 interview with GlobalVillageIdiot, a world music website, Strachwitz would say of his friend Mack: "Without him I don't think I would have ever had the gumption to do all those things."[16]

It was McCormick, an archivist and author, who suggested they try to track down a character from one of Hopkins's most memorable songs, "Tom Moore's Blues." Recorded in 1948, the tune had become an underground anthem for the nascent civil rights movement, with its depiction of the mistreatment of black farmhands by their white employer. They started out not even knowing whether Tom Moore was actually a real person. Imagine their excitement when they asked at a local feed store and were directed to the old plantation owner in the flesh. They met the affable Moore at his office in Navasota, Texas, and had a congenial chat about his plantations. But Strachwitz was more interested in musical leads and asked for the names of any guitar pickers who had played for his farmhands. Moore led them to a local named Peg Leg who hung around a railroad station and seemed to know everybody in the region. Peg Leg then led them to Mance Lipscomb, the son of an emancipated slave who worked on a road crew cutting grass. At age sixty-five, this humble but talented musician would become the debut artist for the new label named for a field hand's holler, Arhoolie. Recorded at home, with Lipscomb surrounded by his wife and grandchildren, that debut record (*Mance Lipscomb: Texas Sharecropper and Songster*, Arhoolie 1001) set the template for subsequent Arhoolie productions: it was done in one take with no overdubs or technical gimmickry and was packaged with informative liner notes, written by McCormick.

Strachwitz and McCormick continued their detective work that summer, seeking what they considered hidden cultural treasures. Armed with a list of musicians provided by yet another informant, British blues writer Paul Oliver, Strachwitz also tried to track down obscure musicians with colorful names such as Little Brother and Black Ace, a steel guitarist whose real name was Babe Kyro Lemon Turner. As he

told an interviewer from the trade journal *Mix Magazine Online* in 2002,

> I just stopped these guys playing dominos on a street corner and asked them, "Any of you ever heard of Little Brother?" And they all looked at me as if I was from Mars, and they said, "What you want with him?" They probably all thought I was the police or a bill collector, and I said, "Well, I got this record by him, and I kind of like the way he plays guitar and sings blues."[17]

That productive summer trip yielded two other early releases: *Black Ace* (Arhoolie 1003) and *Lil Son Jackson* (Arhoolie 1004). The latter featured another of Strachwitz's favorite Texas-style guitarists, Melvin "Lil Son" Jackson, who had retired from music after a car crash several years earlier and was found working the counter in an auto parts store. On subsequent trips to Texas, Strachwitz discovered zydeco music when Lightnin' Hopkins introduced him to his cousin, accordion player Clifton Chenier, who was appearing in Houston beer joints at the time. The meeting led to his first zydeco album in 1961, at a time when the infectious sound with its patois lyrics was barely known outside of Louisiana. Years later, when pop culture caught up with his discovery, zydeco was being used in beer commercials and Chenier was appearing on albums with the likes of Paul Simon. As usual, Strachwitz had been there first.

"He has never done a single thing in his career because it would make money and he has done plenty of things knowing they wouldn't," wrote Joel Selvin in a major profile of Strachwitz published in 2008 by the *San Francisco Chronicle*.[18] "Unlike practically everybody else who wanders into the music business because they love music, Strachwitz never lost touch with that original impulse. All these years later, it's still the music that matters to Strachwitz, the music and the people who make it."

On the Record

by Chris Strachwitz

The record business started slowly during the last two decades of the nineteenth century and took off in the first decade of the twentieth. At first recordings were made, manufactured, and sold on cylinders, with Edison the leader in this field. Soon, however, the flat disc became widely used. Although Edison stuck to his cylinders, he also made flat discs, but they could only be played on his machines, which used the "hill and dale" (meaning up and down) process of picking up the sound from the grooves. The Edison discs were very thick. The sound reproducer, or tone arm, moved the needle, or stylus, up and down (vertically) instead of sideways (horizontally, as was the case with recordings by the other labels, Victor and Columbia).

For most of the first half of the century, music was produced on 78-rpm discs, which means they were recorded at 78 revolutions per minute and played back at the same speed on a turntable. These early discs were essentially singles, usually with one song on each side. The 78-rpm era lasted from the early part of the twentieth century until the middle of the 1950s. Before 1925, recordings were made by the acoustical method. Since microphones and amplifiers had not yet been invented, a horn was used to capture sound waves coming from musicians and other sources, which then directly moved the cutting stylus. This early method did not reproduce the low nor the high end of the sound spectrum.

This all changed in 1925 for most record companies when the electrical process came into wide use. That process is still used today: you record into a microphone and an amplifier transfers the electrical impulse into a wax disc or onto tape—or today into your computer. The 78s were generally ten-inch discs for popular material and twelve-inch discs for classical. In the 1940s albums began to appear; they held from two to four or more 78s and sometimes included liner notes in a small booklet.

In the late 1940s, the invention of the long-play record marked the dawn of the high-fidelity era, not quite as revolutionary as the digital era would be a generation later. Instrumental in the development was Peter Goldmark, a German-Hungarian engineer at CBS, who built on earlier experimentation with recordings at a slower speed. Goldmark had grown weary of the limitations of the old 78 format, which required several discs to play a single piece of classical music. He hated being forced to repeatedly get up and flip sides or switch discs just to hear a complete Brahms concerto at home with friends. The long-play, or LP, basically made it possible to manufacture records with microgrooves, allowing twelve minutes on each side of a ten-inch disc instead of just three minutes on one side of the old 78-rpm of the same size.

The format was introduced by Columbia Records executive Goddard Lieberson in 1948. The firm released 33⅓-rpm recordings in various sizes—seven-inch singles as well as the twelve-inch LP format that now could hold up to twenty minutes per side, five times as much music as the old 78s.

During the 1950s, the LP became the dominant medium for recorded music in album form. But it also triggered a war of speeds. Since RCA was unwilling to pay the licensing fee required by Columbia Records, it introduced the 45-rpm seven-inch single, also made of vinyl. For albums, RCA introduced packages with multiple seven-inch discs, as well as the EP, or extended-play, 45-rpm record, which held up to eight minutes per side. This format was used mainly for pop music, and the discs were marketed in picture sleeves. Eventually the two companies came to an agreement that all albums should be released in the Columbia 33⅓-rpm format and all singles in the RCA 45-rpm format.

These new recordings, pressed on vinyl and recorded with higher fidelity, sounded better than most 78s. Yet the highly touted hi-fidelity invention in the 1950s saw no real change in formats. Major changes came with the introduction of the cassette and eight-track tape configurations, largely designed for use in cars and trucks.

Eventually, of course, the LP began to disappear. This was already evident in the field of Mexican music during the 1980s. With the arrival of the compact disc, or CD, in the middle of that decade, the entire industry changed dramatically and permanently. No more need for pressing plants or album makers. It was the end of an era—the era when sound was reproduced through grooves in a record or from a tape. Eventually, the CD and its digitized signal replaced LPs and cassettes, which almost disappeared from the market. But it too had a short life: by the early twenty-first century the CD was being gradually displaced by the iPod and the enormous amounts of entertainment available on the Internet for download and streaming.

Recording Mexican Music

All three major labels, Edison, Victor, and Columbia, began to make recordings of Mexican music in Mexico City around 1904, but the Revolution scared them and they left by 1910. However, the companies soon discovered that there were many Mexicans in the United States, along with musicians to cater to them. They began recording Mexican musicians in Los Angeles and New York by 1920, using the acoustical method. The real boom began with the introduction of the electrical process; Victor, Columbia, Brunswick/Vocalion, and Okeh as well were making field trips with portable equipment primarily to San Antonio, Texas. Victor had also been to El Paso by 1927, where they recorded the first border music *corridistas*, Hernández y Sifuentes, whose duet vocals with guitars made a big impression on Mexican singers everywhere. In cities like San Antonio, El Paso, and Chicago, the big labels set up mobile recording studios in hotel rooms. But they also built studios in Los Angeles and to a lesser degree in New York, where they began recording mostly Cuban and Puerto Rican musicians.

In the 1930s, with the Great Depression, several labels introduced budget lines, selling records at 25 cents each, a third of the regular price. Victor introduced the Blue Bird line, while Brunswick had the Vocalion label, which was soon taken over by Columbia. Other

Figure 13. The New York–based Okeh record label placed this ad in a San Antonio newspaper, seeking artists for daily recording sessions to be held "here in San Antonio" during two weeks in March 1928. The ad states, "If you have talent to sing or play a musical instrument, YOU ARE THE ONE WE NEED." Photograph courtesy of the Arhoolie Foundation.

Figure 14. Discos Victor, a subsidiary of RCA Victor, began operation in Mexico in the mid-1930s. The text on the illustrated record sleeve promotes records made with "High Fidelity" methods, noting, "They possess a new and surprising tonal realism." Photograph courtesy of the Arhoolie Foundation.

budget labels of the day, such as Okeh Records and the newly founded Decca label, became very active in San Antonio (fig. 13).

These records from the late 1920s and early 1930s are the source of many important local corridos. They were generally recorded in two parts, one on each side of the record, giving singers up to six minutes to deliver the song. This was also the time when many fascinating skits were recorded that give us a real picture of what life was like in that era. Most of the skits were recorded by the husband-and-wife team of Netty and Jesús Rodríguez, who were very popular in South Texas, where they appeared in theaters and tent shows.

As the 1930s went on, the music that was recorded became more stylized and formularized. Even corridos began to sound more arranged and treated more mundane subjects. Shellac, the main material that 78s were made of, became very scarce during World War II and the majors dropped the recording of ethnic music, including Mexican. As Victor opened recording facilities in Mexico by the mid-1930s, joining the then-dominant national label, Peerless,

Mexican stars became popular in the United States. But the demand was hard to meet due to import restrictions (fig. 14).

After the war, small labels sprang up everywhere. In South Texas, Ideal Records was the first major independent, soon followed by Falcon Records in McAllen. Of course there were many labels in Los Angeles, but Azteca was one of the biggest and earliest. By the time 45s appeared, it was even easier to make your own records. Some of the most interesting corridos were released on 45s, especially during the 1960s and '70s, a time of social upheaval for Mexican Americans marked by the Chicano Movement and César Chávez's organizing of field workers.

As I accumulated the vast Frontera Collection, I focused primarily on what I call border music—norteño, Texas conjunto, and Tejano. But the collection also includes many other styles, such as recordings by major

Figure 15. A delighted Chris Strachwitz digs through a haul of rare Cajun 78s purchased from a former juke-box operator in the 1980s. Photograph courtesy of the Arhoolie Foundation.

Mexican ranchera stars, early banda recordings, and pachuco music from Los Angeles.

After 1970, I made repeated road trips through Texas in order to record music for my Arhoolie label. As I drove, I also searched for records. I would visit juke box operators, junk stores, record shops, distributors, even record companies and radio stations. As 78s went out of style, proprietors became willing to sell old 78s cheaply or even give them away (fig. 15). The collection got an exciting boost when I purchased many local and regional items from the collection of radio station KCOR in San Antonio. I collected 45s in a similar manner and from similar sources. Not many years ago I purchased the stock of an old record shop and distribution company in Los Angeles that included lots of Azteca 78s, but primarily we loaded up 75,000 45s and 20,000 LPs, many of which were added to the Frontera Collection. I was lucky to become known among collectors of 78s as the only buyer interested in Mexican discs, and they would sell me items cheaply. On several occasions I was able to purchase incredible collections of old store stock dating back to the 1920s and '30s.

When Professor Guillermo Hernández first encountered my collection in the 1970s, he quickly realized its historical and cultural value. When he planned the next corrido conference at UCLA, he asked me who we could get to perform some corridos live. I said, you are in California: why not try for the biggest stars of this genre, Los Tigres del Norte? He did, and they apparently were impressed by the fact that their music was considered the literature of the people and was being studied by the biggest university in California. Los Tigres not only performed at UCLA's Royce Hall; they also formed a foundation and gave $500,000 to UCLA, of which a good portion has gone to the Arhoolie Foundation to digitize its vast collection of Mexican 78s. I list the recordings I like best in "My Fifty Favorite Mexican and Latin Recordings" (appendix G).

Looking back on recent changes in the record industry that have forced so many labels and record retailers to go out of business, I tell people we had a good hundred years. But I do miss it!

A Century of Corridos
The Musical History of Mexico and Its People

Of the hundreds of genres represented in the Frontera Collection, the corrido is the cornerstone.

Though it has roots dating back centuries to Spain and elsewhere, this distinctive song form is considered quintessentially Mexican, and relatively modern. From the late nineteenth century through the present day, *corridistas* have documented the actions and exploits of the famous, the infamous, and the anonymous everyman. Like newspapers for the literate classes, the corrido is a first draft of history, but in this case written by and for society's downtrodden and dispossessed.

In its simplest definition, the corrido is a ballad or narrative song. However, the genre's unique characteristics—the qualities that distinguish it as uniquely Mexican—have been the subject of study, discourse, and debate for the past century. All corridos are narrative songs, but not all narrative songs are corridos. Researchers and musicologists are still fine-tuning the standards that define the genre. In his 1999 scholarly article "What Is a Corrido?" (reprinted in appendix H), the former UCLA language professor and self-taught corrido expert Guillermo Hernández enumerated the characteristics of the genre, citing specific songs as examples, from the earliest corridos on record to the present day.[1] The vast majority of the corridos used in his study are represented in the Frontera Collection, often with multiple versions of each song. In the next section of this chapter we look at the meaning of those emblematic corridos and analyze the important differences among the versions available in the UCLA Frontera archives.

The fact that most of the songs cited by Hernández can be found in the Frontera Collection testifies to the depth and breadth of this important musical resource. The Frontera Collection is one of the world's most comprehensive repositories of this essential Mexican folk art. Within the archives, almost 4,000 items are listed under the genre of corrido, or one of its various subgenres.[2] That makes it by far the largest of the 2,600 genres identified in the collection.[3] However, the count does not represent 4,000 separate corridos, since some titles are counted more than once, as when the same song is performed by different artists or released on different labels by the same artist.

Chronologically and topically, the corridos in the Frontera Collection encompass virtually the entire one hundred–year lifespan of the recorded genre itself. They touch on topics from the Mexican Revolution to the Gulf War in Iraq, from the assassination of Pancho Villa to the assassination of John F. Kennedy. Since, as some researchers argue, the corrido was born and bred along the US-Mexico border region, it is not surprising that its themes include historic events in both countries. Thus, there are corridos about the Korean War and the terrorist attacks of September 11, about farm labor leader César Chávez and President Barack Obama. Although corridos continue to be written every day, the strength of this collection lies in its extensive holdings of corridos recorded on 78-rpm discs during the genre's golden era, the first half of the twentieth century. The collection also includes relatively recent corridos on 45s, LPs, CDs, and cassettes. This is a testament to the continued popularity of the style, which has enjoyed a commercial resurgence since the 1970s with the so-called narcocorrido, or ballad about drug smuggling. The Frontera archive clearly shows, however, that the narcocorrido is hardly a new phenomenon. As we shall see, it includes many samples of early border smuggling songs dating to the 1920s and '30s, during Prohibition, when distilled spirits and not cocaine were the subject of contraband.

The value of this corrido collection goes far beyond the simple cataloguing of recordings, with their arcane matrix numbers and elaborately designed record labels. Most popular music to some degree provides an expression of a people's sentiments, values, attitudes, and beliefs. But the Mexican corrido carries out this mission explicitly and overtly. It is considered the foremost folk expression of Mexico's rural, working-class culture, precisely the culture brought to the United States by generations of migrants since the Mexican Revolution. In fact, the corrido, by providing a running, real-time commentary on everything from sweeping historical events to personal tragedies, has helped define what it means to be Mexican in the twentieth century. So in this real sense, the corridos of the Frontera Collection provide a vivid, flesh-and-blood portrait of the Mexican character and an eyewitness perspective on the country's tumultuous history. This unique cultural portrait is conveyed through the actions of the genre's heroic protagonists, who can be criminals or revolutionaries, great leaders or simply ordinary men and women swept up by epic events (fig. 16).

The late Jaime Nicolopulos, one of the foremost academic experts on the corrido in the United States, explains the importance of the form:

> The corrido, whether composed orally by anonymous poets among the "popular" classes of society or written in the oral style for a "popular" audience, became one of the principal mediums for the expression of shared values and the celebration, commemoration, or satire of important people and events during late nineteenth and early twentieth centuries, bridging the categories of folklore proper and more or less commercialized popular culture.[4]

The Corrido as Oral History

In a testament to the enduring power of this oral tradition, the Smithsonian Institution organized a traveling exhibition on the corrido that premiered in Washington, DC, in 2002. Titled *Corridos sin Fronteras: A New World Ballad Tradition*, the exhibition featured a website, still operating nine years later, which states, "The corrido stories range in topic from the history of the Mexican Revolution, to a woman who shoots her lover because he is about to leave her, to a local hero who dies attempting to save a town. These ballads have survived centuries and will continue to be passed down to successive generations."[5]

The exhibition was curated by Hernández, former director of the UCLA Chicano Studies Research Center, which served as co-sponsor of the audiovisual show. Hernández, who also organized international conferences on the genre, stumbled into the culture of the corrido by accident. As a student in the early 1970s, he discovered his passion for the subject while

Figure 16. The corrido, or narrative ballad, served as a musical history of the tumultuous events of the twentieth century in Mexico, told from a popular perspective. This sepia-toned photo, circa 1918, shows twin brothers Florencio Estrada (with guitar) and Frumencio Estrada (with accordion), who went on to become military leaders during the Cristero Rebellion, which was sparked by government repression of the Catholic Church. The brothers, Cristero *coroneles* in the state of Durango, were killed in battle in 1936, near the end of the second Cristero conflict. Florencio became the subject of a typically tragic corrido written after his death, "Mañanas de Florencio Estrada." Although this corrido is not in the Frontera Collection, the tale of Florencio arises from the intersection of music and history where the corrido is created. Photograph courtesy of the Arhoolie Foundation.

exploring the physical record collection kept by Strachwitz at his label's headquarters near Berkeley. Three decades later as a faculty member at UCLA, Hernández became the driving force behind the creation of the Frontera Collection. As a result, many of the historic corridos he found so valuable and fascinating have become available to the public at large for the first time in digital form. Never before has so much of this recorded history been accessible to the world with a few keyboard clicks.

The digital archive of these classic corridos became a vehicle for Hernández to preserve and pass on what had always been historically an oral tradition. "Obviously, I didn't grow up with the corrido tradition," Hernández told a 2005 seminar sponsored by the Western Knight Center for Specialized Journalism at the University of Southern California. "I had to discover it through the recordings. It's really the best-kept secret of the Mexican tradition. I compare it to a cathedral or to one of the pyramids, except that this is a musical, verbal [monument], and it's one of the treasures of Mexican culture."[6]

Romance Roots

Because of its historic importance, the corrido is one of the most examined genres in the category of Mexican regional music. The seminal book on the subject is a 1939 study by Mexican musicologist and artist Vicente T. Mendoza (1894–1964). Titled simply *El romance español y el corrido mexicano*, the work remains a reference point for all subsequent serious inquiry in the field. Fifteen years later, Mendoza published another essential work, *El corrido mexicano*, and he continued writing on the subject right up until his death in 1964 at the age of seventy. His final work, published the year he died, is an anthology titled *Lírica narrativa de México: El corrido*.[7]

Most experts agree that the corrido has its roots in the narrative poetry of Europe, transplanted to the Americas by Spanish conquistadors through the *romance español*. "Although the *corrido* did not appear in its present form until the nineteenth century," writes Nicolopulos, "it has clearly identifiable roots that reach back into the heroic, oral-formulaic narrative poetry of the European Middle Ages, particularly the epic *cantares de gesta*, such as the *Cantar de Mio Cid*, and the extensive corpus of popular ballads known collectively as the *romancero viejo*."[8]

That tradition took root and flourished throughout the far-flung Spanish Empire. Thus, as noted by Hernández, Argentina and Chile have the oldest known corridos from the eighteenth century, predating those of Mexico. "It was probably a continental phenomenon, but in Mexico it really exploded as a genre," Hernández told a group of arts journalists during the 2005 seminar sponsored by the Western Knight Center for Specialized Journalism.[9]

The gestation of the genre in Mexico spans the turbulent one hundred–year period between the War of Independence of 1810 and the Mexican Revolution of 1910. The other defining historical event that helped shape the evolution of the corrido was the war between Mexico and the United States, which came midway through the century that separated independence and revolution. All three upheavals imbued the corrido with a growing sense of national identity. The corrido, in turn, helped shape that identity, at least in part, by expressing cultural resistance to occupying forces.

Although there is agreement regarding the ancient roots of the corrido, there has been debate about where precisely the genre originated in Mexico. Mendoza, the musicologist and composer, argued that the corrido was born in the central Mexican state of Michoacán. However, Américo Paredes, one of the leading corrido scholars in the United States, challenged Mendoza's theory, arguing instead that the style had its geographic and cultural origins along the US-Mexico border, where ethnic and cultural tensions became a sort of crucible.[10] Indeed, Paredes believed that the clash of cultures along the frontier between two countries with such disparities of wealth, power, and customs provided the impetus for the unique kind of corrido that developed in Mexico. The genre evolved in reaction to the invasion, the loss of territory, and the descent of the Mexican population into second-class social status.

In his introduction to Paredes's *Folklore and Culture on the Texas-Mexican Border*, Richard Bauman writes,

> For Paredes, the true *corrido* tradition centers around a spirit of heroic bravado, of defiant

manly self-confidence, and this spirit is rooted in the emergent sense of Mexican nationalism "stirred into life by the war with the United States and the French invasion and developed slowly but steadily during the thirty years of Porfirio Díaz's rule, coming into flower with the Revolution."[11]

The bravado and "manly self-confidence" were evident from the very first corrido on record, "El Corrido de Kiansis," about the early cattle drives across Texas to Kansas. Paredes calls it "the oldest Texas-Mexican corrido preserved in a complete form," dating it to the 1860s or early 1870s.[12] In this case, the conflict is not violent but professional, depicting the Mexicans as better cowboys than the hapless gringos.

The cultural clash at the heart of the genre is evidenced in the disparate ways the two sides viewed the corrido protagonists, as heroes or villains depending on one's point of view. To Anglos, they were bandits and outlaws who deserved to be tracked down and imprisoned or killed. To the corrido composers and their audience, they were folk heroes who defended Mexicans against the prejudice and brutality of Anglo society. The early corridos between 1860 and 1910 were populated by modern-day Robin Hoods such as Gregorio Cortez, Joaquín Murrieta, and Juan Nepomuceno Cortina, a Mexican rebel who led guerilla actions against Texas authorities to avenge the mistreatment of his countrymen in the area around Brownsville, Texas.[13] Paredes dubs Cortina "the first corrido hero" to emerge from the Lower Rio Grande Valley.[14]

These ballads of border bandits established the corrido not only as the definer of Mexican identity but as the expression of cultural resistance against the advancing dominant white or Anglo culture driven by the ideology of Manifest Destiny. Through this cultural expression, argues Manuel Peña in his foreword to another Paredes study, "Mexicans were mounting a sustained challenge to their subordination in the capitalist system that had emerged in the southwest by the end of the nineteenth century."[15]

The Frontera Collection has multiple recordings of corridos inspired by many of these Robin Hood–type bandits who became legends throughout the Southwest in the years leading up to the Mexican Revolution of 1910. In at least one case, Strachwitz and the Frontera Collection are credited with sparking contemporary interest in the mythic California figure of Joaquín Murrieta (or Murieta), the nineteenth-century Mexican outlaw whose severed head was paraded on display in mining towns throughout the state. Peña notes that Murrieta "actually came to the attention of modern scholarship in the 1970s" after Strachwitz included a version of the song in a corrido compilation, released on Arhoolie, his independent label.[16] The revival of interest in the defiant Murrieta was also fueled by the surging political and cultural awakening of the Chicano Movement, which embraced him as a symbol of resistance and rebellion against Anglo rule. The corrido in question was performed by Los Madrugadores (The Early Risers), a group that earned its name with its popular predawn radio show in Southern California, which served as an alarm clock for Mexican field workers during the Great Depression (fig. 17). The show also featured commentary by group leader Pedro J. González, who spoke out against the mass deportations of Mexicans at that time. In a case of life imitating art, the message of the Murrieta corrido was reinforced for working-class Mexican listeners when González was himself sent to San Quentin prison on trumped-up rape charges in 1934, the very year Los Madrugadores recorded the song. As American studies professor Shelley Streeby noted, "The story of the unjust

Figure 17. Los Madrugadores (The Early Risers) was a popular group in Southern California led by radio personality and activist Pedro J. González (*center*). González spoke out against mass deportations during the Great Depression and was sent to San Quentin on trumped-up rape charges in 1934. He is flanked by Fernando Linares (*far right*) and Victor Sánchez (*far left*) who, along with Jesus Sánchez, also recorded as Los Hermanos Sánchez y Linares. Also shown are Josefina Rivas (*left*) and La Prieta Caldera (*right*). The photograph, from the collection of Victor Sánchez, was used in a 1983 documentary about González, *Ballad of an Unsung Hero*. Photograph courtesy of the Arhoolie Foundation.

treatment and criminalization of a Mexican immigrant [Murrieta] in the United States must have taken on new and tragic resonances for that working-class audience during these years of intensified nativism and forced repatriation, especially in light of González's harsh experiences with the law."[17]

The Murrieta saga captured the popular imagination in the 1930s, decades after his death. The daring bandit, often pictured with long dark hair blowing in the wind, was the subject of alarmist newspaper articles, dime-store novels, and a book that became a Hollywood movie, *The Robin Hood of El Dorado*, released in 1936.[18] Still, not much is known about

Murrieta, who came from Sonora as a young man to join the California gold rush. The corrido chronicles his transformation from an immigrant searching for fortune to an outlaw seeking revenge on "vain Anglos" for killing his wife and his defenseless brother in cold blood. Though he admits killing thousands in revenge, he explicitly decries the "unjust" laws that label him a "bandido" ("Ay, que leyes tan injustas por llamarme bandolero"). Instead, he sees himself as the prototypical Robin Hood, robbing from the "avaricious rich" and "fiercely defending the poor and simple Indian."

The Frontera Collection has three versions of the corrido of Joaquín Murrieta recorded in two parts on 78-rpm records, all by some incarnation of Los Madrugadores. The 1934 recording on the Vocalion label was also released on Columbia with somewhat better fidelity. A slightly different version (same lyrics, different arrangement) was released on Decca by Los Hermanos Sánchez y Linares, composed of the two original members of Los Madrugadores, the brothers Jesús and Víctor Sánchez, along with Fernando Linares. The group now has its own compilation CD on Arhoolie, *Pedro J. González and Los Madrugadores, 1931–1937* (Arhoolie 7035), which features the two-part Murrieta corrido.

For Peña, this corrido perfectly exemplifies the genre as a vehicle for expressing the Mexican side of the interethnic clash with the dominant and abusive Anglo culture:

> "Joaquín Murrieta" does conform to the classical corrido of intercultural conflict so unique to the Southwest Border: it depicts a larger-than-life hero who either defeats the Anglos or goes down before overwhelming odds. This corrido, if its origin can ever be pinpointed, may yield proof that the Californios—themselves experiencing pressure from the Anglos—were in the vanguard in realizing this important folk music genre.[19]

In these heroic corridos, the larger cultural conflict is often dramatically played out in the dialog between the protagonist and his enemies, especially the hated Texas Rangers, referred to as *rinches* in the phonetic vernacular of border language. Among the most notorious of these heroic outlaws is Gregorio Cortez, a Mexican American rancher who shot and killed a Texas Ranger in what he considered self-defense. The incident, which took place in 1901 in Gonzales, Texas, was enflamed by a linguistic misunderstanding between Cortez and a translator for the pursuing Texas Ranger. This deadly failure to communicate underscored the tension between the increasingly marginalized Mexican American population and the overtly racist Anglo power structure in the border's cultural hot zone.

The story of Gregorio Cortez, documented on the front pages of newspapers in both languages, is the quintessential stuff that corridos are made of, reflecting the epic clash of opposing forces. The truth of this outlaw's life is more fabulous than fiction, and it contained more twists and turns than even a long corrido could recount. It is told in detail by Paredes in his 1958 book "*With His Pistol in His Hand*": *A Border Ballad and Its Hero*.[20] The book became the basis for a 1982 television movie, *The Ballad of Gregorio Cortez*, starring Edward James Olmos. The corrido stops with the hero's capture following one of the biggest manhunts in US history, but there's much more to the story. Cortez was almost lynched while in jail, and his case provoked mob attacks on the Mexican population of the Rio Grande Valley. The racial tensions were inflamed by a sensationalist Anglo press that called Cortez an "arch fiend" and lamented the fact that he had not been lynched. He was convicted, exonerated on appeal, tried again, and eventually sentenced to life. He married while serving his sentence and managed to turn the entire upper floor of the jail into his private "honeymoon suite," with the help of sympathetic guards. Amazingly, he was pardoned by the Texas governor after an appeal for clemency from a most unlikely source, Abraham Lincoln's daughter. He was released and then remarried for the fourth and final time shortly before dying in 1916, officially of pneumonia though his family always believed he was poisoned.

It's not hard to see how such a story would become the stuff of legend and how a ballad about it would be passed down through generations. More than one hundred years after the confrontation that propelled this anonymous farmhand into the history books, people are still singing his praises. Strachwitz personally witnessed that enduring appeal one day during the 1960s, when a Swedish record distributor came to visit him in California. At the time, Strachwitz himself was just starting to discover this grassroots music of working-class Mexican Americans, attracted by the passion he perceived in the music and the emotional reaction he witnessed among its fans. Strachwitz decided to introduce his guest to the genre by taking him to a cantina in the Mission District, the famed Latino barrio in San Francisco, where a Texas-style conjunto was performing. To his amazement, the second song in the band's set was the classic corrido of fugitive folk hero Gregorio Cortez. The nascent corrido collector noticed how enthusiastically the audience responded, half a century after the incident that inspired the song and a world away from the Wild West frontier where the tale originated.

"It was quite extraordinary," says Strachwitz. "Corridos have an amazing life. They are written about events that took place decades ago, but they still resonate with people as if they were hearing them for the first time."[21]

For a hardcore, beat-the-bushes record collector like Strachwitz, discussions about where, geographically, the corrido evolved are not just academic exercises. The answer tells us why he was able to acquire so many recorded corridos during his record-hunting days in the United States. His early interest in the blues had already made him familiar with the border regions of the Southwest, especially Texas. His domestic musical explorations therefore placed him at the center of the corrido's theater of action. That made it possible for him to branch out and explore this seemingly "foreign" song style, which actually was another branch of the US roots music he so cherished.

Two factors, one historical and one technological, converged to turn the American Southwest into a recording mecca for the Mexican corrido. In his summary of these developments, Nicolopulos notes that early recording equipment was so bulky, cumbersome, and expensive that it remained anchored in New York during the infancy of the recording industry. During the first decade of the 1900s, only a handful of corridos were recorded in New York by the three major record labels at the time, Victor, Columbia, and Edison. In Mexico City, where US labels also set up the first recording studios, production was "geared to the tastes of the ruling classes," Nicolopulos notes. The combination of social prejudice and high recording costs made recording prohibitive for a genre that was considered inferior and low-class. Despite these early obstacles, at least three dozen corridos were recorded in Mexico before 1910. Notably, Herrera Robinson in Mexico City recorded two famous corridos— "Ignacio Parra" and "Heraclio Bernal"—about rebels during the prerevolutionary dictatorship of President Porfirio Díaz. The artist waxed them on cylinders for the Edison recording company but, significantly, failed to re-record them later for Victor and Columbia, as he did for much of the rest of his repertoire. The fact that the artist abandoned these rebel ballads, Nicolopulos argues, proves that the seditious undercurrent in corridos was well understood in the capital, the center of both political power and the recording industry. In other words, corridos were censored as a voice of dissent.[22]

The Mexican Revolution of 1910, the first peasant uprising of the twentieth century, overthrew the thirty-year oligarchy of President Díaz, who was known for his affinity for European, especially French, culture. The ensuing twenty-year civil war forced a mass migration of Mexico's poor north into the United

Sates, as people fled the chronic violence and sought some social stability. One side effect of this mass displacement was the creation of a market for the corrido that was immune to the upper-class sensibilities and censorship of centralized power in Mexico City. During the same period, meanwhile, a technological revolution was working to overthrow the old mechanical methods of sound recording. With the advent of the electrical recording process in the 1920s, recording equipment became less expensive and much more mobile. As a result, record labels could more readily take their recording equipment to the places where their artists and audiences were located.

These social and technological developments set the stage for the golden age of corrido recordings, between 1928 and the 1940s. Cities across the Sunbelt—El Paso, San Antonio, Los Angeles—became the new capitals of corrido recordings. By then, the US recording industry had already shown an appetite for what was known as vernacular music, made for low-income blacks and whites alike. The industry's interest was piqued by the unexpected success of so-called race records, beginning with the first recordings made in 1920 by black vaudeville artist Mamie Smith, which were runaway hits at the time. Seven years later, talent scouts from New York record labels sent to Tennessee discovered two of country music's original superstar acts, Jimmie Rodgers and the Carter Family, in a single audition.

As in the black and country music markets, the recording of Mexican music was partly spurred by furniture retailers in Mexican American barrios who sold record players as incentives for customers to visit their stores. One sign that the marketing strategy worked was uncovered by researchers looking at immigration and repatriation patterns. They found that one of the items most frequently carried by migrants returning to Mexico during the 1920s was the phonograph.

For corrido composers and performers on the US side of the border, these changes gave them a creative advantage they did not have in their native country—freedom of expression. As Nicolopulos puts it, "The shift of technology across the border had created the discursive space necessary for the expression of sentiments that could not have been undertaken in Mexico."[23]

Decoding Corridos

In the annals of US folklore, there are countless examples of songs with working-class themes, a tradition carried into the twentieth century by such contemporary artists as Bob Dylan and Johnny Cash. Many tunes tell of the hardships and heartbreak of coal mining, for example, such as "16 Tons" by Tennessee Ernie Ford. And there was a popular wave of topical songs in the 1920s, sparked by the success of Vernon Dalhart, a classical tenor who became the country's first country music star. Dalhart's 1924 hit "The Wreck of the Old 97," about the 1903 derailment of a mail train in Virginia, has parallels in Mexican corridos about similar disasters, such as floods and earthquakes. And his 1925 worldwide smash "The Prisoner's Song," its lyrics carved on the wall of a Georgia jail cell by an inmate, unleashed a wave of popular prison songs, directly influencing many Mexican corridos that picked up on the trend.

Still, Strachwitz finds little in US roots music to compare with the corrido. There are no US musical counterparts with the corrido's distinct combination of elements: (a) journalistic structure, with its who-what-where-when details of time and place; (b) direct dialog between protagonists and/or observers; (c) a clash of opposing forces—heroes versus oppressors, people versus Mother Nature, man versus his own destiny; and (d) lasting impact and relevance over generations. In this regard, Strachwitz says, "I haven't encountered anything close to the Mexican corrido."[24]

The fascination expressed by Strachwitz, a German postwar immigrant, echoes the wonder described half a century earlier by American adventurer and historian Edward Larocque Tinker. The urbane New York author first heard a corrido performed live when he occupied a front-row seat to history—on the battleground during the Mexican Revolution. In 1915 Tinker was a civilian observer with Pancho Villa's troops during the fabled Battle of Celaya, a major defeat for Villa that signaled a turning point in the civil war. On the evening after the battle, Tinker describes hearing voices and guitars as he wandered among the boxcars where Villa's tired, bedraggled troops were quartered. Looking for the source of the music, he came upon a group of men and women around a campfire, "listening in the moonlight like fascinated children to the singing of three men." He gives the following account:

> I too was fascinated and thought they sang some old folk tale. As verse after verse, however, took the same melodic pattern I suddenly realized that this was no ancient epic, but a fresh minted account of the battle of the day before. . . . It was a *corrido*—hot from the oven of their vivid memory of the struggle between Villa and Obregón—the first one I had ever heard.[25]

Of course, not everyone has the chance to be an eyewitness to the events that inspire corridos. As José Eduardo Limón observes, these events are of particular interest to the corrido community; they "capture and articulate this community's values and orientations."[26] But for outsiders, be they other Mexicans or foreigners, the exact nature of an event and therefore its significance are not always clear from the lyrics. Many corridos, for example, tell of local heroes involved in events that remain entirely parochial. Sometimes the lyrics provide only a sketchy story that presumes the listener knows the facts not stated explicitly. Many examples of such anonymous corridos exist on the Orfeo label, a small and obscure record company based in Monterrey, Nuevo León. The Frontera Collection contains the only existing copies of several Orfeo recordings, including rare tracks by Eugenio Abrego and Tomás Ortíz, both individually and as Dueto Abrego, before they emerged as the legendary norteño conjunto Los Alegres de Terán (fig. 18).

Orfeo recorded local corridos during the early 1950s, all with a local theme and a local hero involved in events that history has overlooked or forgotten. The Frontera Collection has seventeen corridos on Orfeo titled simply with the name of the protagonist in each: Mario López, for example, whose pockets were rifled and shoes stolen after he was murdered in 1953; Ezequiel Rodríguez, who was killed the day before Christmas Eve, 1941; and José Rentería, killed just before high noon on one June 15 in a shootout with a rival, Erasmo Salina.

In the latter song, which was written by Ortíz and accompanied by the Dueto Abrego, the two rivals call each other out for some unstated reason. They walk safely away from other people, pull their pistols, and fire. The duel leaves Rentería dead, and still anonymous to the listener. In the UCLA database, the label note pithily sums up the substance of the song: "It sounds like it was a classic showdown." After Salina confesses to the killing, calling it self-defense, the song ends with a verse that gratuitously adds import by linking the killer with a famous revolutionary: "Soy de Durango, muchachos, donde nació Pancho Villa. Aquí termina el corrido de ese Mayor Rentería." (I'm from Durango, boys, where Pancho Villa

LOS ALEGRES DE TERÁN
Eugenio Abrego, accordion
Tomás Ortiz, bajo sexto

10341 San Pablo Ave.
El Cerrito, Ca.94530   Photo by Susan Titelman

...rom the film

CHULAS FRONTERAS

BRAZOS FILMS

Figure 18. Legendary norteño duo Los Alegres de Terán, in a promotional still from the Les Blank film *Chulas Fronteras*. The 1976 documentary helped focus attention on the neglected music of the US-Mexico border that is at the heart of the Frontera Collection. Shown are Tomás Ortiz (*left*) and Eugenio Abrego, performing with an unknown bass player. Photograph courtesy of the Arhoolie Foundation.

was born. Here ends the corrido of that Major Rentería.) In similar sketchy fashion, the Orfeo corridos recount the tragic fates of other men—Gil Treviño, Juan Osuna, Agustín Jaime, Manuel Cantú, Agapito Casanova, Roberto Reyes, and so on.

"They don't seem to have much of a point to them," said Strachwitz in a 2005 interview.

To the average listener, it'll just say, "Well, this guy went to the cantina and he was sitting there, and—bam, bam!—the police came and shot him." That may sound like any average cantina fight but it's hardly ever just that. Each

one of them has a much deeper meaning than what you think. The people involved are usually well-known figures of some kind [caught up] in a special event that took place. And that's the big mystery very often. You see, the people there are familiar with the stories and we are not.[27]

Most of the time, the historical facts surrounding a corrido are shrouded by the conventions of the art form and the passage of time. In one rare case, however, UCLA's Hernández researched and documented the historical events surrounding a famous early corrido called "El Contrabando de El Paso,"

Figure 19. "El Contrabando de El Paso" by Leonardo Sifuentes and Luis Hernández, released in 1928 by the Victor Talking Machine Company, was a precursor of the modern narcocorrido and the subject of a research paper by Guillermo Hernández, professor of Chicana/o studies at the University of California, Los Angeles. Photograph courtesy of the Arhoolie Foundation.

considered a precursor of the popular narcocorrido of today.[28] It was first recorded in 1928 by the duo of Leonardo Sifuentes and Luis Hernández, pioneer corridistas from El Paso, Texas, for the New Jersey–based Victor label (fig. 19). Although the composer is not credited, the song is written as the first-person account of a prisoner who describes being transported from El Paso to the federal penitentiary at Leavenworth, Kansas, where he was to serve a sentence for smuggling. The exact type of contraband is not specified, but the song was written at the height of Prohibition (1920–33), when smuggling liquor from Mexico was a booming underground trade. Today's modern narcocorridos, which some contend glorify the drug trade and lionize traffickers, boast much more explicit descriptions of smuggling and the violence surrounding it.[29] By contrast, "El Contrabando de El Paso" was a cautionary tale,

ending with the imprisoned composer lamenting his own bad luck.

Using classic investigative techniques, Hernández unearthed the likely composer, a man named Gabriel Jara Franco who was incarcerated at Leavenworth prison at the time. Hernández examined prison records that logged a series of correspondence between the prisoner and Leonardo Sifuentes, half of the musical duo that first recorded the song. Relying on sketchy information in the lyrics, Hernández even re-created the likely itinerary of the prisoner train, stop by stop. In his case study, "En busca del autor de 'El contrabando de El Paso'" (In Search of the Composer of "El Contrabando de El Paso"), Hernández concludes that neither Jara nor his family ever saw a dime of royalties for the song; these would add up to millions in the eight decades since he wrote it, given that it has been recorded many times over the years.[30] The Frontera Collection lists dozens of versions of the song, including relatively recent renditions by Los Alegres de Terán (1975) and Lorenzo de Monteclaro (1976), the latter on the Los Angeles–based Fono-Rex label. Most of these versions list the song as public domain; some use an alternate spelling in the title, "El Contrabando del Paso," substituting a contraction for the proper name of the Texas border city.

The most significant versions continue to be the early ones, recorded as two-part corridos on 78-rpm discs. The archive lists five such versions on different labels, including the original by Hernández y Sifuentes on the old Victor label with the scroll design and the logo of the gramophone and the dog above the slogan "His Master's Voice." Over the years, Strachwitz collected five copies of this same record, but the notes indicate that one copy is extremely damaged and another has a manufacturing error, with two B sides. The collector's strategy of buying old 78s in lots yielded the multiple copies and ensured that at least one version of this historic recording would be in good condition.

Recording corridos in two parts was a common practice in the early years of the recording industry. Before the introduction of the long-play record in the 1950s, songs were limited in length by the amount of music that could fit on one side of a 78-rpm record, which was essentially a single. So corrido composers were constricted by the technology of the day. They could only fit so much of the story, only so many details, on one side of the old shellac records. To tell the whole story and get to the all-important climax where the protagonist often dies heroically, they had to use both sides of the record. The listener would play side A, then flip the record over and finish the story on side B.

"The local people knew the story, but they wanted to hear the ending, how bravely the guy died and all that," says Strachwitz. "That's the part they wanted to hear, the part where he dies, because that's the redeeming part."[31]

These two-part corridos became a special focus of Strachwitz's record hunts throughout the years (see "Two-Part Corridos in the Frontera Collection," appendix I). He picked up every two-part corrido he could get his hands on. The Frontera Collection boasts 183 two-part corridos, including five of the six recorded about the celebrated case of Juan Reyna, a prisoner who committed suicide in his San Quentin prison cell in May 1931, just five months before his scheduled parole date. The case received so much sensational press coverage in its day that Nicolopulos calls it "the 1930 Hispanic equivalent of the Rodney King trials of our own time."[32]

Reyna, a young Mexican American, was picked up by police in Los Angeles after a traffic accident. While in custody in the back seat of a patrol car, he disarmed a police officer and shot him in the head with the officer's own gun. The prisoner claimed self-defense and the case became a cause célèbre in the community, inflamed by accounts that police had used racial insults against the suspect before he fired. The trial made front-page news for days in *La Opinión*, the city's Spanish-language newspaper. The song in the Frontera Collection with the most detailed, reportorial version of events is the "Corrido of Juan Reyna" by Los Hermanos Bañuelos (Vocalion 8383), written by Luis M. Bañuelos. This version, which refers to police as "chotas," Mexican slang for cops, hews faithfully to the facts of the case, including the courtroom fistfight between the prosecutor and the defense attorney, described separately in a book by Arizona State University historian Edward J. Escobar.[33] However, the song does not include the grisly detail that Reyna had "slit his jugular" in his jail cell, as recounted in "Suicidio de Juan Reyna" (Vocalion 8425), written by F. Galindo and performed by the duet of Nacho y Justino. Regardless of composer, however, all the Frontera versions of the corrido enshrine Reyna as a hero for defending not only himself, but also the honor of the Mexican people in general. In this sense, the crusading corrido serves as a counterbalance to the sensationalist yellow press of the era, including the *Los Angeles Times*, which tended to inflame racial antagonism against the city's Mexican minority.

When dealing with longer corridos, some recordings inexplicably restricted the narratives to one side, truncating the story or eliminating the climax altogether. Strachwitz discovered the inherent limitations of the one-sided corrido with a recording of "La Delgadina," a heart-wrenching tale of father-daughter incest. The tragic song tells of a lovely and noble young woman who pays the ultimate price after refusing her father's sexual advances. The version by the Cuarteto Carta Blanca (Vocalion 8677), however, ends on one side of the record with her father ordering servants to imprison his daughter for her refusal. He orders them to lock her up tight so her cries won't be heard. ("Remachen bien los candados, que no se oiga su vocina.") Strangely, the song ends without ever reaching its tragic conclusion. Instead, side B features the unrelated track "En el Rancho Grande." Ironically, famous Texas singer Lydia Mendoza, who made her first recording with her family as the Cuarteto Carta Blanca quartet (fig. 20), herself went on to record a more complete version of the song under her own name for the Bluebird label (2989), this time including the tragedy's denouement. In part 2 on side B, Delgadina pleads for a glass of water because she is dying of thirst. When her father finally relents, the servants find Delgadina already dead, "with her little hands crossed, her little mouth wide open" ("con sus manitas cruzadas, su boquita bien abierta").

"Delgadina" is a corrido with direct roots in the romances of medieval Spain. In some traditional versions of the song, the first verse refers to the philandering father as a king who has three daughters, Delgadina being the youngest. This opening reference to royalty does not appear in any of the seven versions of the song contained in the Frontera Collection. By some convention of time, these twentieth-century versions all skip straight to the second verse. They refer only to Delgadina's father, not to any royal ranking, though most keep the reference to his eleven servants as a clue to his social status. Also, they all set the same stage for the tragedy when the father instructs Delgadina to put on her silk dress and accompany him to Mass, clouding his true intentions with hypocrisy. He makes his sinful proposal to her after the service. (In some versions, the father invites his daughter to Mass in Morelia, Michoacán;

Figure 20. This portrait of the fabled Mendoza siblings was taken in the 1950s. The family launched its recording career in San Antonio as the Cuarteto Carta Blanca in 1928, led by their parents, Francisco and Leonor Mendoza. The original quartet included Lydia Mendoza (*bottom left*), who went on to a celebrated solo career as "La Alondra de la Frontera" (The Lark of the Border). Her sisters, María (*bottom right*) and Juanita (*standing*), also performed as a popular duet, Las Hermanas Mendoza. Their older brother, Manuel (*top*), often toured with them. Photograph courtesy of the Arhoolie Foundation.

others say the state of Durango.) Curiously, three of the seven versions credit three different contemporary composers; the other four properly give no composer credit, since the true author is unknown.

The most complete version in the Frontera archives is by the artist known only as El Cancionero Solitario, or the Solitary Songster, a stage name that poetically evokes the itinerant troubadours who first popularized this style of music. In this version (Bluebird B-3409), featuring solo voice and a single guitar accompaniment, the lyrics make one passing reference to the father as king, when Delgadina addresses him directly to respectfully refuse his proposition: "Papacito de mi vida, eso sí no puede ser, porque tú eres rey, mi padre, y mi madre tu mujer." (Dearest Papa, this cannot possibly be, because you are king, my father, and my mother is your wife.)

Other versions contain the same line, but drop the word "rey," or king. But the most interesting detail offered by this version comes when Delgadina asks for water while imprisoned. In all the other versions, she only asks her father, who complies too late to save her. But here, Delgadina seeks to quench her thirst by first appealing to her mother and her sister, and they both refuse before she turns to her father as a last resort. The women's refusal to help underscores the patriarch's total dominion over his family. The mother's response adds to Delgadina's pain and to the depth of the tragedy: "Delgadina, hija mía, no te puedo dar el agua." (Delgadina, my daughter, I cannot give you water.) She refuses her daughter's plea because she's afraid of what her husband might do to both of them. When the father ultimately gives in, he orders his servants to take her water in a glass of crystal on a gilded plate, a symbol of his wealth and his mercy, which becomes a mockery in the face of her cruel death by deprivation.

The many variants in the versions of this corrido continue to be the subject of formal analysis and research among historians and musicologists.[34] In her 1999 book *The Decolonial Imaginary: Writing Chicanas into History*, Emma Pérez offers a feminist perspective on the old verse. Through her analysis of four cultural figures—Delgadina, La Malinche, the Indian woman Silent Tongue, and Tex-Mex singer Selena—Pérez suggests a "third space

feminist perspective" that "unveils women's desires through their own agency."[35] In the case of Delgadina, tragically, "only in death is she free." Pérez writes:

> The father's desire leads to tragedy for both father and daughter. . . . Delgadina, like any other young woman, was supposed to have hidden her sex. She is to blame for having a sexed, female body that a man will desire. Yet as a sexed woman, she enters a double bind. There is no way she can guard her sex enough from male seducers. By becoming a woman, she has already failed; despite the fact that she refused her father, opted for imprisonment, and finally dies, she is still blamed because she caused her father to desire her. The patriarchy is not blamed, however. It is left intact.[36]

Today, new versions and interpretations of "Delgadina" appear on the Internet, a modern-day amplifier of the ancient oral tradition that gave rise to corridos. Several versions are now posted on YouTube, the popular video site, including some by contemporary recording artists such as Irma Serrano and the San Jose–based group Los Humildes. The most revealing YouTube version is perhaps the least professional. It was posted by a soft-spoken man named Gilberto; based in Mexico, he joined YouTube in 2007 and goes by the moniker tubero9999. The sixty-eight-year-old with gray hair and beard films himself as he strums his guitar and sings a long version of the song, including the verses about the mother and sister refusing Delgadina's dying pleas. This scruffy, apparently working-class performer, seen in his modest surroundings, best captures the spirit of the troubadours of old with this brief self-description on his YouTube channel: "Estudioso de la música, sin mas ambiciones." (A student of music, with no further ambitions.)

The long legacy of "Delgadina," from oral tradition to recorded song to YouTube video, underscores the enduring appeal of the Mexican corrido as a genre, now well into its second century. Hernández artfully explained that appeal at the end of his essay on "El Contrabando de El Paso," the corrido whose once anonymous composer would have remained so were it not for the professor's passion for the art form and his efforts to understand its timeless popular attraction.

"Just as happens with other unforgettable corridos, various generations continue to sing 'El Contrabando de El Paso' because in the lyrics and melody there is a series of codes that manage to touch the most sensitive chords in lovers of the genre," Hernández writes. "Gabriel Jara, although unknown and forgotten, recovers for the rest of us a touch of human existence and sensibility. That is, perhaps, all we can ask of art in any time or place."[37]

Thirty Corridos that Define the Genre

In his essay "What Is a Corrido? Thematic Representation and Narrative Discourse," Hernández explored the themes, style, and structure of corridos throughout history, using thirty songs as examples to illustrate his points.[38] He cited many of the songs from various books and studies about the historic narrative genre. A review of these songs shows that almost all are included in the Frontera Collection, many in various versions. With these thirty songs, Hernández was able to tell the full story of the corrido—its history, stylistic structure, and thematic makeup. Now, researchers and students of the style can access the songs themselves to bring this history to life.

What follows is a guide to the thirty songs, grouped as they are in the essay—that is, clustered according to the particular theme or feature they illustrate. There is also a brief analysis of the variations in the versions found in the Frontera Collection in cases where a significant distinction is relevant. A complete list of the corridos included in this section can be found in appendix J, "Thirty Corridos that Define the Genre," along with a brief description of the literary qualities they exemplify.

Theme: Character

The Heroic Protagonist: "El Nuevo Corrido de Madero"

Performer: Camacho y Pérez
Label: Okeh 16696 / Columbia 4863 /
Vocalion 8696

The version of this famous corrido that is sung by the duo of Camacho y Pérez appears on three labels in the collection: Okeh, Vocalion, and Columbia. They are separate releases of the same recording made by the duo in Los Angeles around 1930. Manuel Camacho, half of the team, is credited as the author. As with many early corridos, the accompaniment is simply two guitars.

Hernández selected this corrido to illustrate the character of the corrido protagonist, "who generally serves as a model of conduct under extraordinary circumstances." In this song, Francisco Madero, Mexico's first revolutionary president, is depicted as a courageous man—"tan hombre." After overthrowing Porfirio Díaz, he goes immediately to the prisons and releases the inmates, who were, presumably, held unjustly by the dictator's administration. The bold act establishes Madero's character in the second verse, and the corrido goes on to tell of the political betrayals and intrigue that eventually cost him his life. His heroic death is recounted in another corrido, "El Cuartelazo," discussed below.

Moral Authority: "Gregorio Cortez"

Performer: Trovadores Regionales
Label: Vocalion 8351, Parts 1 and 2
Performer: Timoteo Cantú and Jesús Maya
Label: Ideal 294-A

As we have seen, this seminal corrido tells the story of a Texas Mexican folk hero who shoots a sheriff in what he considers self-defense, then eludes capture before finally surrendering voluntarily. The song is used here to illustrate the establishment of the protagonist's character in contrast to that of his opponents. Although the killings committed by Cortez are not glossed over in the lyrics, he expresses remorse and justification: "No siento haberlo matado . . . la defensa es permitida." (I'm not sorry I killed him . . . self-defense is permitted.) By contrast, his pursuers are depicted as mercenaries who hunt him for money, led by "perros jaunes," or hound dogs.

"The protagonist's defeat is generally a tragic, although heroic, event," writes Hernández. "Like other corrido figures, Cortez demonstrates moral authority despite his vulnerable situation."

The two Frontera versions of the song stick faithfully to the lyrics, but with different styles. The release by Trovadores Regionales on Vocalion is the first recording of the famous corrido, according to Strachwitz. It is a two-part corrido with guitar accompaniment, which was common in the late 1920s and the 1930s. The extreme surface noise is the result of wear on the record.[39] The release by the duo of Maya and Cantú has a more contemporary, post–World War II sound but much less narrative detail; it features the conjunto-style accompaniment of Narciso Martínez on accordion.

Humor and Sarcasm: "Corrido de Yurécuaro y Tanhuato"
Performer: Hermanos Bañuelos
Label: Brunswick 41192
The title of this corrido refers to the names of two rival towns in the western Mexican state of Michoacán, Morelia and Guadalajara, which are engaged in battle. (The first town is spelled incorrectly on the Brunswick label as "Yurecuardo," an error reflected in the

database.) This is another two-part 78 recording, with the unusual accompaniment of a *salterio*, or dulcimer. As with many corridos loosely based on historical events, the exact causes of the conflict are not specified, though the lyrics detail specific strategies and actions, such as cutting off water to one town. The presumption is that the listener is sufficiently familiar with the facts and historical context to make sense of the story.

Hernández cites the song as an example of humor used to highlight character qualities. One verse, for example, ridicules the fighters on one side who get scared and turn to run, crying like little kids ("llorando como chiquitos"). Writes Hernández, "Often the negative qualities demonstrated by the enemy merit irony and sarcasm from the narrator. Running in the middle of battle is a mark of cowardice."

On a side note, this corrido is unusual in that the narrator reveals his identity at the end. After describing the taking of prisoners en masse and their forced march through the streets like a procession, the narrator delivers a farewell in the last verse, which is customary. Then, in a kind of punch line, he identifies himself as one of the prisoners who wrote the song: "Aquí va la despedida; escúchenla, compañeros. Estos versos los compuso uno de los prisioneros." (Here goes the farewell; listen up, comrades. These verses were written by one of the prisoners.)

Female Narrator: "Corrido de Jesús Leal"
Performer: Trío Nava
Label: Columbia C4054
Performer: Lupe Martínez and Pedro Rocha
Label: Vocalion 8263, Parts 1 and 2
Performer: Los Alegres de Terán
Label: Tico M-10-3683 and Columbia 3683-C
Performer: Lorenzo de Monteclaro
Label: Fono-Rex Records FR-500-A
Performer: Hermanas Segovia
Label: Ideal 508-B

This is another corrido about a folk hero from Michoacán, a gunslinger who is on the run and making fun of his pursuers. Again, the song sets up a contest between the protagonist who is taken prisoner and his captors, led by Felix Alba. The most complete version, as usual, is the two-part corrido, in this case performed by the duo Pedro Rocha and Lupe Martínez with guitar accompaniment (fig. 21). The version by Los Alegres de Terán is shorter, eliminating some verses from the narrative.

At the end, the narrator once again is identified as the composer, a young woman from Tepic ("una joven de Tepic"). Hernández notes that the gender of the narrator remains the same in subsequent recordings, even when the singers are men, which is most often the case. "This shift in narrative voice, from composer to performer, may modify a narrative," Hernández notes. "In 'Jesús Leal,' this shift accentuates the narrator's awareness of the act of creation ('estos versos te compuso / una joven'), demonstrating, as MacDowell has noted, the genre's capacity for reflexivity."

However, the identity of the narrator, and thus the issue Hernández describes, disappears altogether from all but one of the versions of the song contained in the collection. Only the longer two-part corrido by Rocha and Martíne concludes with the line identifying the young female narrator. Oddly, even the version by the female duo of Hermanas Segovia drops the narrator's identity, though they, as females, are the only performers who could have legitimately claimed the credit.

The differences in song length and content, however, may be the result of recording industry practices. Strachwitz notes that, at least in part, the era in which these versions were recorded determined the length and format. In the early period, when the Trío Nava record was made, most corridos were limited to one

Figure 21. Pedro Rocha (*left*) and Lupe Martínez were a popular and influential duet in San Antonio in the 1930s, during the golden age of the recorded corrido. The Frontera Collection includes several two-part corridos by Rocha and Martínez, including "Corrido de Jesús Leal," which has lyrics from the perspective of a female narrator, although the singers are male. Photograph courtesy of the Arhoolie Foundation.

side of the disc as one-part corridos, with few exceptions. Next, chronologically, comes the Vocalion disc by Rocha and Martínez, recorded in two parts during the golden age of the recorded corrido. "All the others are post WW II when records became largely juke box and radio fodder—and thus only on one side of the record and if possible even less than 3 minutes," notes Strachwitz.[40]

Women as Protagonists: "Contrabando y Traición"
Performer: Armonía del Norte
Label: Cash 1040-A
Performer: Los Fronterizos de Nuevo Laredo
Label: Disa-87-A
Performer: Gerardo Reyes
Label: Caytronics CY-8179-A
Performer: Felix H. Morales
Label: Exito Regional Records ER-113-A
Performer: Dueto Carta Blanca
Label: Akron 304

This is considered one of the original tunes that launched the narcocorrido craze of recent decades. The story of a female smuggler who kills her cheating partner and makes off with the bounty of their illegal trade has spawned a book and a movie. The most popular version, the smash 1974 recording by Los Tigres del Norte, appears in the Frontera Collection in three formats (LP, CD, and 45-rpm single), including the release on their original label, Fama Records of San Jose.[41]

Hernández cites the song as a milestone in the portrayal of women in corridos. As the protagonist, Camelia is clearly as cunning and ruthless as her male counterparts. She kills her partner, Emilio, with seven shots and makes off with the proceeds from their drug deals, again making fools of her pursuers, who captured neither her nor the money:

> Sonaron siete balazos,
> Camelia a Emilio mataba;
> la policía sólo halló
> una pistola tirada,
> del dinero y de Camelia
> nunca mas se supo nada.

"Previous heroines of corridos were, frequently, negative models who were censured for violating codes of behavior," Hernández writes. "A new day for the role of gender in the corrido is also marked by a narrative voice that blames Emilio for his fate and does not condemn Camelia."

Heroic Horses: "El Potro Lobo Gateado"
Performer: Agapito Zúñiga
Label: Discos Escorpion ES-186-A
Performer: Rancheros del Norte
Label: Del Valle DE-209+
Performer: Chelito Velasco
Label: Texas 1022B
Performer: Trío Los Aguilillas
Label: Columbia 6277-X and Columbia 1150-C
Performer: Gaytán y Cantú
Label: Ideal 232
Performer: Carmen y Laura
Label: Ideal 011
Performer: Mariachi México del Norte
Label: Aguila 5005-A

In the world of corridos, tales of heroic horses are second only to tales of heroic people. This country tale of a horse swap leading to a heavy-betting horse race has been recorded by Mexico's top stars, such as Vicente Fernández and Antonio Aguilar. The Frontera Collection contains seven versions of the song, whose arrangements range from the polka style of Gaytán y Cantú (with Narciso Martínez Conjunto) to the traditional ranchera sound of the Mariachi México del Norte. One recording features Agapito Zúñiga on the piano accordion (fig. 22).

Hernández cites the song as an example of how protagonists portrayed in corridos may be human or animal, "as long as their treatment conforms to its heroic canons." In "El Potro Lobo Gateado," whose title refers to the color of the winning horse, the animal is as much a hero as its rider.

However, the lyrics cited by Hernández describing the horse's extraordinary prowess are not included in most of these recorded versions. The only recording with the exact verses he cites is the one by Mariachi México del

Figure 22. Agapito Zúñiga (*left*) recorded many corridos on a range of topics, from horse races ("El Potro Lobo Gateado") to the 1969 Apollo moon landing ("Astronautas en la Luna") to the 1970 hurricane that devastated Corpus Christi, Texas ("Desastre del Huracán Celia"). A top songwriter and performer in the Frontera Collection (see appendixes D and E), Zúñiga is among the few Texas conjunto artists to play the piano accordion, as seen here in a studio portrait with an unidentified fellow musician. The photograph was taken in Matamoros, Mexico, in the 1950s. Photograph courtesy of the Arhoolie Foundation.

Norte. In these stanzas, the charro brags that his horse is "like lightening" and is bound to win; the only thing he needs is "wings to fly on the wind" ("nomás alas le faltaban para volar por el viento").

Interestingly, the Lobo Gateado wins in all versions of the corrido, but not always in the same way. In the most heroic version cited by Hernández, the horse disappears into a cloud of dust and winds up at the finish line. But in the other versions, the underdog aspects of the story are underscored. In these versions, the Lobo Gateado is left behind in the dust at the starting gate, but he winds up winning by three heads, vindicating the decision by the charro who took a chance on buying him in the first place.

Theme: Values and Qualities
Courage: "Arnulfo González"
> *Performer: Lalo González*
> *Label: Capitol 71034*
> *Performer: Conjunto de Los Hermanos Banda*
> *Label: A D 10016*
> *Performer: Pedro Yerena and Juan Montoya*
> *Label: Bego BG-359*
> *Performer: Conquistadores*

Label: Victor 70-7998-A
Performer: José Alfredo Jiménez
Label: Seeco 12060B / Columbia 3512-C
Performer: Conjunto Hermanos Garza
Label: Discos Dominante DD-690-B
Performer: Trío Calaveras
Label: Victor 23-5198-B
Performer: Timoteo Cantú
Label: Ideal R-152
Performer: Juan y Amalia Mendoza ("Dueto Tariácuri")
Label: Columbia 3458-C
Performer: Juanita y María Mendoza
Label: Azteca 5047
Performer: Montañeses del Alamo
Label: Anfión 10-111-A

Hernández begins his discussion of values in the corrido tradition with a song about a violent duel between two men, Arnulfo González and an unnamed official of the rural police, a force that ruthlessly defended the dictatorship of Porfirio Díaz. To some, it may seem an odd choice to illustrate the valued qualities of the genre's protagonists, considering the needless and deadly confrontation at the heart of this story.

The confrontation starts when the rural policeman takes offense at the way González is looking at him. That leads to the duel in which the policeman first is shot, then sets a trap as he pretends to lie dying. As a final request, he asks González to finish him off, rather than leave him to die slowly. When González obliges and returns to deliver the final shot, the policeman unleashes a surprise attack and shoots González dead first: "¡Qué bonitos son los hombres que se matan pecho a pecho, cada uno con su pistola, defendiendo su derecho!"

It is a macho story that could apply to some modern-day street gangs. Yet Hernández does not focus on the men's short fuses or their conceit, violence, and trickery. He argues that the song emphasizes courage, one of the qualities most commonly attributed to protagonists. In "Arnulfo," both opponents are praised for their bravery in hand-to-hand combat, regardless of who is right or wrong. In fact, men who shoot each other point-blank ("pecho a pecho," chest to chest) to defend their honor are considered beautiful ("bonitos"), a word usually reserved for women. The number of versions of this corrido in the Frontera Collection—seven 78s and three 45s—is evidence of the enduring popularity of these values.

Virtue and Villains: "La Toma de Zacatecas"
Performer: Bernardo San Román y Luis Vera
Label: Okeh 16325
Performer: Dueto Los Errantes
Label: Camden 95-4
Performer: Luis Hernández and Leonardo Sifuentes
Label: Victor 81653-A & B, Parts 1 and 2

The lyrics vary substantially among these three versions of "La Toma de Zacatecas," a corrido about one of the most important military victories of the Mexican Revolution. Verses are missing or rearranged and wording is changed. However, all three contain the biting political critique highlighted by Hernández.

In part, the song ridicules Victoriano Huerta, the counterrevolutionary figure who spearheaded the coup against President Francisco Madero, the martyred revolutionary president lionized in "El Nuevo Corrido de Madero." This battle, led by Pancho Villa and his Division del Norte, represented a key victory leading to the ouster of Huerta, Villa's nemesis. "Enemy characters are often denigrated, and the negative representation of their values and qualities stands in contrast to the virtues of heroic opponents," writes Hernández.

Here, Hernández notes, Huerta is portrayed as a corrupt drunk ("borracho") who was weak in battle and whose defeat would cause him to be even more bowlegged, with "patas chuecas" (literally, crooked legs). In the immediate aftermath of the 1914 battle, this corrido took on particular importance in disseminating the news because Huerta banned newspapers in Mexico City from reporting on his defeat, as Jaime Nicolopulos notes.[42]

The two-part 78-rpm recording by Hernández y Sifuentes contains a line that is missing from the other two versions but which underscores the contrasting qualities between the hero and his enemies. Villa is said to have spared the life of his prisoners, giving them clothing and money: "Fíjense lo que hacía Villa con el que hacía prisionero. Les perdonaba la vida, les daba ropa y dinero."

The only 45-rpm recording among these versions, by Los Errantes, once again raises the thorny question of corrido authorship. This version, backed by a conjunto with accordion, credits Tony Vélez as the composer, although the earlier versions do not identify the songwriter. Some Mexican sources cite the author as anonymous. Vélez kept the credit, and the publishing rights, in other recent recordings of the song, including one made by famed Mexican singer and movie actor Antonio Aguilar. It is hard to fathom how the real author could have emerged decades after the song was written to claim songwriting credits and royalties.

"In the music business, both in the US and Mexico, it has long been a practice for various composers to claim credits for songs in the public domain," notes Strachwitz. "Today, it is more common for some to take arranger credits, but you can't collect as much. It is greed!"[42]

Satirizing the Enemy: "Corrido de Inés Chávez García"
Performer: Hermanos Bañuelos
Label: Vocalion 8312, Parts 1 and 2
Performer: Trío Iglesias – Calvo – Silva
Label: Universal 4103-A & B, Parts 1 and 2

This rather obscure corrido once again underscores the contrasting qualities in corrido characters. However, in this case, the song makes just a passing, ambiguous reference to the secondary character, Rafael Espinoza, who asks to join forces with the title's protagonist, a revolutionary general, whose "valor was second to none." In an early verse, Chávez dismisses Espinoza's overture with a single, contemptuous line: "What do I need you for?"

The rejected recruit is never mentioned again in the song, nor is the listener given any specific clue as to why he was not fit to serve. The dismissive treatment signals what Hernández calls the song's "satirical intent," drawing a contrast between the heroic leader and the useless wannabe.

"Local contemporaries—who knew Rafael Espinoza and the reasons for such disdain—must have appreciated the scene and fully comprehended its significance," writes Hernández. "Narrators frequently include such revealing textual and contextual details that describe the roles and reputations of the characters represented." The full meaning and message, however, is left for subsequent generations to decipher.

The main difference between the two 78-rpm versions in the Frontera Collection is the tempo. The Bañuelos recording is slower and has a slightly clearer sound. There is a discrepancy, however, in the spelling of the protagonist's first name in the title. The New York–based Vocalion label spells it "Ines," while the Universal label, based in El Paso, Texas, goes with "Inez." Historians identify the general who operated mainly in Michoacán as José Inés Chávez García. But far from a hero, he is described as a bloody and barbaric bandit who earned a nickname comparing him to Attila the Hun.

Taking Sides: "La Derrota de Villa en Celaya" or "La Toma de Celaya"

Performer: Pedro Rocha y José Angel Colunga
Label: Decca 10141, Parts 1 and 2
Performer: Hermanos Bañuelos
Label: Brunswick 41169 Side A & B /
Columbia 3463X Side A & B
Performer: Cancioneros de los Santos
Label: Columbia 3958-X

Just as corridos can enshrine heroes, they can serve to dethrone them. In this ballad about the humiliating defeat of Pancho Villa at Celaya, the revolutionary hero is cut down to size. "While admiring composers created a cycle of corridos representing Francisco Villa as a heroic protagonist, his opponents painted him with the ridiculousness associated with enemies," notes Hernández.

The belittling begins when the revolutionary hero is referred to by his real surname, with a warning not to brag nor be so sure of his victories:

No te las eches Arango
ni te las vayas a echar,
ni las cuentes tan seguras
que las más hechas se van.

(Don't flatter yourself Arango
nor count on the outcome,
even sure things slip away.)

The song goes on to ridicule his fighters:

Decían los pobres villistas
—Ya no semos tan temidos,
por dondequiera rodamos,
parecemos armadillos.

(We are no longer so feared,
wherever we roll,
we look like armadillos.)

The final blow is delivered with a word play on the verb *tomar*, which means both "to drink" and "to take." Thus: "Ya se les afiguraba a esa pobrecita gente que tomaban a Celaya como tomar aguardiente." (Those poor pitiful

people figured that taking Celaya would be as easy as drinking firewater.) The line elicits a subtle but audible chuckle from the two singers, Pedro Rocha and José Angel Colunga, who seem to be enjoying the diminishing of Pancho Villa, who at the end confesses that his enemies are "too much for me."

A different corrido, not mentioned by Hernández, gives a much more sympathetic perspective on Villa's defeat at Celaya. This corrido, in fact, avoids the use of the word defeat (*derrota*) in the title. It's called "La Toma de Celaya," or The Taking of Celaya, a two-part corrido by Los Hermanos Bañuelos (fig. 23). (These versions on Brunswick and Columbia are two distinct recordings with separate matrix numbers.) This corrido still portrays Villa as a brave revolutionary hero and laments his defeat as a tragedy. Rather than end with ridicule, this song ends with Villa ordering his troops to fall back to Torreon where they can regroup, suggesting he's ready to fight on another day.

Figure 23. "La Toma de Celaya" by Los Hermanos Bañuelos, a 78-rpm release on Columbia, presents a heroic portrayal of Pancho Villa, in contrast to other corridos that mock the revolutionary leader for his defeat at Celaya. Photograph courtesy of the Arhoolie Foundation.

Like narcocorridos in modern times, the corridos of the revolution favored one side or the other, depending on the author.

Theme: Time and Setting

Where and When: "Arturo Garza Treviño"
    Performer: Leonel Olivares
    Label: Akron 335
    Performer: Timoteo Cantú y Jesús Villa
    Label: Ideal 661-A
    Performer: Cancioneros del Bajío
    Label: Falcon A208
    Alternate Title: "Kilómetro 1160"
    Performer: Conjunto de Los Hermanos Garza de Monterrey, N.L.
    Label: Discos Dominante DD-619-B

Fans are accustomed to hearing their favorite corridos open by establishing the time and place of the events that are recounted in the song. This matter-of-fact introduction is the signal that a dramatic story is about to unfold, and audiences respond with a sense of anticipation that is renewed with every listening. In the above-mentioned corrido about the Battle of Celaya, the song starts by telling us when Villa departed from his base in Torreón. The year is given as 1915. The day is Holy Thursday. The time is "in the morning": "En mil novecientos quince, Jueves Santo en la mañana, salió Villa de Torreón a combatir a Celaya."

Time and setting are crucial elements of a corrido because "geography and chronology imprint a sense of realism that provides historical credibility and relevance to the actions of the characters," notes Hernández. "Commonly mentioned corrido settings include the plaza, street, dance hall, bar, or battlefield. Natural settings are frequent: a road, a sierra or a hill, a mine, or an agricultural field. Although less usual, the portrayal of an official setting also occurs, such as a church, a military installation, or an office."

Sometimes the time and setting are not so specific. In referring to the corrido about the death of Arturo Garza Treviño, Hernández notes that the scene "only provides a point of reference." In the opening line of these four Frontera Collection versions, the song indicates the exact marker on the highway, kilometer 1160, where the protagonist drove his car off a highway and later died: "Kilómetro once sesenta, carretera nacional."

"To experienced corrido listeners," Hernández writes, "such outlines are sufficient, since previous knowledge and imagination help recreate the suggested scene." However, in this case, Hernández understates the importance of the location provided in the opening lyric. On long open stretches of many Mexican highways, the posted kilometer signs, comparable to mile markers in the United States, are the only indication of the geographic location along the road, measuring from its starting point. In this corrido the kilometer sign not only indicates the location of the crash, but also alludes to the isolation in which the hero met his untimely death. Another line notes that God was the only witness to the scene ("Solo díos presencio el cuadro"). Later, the location is elevated almost to holy ground when the narrator notes that it was there, at "the 1160," where the protagonist "paid for all his offenses." That verse gives the song's only clue to the identity of the main character, Arturo Garza Treviño, noting that he was a true friend but also a convict: "Era amigo del amigo, otras veces fue convicto, pero en el 1160, pagó todos su delitos." Strangely enough, the version by Cancioneros del Bajío attempts to sanitize, perhaps, the biographical data by changing "convicto" to "cumplido," converting the protagonist from a convict to a man of his word. That, however, leaves the listener wondering what his "delitos" or offenses may have been.

Contrary to the suggestion by Hernández that the time and setting are vague in this song because listeners fill in the blanks, the cold, impersonal highway number poetically evokes the tragedy of the accident. The significance of the isolated location is heightened by the contrast to the doomed driver's anxious anticipation of arriving at his destination of Nuevo Laredo. That highway marker is so important, in fact, that one of the Frontera versions changes the title of the song from the name of the protagonist to the place where he died. Otherwise, the version titled "Kilómetro 1160," by Conjunto de Los Hermanos Garza, follows the lyric faithfully.

Theme: Language

Corridos are so full of regional idioms, slang, and colloquial expressions that even experienced listeners sometimes need to have reference books handy to interpret the meaning. Corrido lyrics often reflect local dialects and contain linguistic anachronisms in use at the time they were written. Writes Hernández:

> Their vocabulary is often distinctively regional and follows Mexican Spanish rural traditions. . . . The pronunciation and inflection of performers will parallel local dialectal tonalities serving as a marker to corrido audiences that the message conveys their social and cultural assumptions. . . . The listener, therefore, is expected to possess knowledge of local linguistic customs in order to appreciate nuances in a narrative.

The range and variety of vernacular language used in corridos could fill a dictionary, from the Anglicisms of the border region to the Afro-mestizo conventions of speech in the Costa Chica region of the southwestern state of Guerrero. In "Filadelfo Robles," a Costa Chica corrido cited by Hernández, the lyric refers to the protagonist's "sombra pesada" (heavy shadow), a concept, inherited from African

spiritual belief, suggesting an individual's status. The song also refers to the man's "broza," a regionalism that means "gang" or "group." Thus, as the song says, "Ese Filadelfo Robles tenía la sombra pesada. El andando con su broza ni los perros le ladraban." (Filadelfo Robles had a heavy shadow. When he was about with his gang, not even the dogs barked at him.)

As an example of Spanglish creeping into corridos, Hernández returns to "El Contrabando de El Paso," the prisoner song. In what he calls "linguistic borrowings," the song mentions a "dipo" (depot), a "coche" (coach), and a "corte" (court).

Poetic Rhythm: "Rosita Alvírez"
   Performer: Conjunto de Los Hermanos Banda
   Label: A D 10016
   Performer: Juan y Amalia Mendoza "Dueto Tariácuri"
   Label: Columbia 3458-C
   Performer: Trío Calaveras
   Label: Victor 70-7518-B
   Performer: Hnos. Barrón
   Label: Disa 189-B
   Performer: Fernando Rosas con Mariachi Vargas de Tecalitlán
   Label: Imperial 163-B

Regardless of idioms, slang, or colloquialisms, corrido lyrics hew to formal poetic patterns and rhythms. "The poetic form is customarily based on variable octosyllabic quatrains with a rhyme scheme that coincides in the even lines, as is customary in the copla," states Hernández. He cites the following verse from the corrido "Rosita Alvírez":

A-ño-de-mil-no-ve-cien-tos,	A 8
muy-pre-sen-te-ten-go-yo,	B 8
que en-un-ba-rrio-de-Sal-ti-llo,	C 8
Ro-si-ta-Al-ví-rez-mu-rió.	B 8

All five versions in the Frontera Collection stick faithfully to this structure, with minor word variations. What is most interesting, however, is that the songs all have vastly different arrangements and instrumentations. They range from the standard conjunto norteño of Los Hermanos Banda, to the refined guitar and harmonies of Trío Calaveras, the rousing mariachi of the Mendozas and Fernando Rosas, and finally the bouncy Tex-Mex cumbia of the Hermanos Barron.

The song, about a woman who is shot and killed after refusing a man's advances at a dance, is also interesting for what it says about the place of women in some sectors of Mexican society. There is even a suggestion in one line that the victim is responsible for her own fate, though the line is not included in all versions. (This aspect of "Rosita Alvírez" is discussed further in chapter 6.)

Hernández notes that there are many variations on the standard poetic structure of corridos such as "Rosita Alvírez." Some have more or fewer syllables; others have slightly different rhyming patterns. However, these variations have tended to disappear over time, as counterintuitive as that may sound.

> Irregularities are more common among older corridos whose oral diffusion increases the possibility for the creation of variants. In contrast, contemporaneous corridos are generally transmitted through electronic means of production and communication and, therefore, tend to maintain a single narrative textual version and regular metrics. This poetic tendency in modern corridos also influences their linguistic conventions: they are products of popular culture rather than oral tradition.

Narrative Discourse

Hernández identifies seven distinct narrative sections of the corrido: fate, pursuit, challenge, confrontation, defeat, judgment, and farewell. He goes on to enumerate the various elements that each of these narrative sections can contain:

> Fate encompasses anticipation, omen, and chance. Pursuit may involve plans, coercion, chase, and escape. Challenge may take the form of ridicule, offense, defiance, provocation, aggression. The confrontation may be a duel, a battle, an attack, or a skirmish. Defeat may comprise capture, imprisonment, sentence, execution, and death. The judgment involves thought, reflection, deduction, advice, experience, and lamentation. The farewell encompasses remembrance, memory, nostalgia, and reputation.

It is rare to find a corrido that contains each and every narrative section, Hernández explains. However, without a minimum presence of these narrative sections, especially challenge, confrontation, and defeat, the researcher argues that a song may "lack the emotional power characteristic of the genre and may be excluded from its corpus." The researcher then provides a sample of songs that illustrate each theme.

Fate: "El Corrido de Reyes Ruiz"
Performer: Los Montañeses del Alamo
Label: Columbia 1601-C
Performer: Hermanos Yáñez con el Conjunto de Narciso Martínez
Label: Ideal 573

This song provides a simple but essential lesson regarding fate. The protagonist, Reyes Ruiz, decides to ignore his mother's advice to refrain from attending a September 16 (Independence Day) festival and is murdered as a result. Without explaining her premonition, his mother warns him not to attend and adds that he can go another day: "ahí irás en otra ocasión." In the lyrics cited by Hernández, even his friends caution him to listen to his mother's advice: "Lo mejor será no ir, si tu madre te lo evita, no sabes tu porvenir." (It's better if you don't go; if your mother is preventing it, you can't know what may happen.) The protagonist defies his mother's premonition and goes anyway. He stops to drink, then gets in a fight for reasons unexplained. The confrontation leads to a rumble on the outskirts of town during which he gets stoned, then stabbed, and dies.

The two versions in the Frontera Collection, both on 78-rpm recordings, differ in their details of what happens. Significantly, the one by Hermanos Yáñez actually makes no mention of the mother's warning, removing the element of "fate" from the narrative altogether. In fact, there is no mention of the mother at all in this version, and the friends have no dramatic role; they are just present. The song starts with Reyes Ruiz getting into a bar fight with a character named Plutarco, who doesn't appear in the other versions. It's Plutarco who has speaking lines, saying he's reluctant to fight in the center of town and convincing the others to take the fight to the outskirts. (In the other Frontera version, these lines are spoken by Reyes Ruiz himself after the fight starts.) After the protagonist is stoned and stabbed, Plutarco runs away, promising never to return to Ruiz's town ("a tu tierra")—a rather empty gesture at that point.

The Colombia recording by the famed Montañeses del Alamo hews more closely to the original corrido (fig. 24). In this case, however, there is no mention of a September 16 celebration. Reyes is having dinner at home when three friends show up and invite him to a fandango, or party. The mother then issues her warning, but the friends don't support her as in the version cited by Hernández. They simply leave with the protagonist and stop at the cantina, where the fateful fight ensues. Interestingly, though, the fight in this song takes place between Reyes Ruiz and his friends, again for no specific reason beyond the drinking. Their conflict is foreshadowed in the first verse, which establishes that Reyes will be killed in a fight "three against one." He then tells his friends he'll fight them outside of town, leading to this gruesome verse:

> Se fueron a la orilla,
> se agarraron a pedradas.
> Se acercaron poco a poco,
> hasta darse puñaladas.
> Luego que lo apuñalaron,
> se sentaron a chupar,
> mirando de carcajada,
> ver a Reyes penar.

> (They went to the edge of town,
> they laid into each other with rocks.
> Little by little they got closer,
> until they started stabbing each other.
> After they stabbed him,
> they sat down to drink,
> cackling with laughter,
> watching Reyes suffer.)

This harsh ending makes the mother's warning all the more tragic. Remember, in this song, the three murderous friends visited the victim's home, where he was having dinner with his mother. Instead of heeding her, he goes with the traitors to drink. As Hernández explains, "The identification of a vice will be an indication that tragedy is awaiting a culprit; usually recklessness or breaking the norms of good conduct causes the unfortunate end."

Pursuit: "Belén Galindo"
Performer: Trovadores Norteños
Label: Ideal 868-A

To illustrate the element of pursuit, Hernández cites two of the most popular corridos in history about legendary bandit-heroes from the late eighteenth century. "Gregorio Cortez," in which the protagonist is pursued by Texas Rangers, has been discussed in detail above. "Heraclio Bernal," about a bandit from Sinaloa considered a prerevolutionary figure, is one of the most recorded corridos of all time, with thirty-six separate releases on 78, 45, LP, and cassette by a total of twenty-three artists in the full Frontera Collection.

Figure 24. Los Montañeses del Alamo was a Mexican regional ensemble with a distinctive instrumentation featuring flute and sax, but no accordion. Founded in the 1930s near Monterrey, Mexico, Los Montañeses del Alamo performed frequently at the famed sombrero-shaped restaurant outside the city, El Sombrero Charro (see figure 47). They recorded many corridos included in the Frontera Collection. Photograph courtesy of the Arhoolie Foundation.

"A common scene in corridos portrays a heroic protagonist who is chased by a group of enemies under overwhelming and unjust conditions," writes Hernández. "The picture of a humble and vulnerable man who successfully evades his ferocious pursuers provides [the protagonist] with a larger-than-life stature."

In many cases, the pursuit is a real chase and the corrido provides the specifics: the capture, the escape, the harrowing conditions, the strategies, the thoughts and statements of both the pursuers and the pursued. However, Hernández notes, sometimes "the persecution takes a symbolic form that involves the coercion or intimidation of the protagonist by someone who has a higher position of authority or social and political prominence." Such is the case of the lesser-known corrido about Belén Galindo, an innocent young bride who falls victim to her mother-in-law's evil plot to alienate her from her husband.

In the version by Los Trovadores Norteños, the only one contained in the Frontera archives, we learn at the start that "the poor Bélen Galindo" was stabbed to death just three days after her wedding. The twisted scheme is revealed in the first few verses, as the wicked mother-in-law offers her son's wife an illicit proposal. Implying with a wink that the young woman is the cheating kind, "la suegra" suggests an affair with a wealthy suitor who will "give you money to spend" ("te da plata pa' gastar"). Incensed, the young woman righteously rejects the offer, standing up to her mother-in-law with moral indignation:

> Quítese de aquí, Señora,
> no me venga a molestar.
> Usted me levanta falsos,
> y yo no le doy lugar.
>
> (Get away from here, Madam,
> don't come to bother me.
> You're telling lies about me
> and I give you no reason for that.)

Interestingly, the lyric quoted by Hernández adds a significant twist to the young woman's retort. Instead of accusing the mother-in-law of lying, in this version, titled "Mañanas de Belén Galindo," the young wife proclaims her innocence: "Mire que yo no soy de ésas, no me doy ese lugar." (Look, I'm not that kind of woman. I don't put myself in that place.)

Notice the similar turn of phrase in the final lines of both versions, each defending honor from a different angle. In the Frontera recording, the daughter-in-law puts the mother in her place by asserting that she gives no cause or quarter for the accusation: "y yo no le doy lugar." In the other version, she puts herself in a virtuous place by asserting she would never cross that line: "no me doy ese lugar." In either

case, she expresses indignation to protect her unimpeachable character.

This is not enough to prevent the tragedy. Incensed at being rebuffed, the mother-in-law tells her son, Polo, that Belén is cheating on him. Polo angrily confronts the innocent woman and stabs her to death, but quickly regrets his crime and laments his wife's dead body.

In a common convention of the day, the song genre is identified on the label as a "tragedia," a tag justified by the lovers' sad fate:

> Por un falso de su suegra
> Belén está en el panteón,
> y Polito por su crimen
> fue a parar a la prisión.
>
> (For her mother-in-law's lie
> Belén is in the cemetery,
> and Polito for his crime
> wound up in prison.)

Obviously, the story is meant to arouse moral outrage in the listener, as Hernández points out: "The coercion demonstrated toward the main character also produces a double response on the part of the listener: sympathy toward the misfortunes of the protagonist and a deep sense of antagonism for the injustices perpetrated by the oppressors."

Challenge: "Ignacio Parra"
Performer: Trío Nava
Label: Columbia C4059

Hernández cites this corrido about yet another prerevolutionary figure as an example of the courage of protagonists in facing challenges, even those that could lead to their deaths. Yet, in this rendition by Trío Nava, the only one to date in the UCLA database, all the rich details that highlight that bravery are missing.[44] Instead, we get a bare-bones story about an admired man with a big heart ("de mucho corazón") who is targeted by authorities and quickly shot dead. At the outset, the hero's courage in confronting his enemies is established, but in general terms:

Ignacio Parra decía
que era hombre y no se rajaba,
que montado en su caballo,
solo con Dios no peleaba.

(Ignacio Parra would say
that he was a real man and didn't back down,
that once mounted on his horse,
he'd fight with anybody but God.)

In the broader lyrics cited by Hernández, however, Parra displays defiance in the face of specific dangers. Playing to the listeners' expected approval, he heaps scorn on his pursuers, mocking as pitiful the inept soldiers of the powerful Porfirio Díaz and daring the dictator to send him some better ones ("que les mande otros mejores").

In other words, to the feared federal military, Parra taunts, "Is that all you've got?" Today, that kind of David-versus-Goliath gumption is immediately understandable to fans of Bruce Willis action movies. But in prerevolutionary Mexico, it was tantamount to a war cry for the masses.

"The pride and courage of heroic protagonists justify their open defiance of their enemies," explains Hernández. "Such boldness, however, must not be interpreted as arrogance or vanity, flaws of character usually ascribed to enemies. That is, the challenge serves to mark offended righteousness, highlighting the vices of opponents and asserting the positive values guiding the actions of favored characters."

Even though the Trío Nava version on Columbia is skimpy on narrative details, Hernández considered it historically quite valuable. "This [78-rpm] record was found only recently but astonished and delighted Guillermo," notes Strachwitz. "Prior to finding this one, the only other version we had was one by Los Alegres de Terán, in which Parra is portrayed as a bandit whose death is cheered. This one was apparently a revelation because, even in the early 1920s when this record was made in New York, it gave the people's side of him, in contrast to later versions."[45]

Confrontation: "Valente Quintero"
  Performer: Trío Los Tucanes
  Label: Continental 147-B
  Performer: Angelina y Toño con el Mariachi Güitrón
  Label: Peerless 2354
  Performer: Balboa Brass de Manny Quintero
  Label: Bego BG-668
  Performer: Dueto Azteca con el Mariachi Reyes de Chapala
  Label: Aguila 264
  Performer: Hermanos Yáñez
  Label: Falcon A156
  Performer: Carmen y Jaime con Los Montañeses del Alamo
  Label: Ideal 032

In the typical corrido, Hernández explains, the core confrontation can include a contest between race horses ("El Moro de Cumpas") or a clash with Mother Nature, as in the corrido about the deadly flood when a dam failed in Santa Clarita, California, in 1928 ("La Inundación de California," Cancioneros Acosta, Columbia 4883-X). But there's no better way to illustrate the element of confrontation in corridos than with an old-fashioned gun duel between two military men, as in the oft-recorded "Corrido de Valente Quintero."

Second lieutenant Valente Quintero, who fought with Madero's revolutionary forces, and major Martín Elenes squared off with deadly results in 1921. There were no heroics or high-minded principles involved, however. The two men were drunk and fought over the music they demanded to hear at a party.

The six versions in the UCLA database are remarkably similar. The song starts when

Valente Quintero straps on his "carrillera" (bandolier) and heads out to another town. His girlfriend warns that his military rival is drunk and something bad is likely to happen. Nevertheless, Valente goes and immediately demands that the band play a tune called "El Toro," much to his rival's displeasure, since he was enjoying his own "música de viento," or wind instrument music.

Valente exhibits defiant bravado as he tells the band, "Si el mayor paga con plata, yo se los pago con oro." (If the major pays with silver, I'll pay you with gold.) When the band director claims they don't know the song, Valente then asks for that other rebel corrido, "Heraclio Bernal." That enrages Elenes, who emerges to tell Valente "you are not a man." Of course, those are fighting words and the two men walk away, "arm in arm" (or "hand in hand," depending on the version), to fight the duel. By the time police arrive at high noon, both men are dead. That's the only mention of time in the song, indicating perhaps that the two rivals had been drinking all night.

In most versions, shots are fired and it's all over. Only one of the six Frontera recordings—by Trío Los Tucanes on the Fresno-based Continental label (fig. 25)—gives specifics of how the two men died. And it's quite dramatic:

Valentín cayo primero,
dándole cuenta al Creador.
Entre la vida y la muerte,
le dio un balazo al mayor.

(Valentín fell first,
giving account to the Creator.
Between life and death,
he fired a bullet that hit the major.)

Concludes Hernández: "The genre can be considered as epic-tragic because it poses a denouement that cannot admit of a happy resolution for both adversaries."

Figure 25. "Valente Quintero" by Trío Los Tucanes, a corrido about a man who is killed at a dance, was released on Continental, a label based in Fresno, California. Photograph courtesy of the Arhoolie Foundation.

Defeat: "El Cuartelazo"
  Performer: Hermanos Chavarría
  Label: Columbia 4372-X, Parts 1 and 2
  Performer: Dúo Atasoseno
  Label: Columbia 4180-X
  Performer: María y Juanita Mendoza
  Label: Azteca 5052

"El Cuartelazo," or coup d'état, recounts the final days of Francisco Madero, the first president to take office after the Revolution of 1910. All three versions in the Frontera archives tell the same general story, with more or less detail. All of them include the verse in which an opposing army officer, the nephew of deposed dictator Porfirio Díaz, orders Madero to resign or face execution. Madero defiantly refuses, setting up his tragic downfall. Additional verses expanding on Madero's principled resistance are offered only in the 78-rpm version by Hermanos Chavarría, which is a two-part corrido and thus has more time to tell the story.

This version adds two verses that make Madero seem even more heroic, and his death even more tragic.

> Madero estando en palacio,
> dice, "Qué ingrata es mi suerte.
> Doy la vida por el pueblo,
> yo no le temo a la muerte."

> Madero les contestó,
> "No presento mi retiro.
> Yo no me hice presidente,
> fui por el pueblo elegido."

> (Madero, from the presidential palace,
> says, "How undeserved is my fate.
> I give my life for the people,
> I do not fear death."

> Madero answered them,
> "I will not resign.
> I did not make myself president,
> I was elected by the people.")

In addition, the two-part recording on Colombia is the only one of the three to contain this key line, which is quoted by Hernández in his analysis:

> Señores, les contaré
> lo que en México pasó:
> que una bola de asesinos
> a Madero asesinó.

> (Gentlemen, I shall tell you
> what has occurred in Mexico:
> that a bunch of murderers
> have killed Madero.)

The other two versions omit the line, removing the direct expression of outrage.

Still, all versions recount the horror of the ten-day siege to depose the doomed leader, describing the fear that gripped the city and the scenes of dead and injured on the streets. Curiously, there are variations in the description of which part of the populace reacts with tears. When government forces start bombing the Citadel (La Ciudadela), the Dúo Atasoseno notes that people were crying ("estaba gente llorando"). But the rendition by sisters Juanita and María Mendoza (figs. 26, 27) notes only that "the women were crying" in reaction to the same assault:

> Otro día por la mañana,
> las mujeres llorando,
> de ver la ciudadela
> Que la estaban bombardeando.

Perhaps this and other minor differences were enough to justify a songwriting credit for Leonor Mendoza, the matriarch of the famous musical family from San Antonio. The questionable composer credit is listed on the Azteca label, based in Los Angeles, though the other two labels don't identify a songwriter, as is frequently the case with historic corridos. Whether she wrote it or not, this version does get extra points for getting the dates correct. While the other two versions establish the year in question as 1911 and 1912, respectively, the Mendoza family version pegs it at 1913, the

Figure 26. Juanita and María Mendoza, of the famed Mendoza family of San Antonio, performed as the popular duo Las Hermanas Mendoza. The Frontera Collection contains scores of performances by the sisters on Río, Ideal, and other independent labels. Their recordings include the well-known corrido "El Cuartelazo," about the coup that overthrew Mexico's first revolutionary president, Francisco Madero. Photograph courtesy of the Arhoolie Foundation.

Figure 27. "Tú Eres Culpable" (You Are To Blame), a romantic ranchera written by Daniel Garzés and performed by Juanita and María Mendoza, was recorded on Rio, one of many independent labels in the Southwest. The company was run by businessman Hymie Wolf in offices behind his popular record shop in San Antonio. The label design featured a cowboy lassoing a bucking bronco. Photograph courtesy of the Arhoolie Foundation.

actual year in which Madero was overthrown and executed.

"The defeat of one of the opponents is an important turning point in corrido narratives," writes Hernández. "These courageous but fatal conditions often provide corrido protagonists with an aura of martyrdom. Thus, a national figure of the stature of Francisco I. Madero, murdered for political reasons, is portrayed as a victim of heartless enemies."

Judgment: "Carga Blanca"
  Performer: Los Cuatesones
  Label: Corona 2032 and Corona 2331
  Performer: Los Cuatezones
  Label: Del Bravo Records DB-102-B / Bravo Records BO-9028-B
  Performer: Lydia Mendoza
  Label: Corona C-2403-B

Performer: Juan Montoya y Pedro Yerena
Label: Norteño 62
Performer: Los Caporales
Label: D.L.B. 696-A
Performer: Los Montañeses del Alamo
Label: Del Bravo B-264-A
Performer: Los Alegres de Terán
Label: Falcon 1647
Performer: Los Bravos de Matamoros
Label: Ideal 2320-B

This seminal narcocorrido tells of a drug sale gone bad when the Mexican dealers are betrayed by their buyers on the US side of the border. With traditional accordion accompaniment, the story starts with the dealers crossing the Rio Grande by night and heading straight to San Antonio, to a "house of stone on Calle Navidad." The sale goes off without a hitch until the dealers head home with their cash and are ambushed on the street. A gunfight breaks out on "that night of terror," leaving three dead and two injured. The cash disappears from the scene, but gossip has it—"you know how people talk"—that all the money went back to its original owner.

The original 78-rpm recording of the popular tune is the first one listed above (Corona 2032) by Los Cuatesones, a duo that includes the corrido's composer, Manuel C. Valdéz, an important figure in the San Antonio scene at the time. Valdéz and his partner, Andrés Alvarez, did the vocals and guitar accompaniment on the number, identified on the label as a "tragedia." The duo's other recording listed (Corona 2331) is a re-release as a 45-rpm single. Notice that two more recordings by what appears to be the same duo are actually by different performers, who fudged the distinction by changing one letter in the spelling of Los Cuatesones to produce "Los Cuatezones."

Unlike many other corridos, this story of a classic gangland double-cross is virtually identical in all four versions. (Musically, however, the conjunto accompaniment on the Montoya-Yerena version is an impressive standout, with its accordion background playing almost continuously, rather than just as accents between verses.) All the songs end with a cautionary lesson that Hernández describes as an important element in the genre. "Such commentaries expressed by the performer within the text of the corrido may also highlight the exemplary nature of the events narrated and the role of corridos in prescribing community behavior," he writes. "In 'Carga Blanca,' for example, one of the first corridos to include the topic of drugs, the narrative voice advises against drug trafficking, warning of the negative consequences awaiting the transgressors": "Dejen los negocios chuecos: ya ven lo que sucedió." (Get out of crooked businesses; you see what happened.)

Farewell: "Benjamín Argumedo"
   Performer: Trío Los Aguilillas
   Label: Columbia 6277-X / Columbia 1150-C
   Performer: Los Palillos
   Label: Colonial 45-158
   Performer: Gonzáles y Hernández
   Label: Vocalion 8241 Parte 1 & 2
   Performer: Jimmy Martínez and Trini Martínez
   Label: Del Mar DM-116-B
   Performer: Dueto Hureta-González
   Label: Universal 4050-B
   Performer: Conjunto de Los Hermanos Banda
   Label: A D 10013
   Performer: Maya y Florez
   Label: Ideal 224
   Performer: Morales y Romero
   Label: Decca 10041A-B Primera y Segunda Parte
   Performer: Los Dos Rebeldes
   Label: Bronco BR-152
   Performer: José Luis y Los Maloos
   Label: Capitol 6806

This corrido about a military general who was executed in 1918 has been recorded scores of times since the 1930s. Here it is cited to underscore the nature of the farewell, or *despedida*, in the corrido song tradition. Writes Hernández: "The tragic end met by many of the corrido protagonists is usually formulated as an earthly farewell, often with religious allusions, for a voyage to an eternal world."

> Ya se acabó Benjamín,
> ya no lo oirán mentar.
> Ya está juzgado de Dios,
> ya su alma fue a descansar.

> (Benjamín is now finished,
> you won't hear of him again.
> He's now been judged by God,
> his soul has now gone to rest.)

Conclusion

Throughout its almost 200-year history, Hernández concludes, the corrido has evolved from a strictly oral tradition to a commercially recorded product of popular culture. Yet its central themes and characters have remained relatively unchanged. "Corridos recount stories of heroic and often tragic figures who left us their example as they confronted difficult situations in their communities," he writes. "Many of the names of narrators and characters, as well as their trials and tribulations, remain only in that collective and unofficial history that is the corrido tradition."

Now, thanks to the digital archive he helped create, that tradition is sure to endure for the ages.

Transcending Machismo
Songs of Loss and Love from the Frontera Collection

The late Carlos Monsiváis, Mexican journalist and commentator, did not elaborate on his sweeping assertion that "machismo takes refuge in Mexican country music" ("el machismo donde se refugia es en la canción ranchera"). He made the observation during a 2009 interview on the Dominican television show *Mundos Paralelos*, with Cuban-born host Alfonso Quiñones.[1] Their main topic was the bolero, a genre closer to Monsiváis's heart. His reference to machismo and rancheras was made just in passing.

It's such a common perception that the statement went unchallenged. Yet Mexican folk and country music actually reflects a wide variety of values, attitudes, and beliefs that are incongruent with those typically associated with machismo. I reviewed the themes and content of more than 2,000 recordings in the Frontera Collection, looking for machismo where one would most expect to find it, in love songs of rejection and abandonment. And although the macho response—from murderous rage to debauched despair—can certainly be found in these songs, more enlightened ways of handling rejection are also prominent. In fact, examples of songs with alternative themes, such as acceptance, love, and goodwill in the face of lost love, are so numerous that they constitute a branch of folk wisdom all their own. Rather

than drowning their sorrows in liquor or releasing them in violence, these artists assert a set of principles that could be turned into a modern self-help book on how to handle rejection in relationships with dignity, selflessness, and even a certain worldly detachment. To turn Monsiváis on his head, Mexican folk music is also a refuge for anti-machismo, which is just another way of saying true love.

The subject of machismo in Mexican folk music has been addressed at length by two other prominent observers of Mexican culture, Vicente T. Mendoza and Américo Paredes. Mendoza took up the issue directly in a 1962 essay, "El machismo en México a través de las canciones, corridos y cantares," one of the last works published by the renowned folklorist. In it, he distinguishes between two types of machismo, false and authentic, and cites thirty Mexican folk songs to show examples of each.[2]

Five years later, Paredes took issue with Mendoza's machismo analysis in a rebuttal essay first published in Spanish as "Estados Unidos, México y el machismo." (The article was translated into English in 1970 and appeared in the book *Perspectives on Las Américas*, published in 2003.[3]) Indeed, Paredes does not even agree with the definition of machismo used by his colleague. Instead, he argues that what Mendoza calls authentic machismo in many cases is simply heroism or bravery, traits which are often found in the Mexican corrido but which are also universal. The term *machismo* or *macho*, Paredes writes, does not even appear in Mexican music until the 1940s, when it conveniently rhymed with the name of then Mexican president Avila Camacho.

It is only since the 1940s that Mexico has been so closely identified with machismo in popular culture, Paredes argues. That is when we start to see the emergence of "the *corridos* for which Mexico is known abroad, the same ones cited repeatedly by those who deplore *machismo*."[4] Their popularity was driven by the movies of the so-called golden age of Mexican cinema, through virile singers-turned-actors such as Jorge Negrete and Pedro Infante. As an example of this boastful machismo on steroids, Paredes cites the rowdy, gun-packing song "Traigo Mi 45," of which there are four 78-rpm versions in the Frontera Collection, including one instrumental featuring just the jaunty melody (fig. 28). The chorus states the quintessential quality of the macho, his fearlessness in the face of death: "Quién dijo miedo, muchachos, si para morir nacimos?" (Who is afraid, lads, if we are born to die?)

Paredes dismisses this unbridled expression of machismo as "foolish," a contemporary creation of pop culture for the postwar middle class. But is it really Mexican? Not according to Paredes, who goes on to explore comparable macho qualities in US pop culture. He also ridicules the theory that Mexico's unique brand of machismo is a national trait, conceived five centuries ago in the violent rape of Aztec women by the conquering Spaniards. "It seems," he concludes, "that Mexican *machismo* is not exactly as it has been painted for us by people who like to let their imaginations dwell on the rape of Indian women."[5]

Figure 28. "Traigo Mi 45" (I've Got My 45), a quintessential expression of machismo as fearlessness in the face of death, is performed with bravado by female vocalist Irma Vila and her mariachi. This 78-rpm release on Odeon (Compañía del Gramofono Odeon), located in Barcelona, Spain, features a variation on the iconic Victor design familiar in the United States, with Nipper the dog listening to a gramophone above the slogan "His Master's Voice." In this case, the slogan appears in Spanish, "La Voz de Su Amo," as a banner across the top of the label, consistent with earlier versions of the design. The B-side of the record is Vila's rendition of the traditional Mexican folk tune "Cielito Lindo," the most frequently recorded tune in the Frontera Collection (see appendix B). Photograph courtesy of the Arhoolie Foundation.

Until now, debates such as these about Mexican music and culture have been left to researchers with access to the source materials, such as historic record collections and archives of printed music. But today, thanks to the massive trove of Mexican folklore in the Frontera Collection, members of the general public have the ability to review primary materials in their own homes. A century of Mexican music is now literally at our fingertips, allowing people to come to their own conclusions. Instead of relying on thirty songs selected to support one author's conclusions, any music fan or student can audition thousands of songs, from the most popular to the most obscure, and hear what artists have been saying on any subject.

Although academic discussions of machismo tend to focus on the larger-than-life heroes and anti-heroes of the Mexican corrido, much more can be learned from the actions of the star-crossed lovers, heartbroken suitors, and disillusioned spouses who populate the common love songs of Mexican folklore. After all, the macho is known not only for his exploits on the battlefield and in the barrio but also for his behavior in his relationships with women. In this field, the Frontera Collection reveals a vast array of values that defy any preconceived categories or pat stereotypes.

Love, and all its variants, is one of the top three song subjects listed in the UCLA archive. As of this writing, the searchable database includes twenty-eight subcategories of love themes, from "impossible" and "unrequited" love to the many ways one can express the emotion, through "proclamation," "declaration," "affirmation," "entreaty" and "vow" of love. The themes run the gamut, from the brash and swaggering machismo associated with the rural figure of the Mexican charro to the urbane, philosophical, almost Zen-like reactions to rejection and loss that are the antithesis of machismo. Instead of reacting to rejection with violence and a primal compulsion to control outcomes, the men and women in these love songs illustrate a willingness to move on, to live and let live, and even to wish their ex-partners a happy future, despite their amorous wounds.

Paredes would say that "authentic" machismo has some of these excellent qualities of courage, honor, and self-sacrifice. For purposes of this analysis, however, machismo in Mexican

folk songs is taken to be of the common variety best defined by Felipe Montemayor:

> The folk songs of Mexico are openly tearful and addressed to the woman who has gone away with another man "who is no doubt more of a man than I am" . . . , in which [the singer] openly admits his frustration and failure; as for the rest, they are strings of phrases typical of one rejected, who tries to conceal his humiliation or the scorn directed at him by resorting to aggressive or compensatory forms.[6]

That is a vast generalization that seriously sells short the complexity of human emotions reflected in Mexican folk songs dealing with breakups and heartbreak. Taken as a whole, in fact, the responses expressed in Mexican music, far from being one-dimensional, are more like the famous five stages of grief, though with a cultural twist. They may start with the anger and rage of machismo. But they also pass through what is called *despecho*, or spite, often spiced with a dose of folksy humor, before ending in resignation and acceptance, leaving the future to fate.

A Lo Macho: Dance with Me or Else

To be sure, the Frontera Collection is full of songs brimming with overt and arrogant macho bravado in relation to women. "La Güera Ingrata," a 78-rpm recording by Las Hermanas Padilla (fig. 29) with the Mariachi Azteca, clearly spells out the rural macho mindset in reaction to rejection by a woman. Oddly enough, the song was written by the lead singer of the female duo, Margarita Padilla. The characterization of male dominance, violence, and perhaps even racism is so extreme, however, that it raises suspicion that Padilla may have intended the song as a parody.

The song opens with the macho protagonist declaring himself on a mission of vengeance against the woman who betrayed him, "the

Figure 29. Las Hermanas Padilla, one of Mexico's most famous female duets, performs on more than 350 recordings in the Frontera Collection (see appendix E). Margarita Padilla (*left*), credited with writing the misogynistic "La Güera Ingrata," is seen here with sister María in an exotic promotional portrait for Columbia Records. Photograph courtesy of the Arhoolie Foundation.

Figure 30. This two-part 78-rpm corrido "¡Ay! ¡Que Muchachas!" by Hernández y Sifuentes laments the modern, liberated woman of the 1920s. Photograph courtesy of the Arhoolie Foundation.

ungrateful fair-skinned one" of the title. He rails against her for "taking other men to my very own home." He even asks God to help him locate her, so that he can take his revenge before he dies. The appeal to a higher moral power for help in tracking down the ingrate underscores the self-righteousness of the macho mind. The woman is evil and sinful, so she must be punished, and even destroyed. The chorus then offers the most chilling line of the song, a threat that smacks of medieval honor killings: "Si yo la encontrara, quizás la matara, para con su vida limpiar mi honor." (If I should find her, perhaps I'd kill her, to cleanse my honor with her life.)

In the famous two-part corrido "Rosita Alvírez," the man doesn't hesitate to kill the woman for even the slightest snub. Rosita is shot dead for turning down a thin-skinned macho who asked her to dance. But first the killer warns her to spare his pride in public: "Rosita, no me desaires, la gente lo va a notar." In this and similar songs, women are too coquettish or fun-loving or simply too beautiful for their own good. Even their own mothers warn them: don't go out dancing, but if you must, don't be dumb enough to turn a man down.

In "¡Ay! ¡Qué Muchachas!" (Oh, What Girls!), another 78-rpm record by the duo of Hernández y Sifuentes, modern, liberated women are even berated for having minds of their own (fig. 30). (It sounds quaint today to hear laments about "modern" women in the scratchy, high-pitched tones of this old phonograph record from the 1920s.) The song's litany of complaints about "the girls of today" is so extensive it takes a two-part recording to enumerate them all. Side A opens with the gripe that young women want to get married even before they learn how to cook. If their parents object, we're told, the girls turn into "very demons" and run off to get married anyway. Within a month, they get tired of their husbands and start affairs behind their backs, while the poor men are off working hard to support them. On side B, we hear that these "cousins of Satan" get together to gossip with their friends and brag about their infidelities. When husbands leave for business trips, the wives invite their lovers to the home. This song ends with a sly, winking warning to male listeners:

> No se les olviden los buenos consejos:
> ustedes acá en la bola,
> y otro allá con su mujer.

> (Don't forget this good advice:
> while you're here with your buddies,
> your wife's out with another man.)

El Despecho: Getting Things Off Your Chest

There's a word in Spanish, *despecho*, that encompasses a wide swath of reactions touched off by rejection in a relationship. The common definition is spite or vengeance, but dictionaries also describe it as a general feeling of resentment as a result of a betrayal, abandonment, or personal slight. So the word also connotes indignation, wrath, dejection, defiance, despair, and dismay. The roots of the word reveal its cathartic nature. *Pecho* is the Spanish word for chest. Thus, *des-pecho* suggests getting something off one's chest.

Despecho is considered part of the macho psyche, though women can certainly act out of spite as well. Men, however, are usually the ones who unleash explosive violence and kill out of *despecho*, as we've seen. And it's always men who can be found drowning their sorrows in cantinas. *Despecho* is culturally specific as well. Although spite and despondency

are universal human reactions (even cowboys drown their sorrows in their beer), *despecho* is considered uniquely Latin American.

"The United States is the culture of 'moving on' and 'shaking off' a heartbreak and/or unrequited love," writes Dr. Carolina Acosta-Alzuru, who specializes in cultural studies at the University of Georgia. "In contrast, in Latin America we have the tendency of not moving on until we have wallowed in our sadness for a good while. That is '*despecho*.' And there's no better company for a good '*despecho*' than a bolero, tango or ranchera."[7]

As we shall see, the notions of "shaking off" a bad relationship and "moving on" can also be commonly found in Mexican music. Yet, there's no doubt that *despecho* appears much more often as a theme in the Mexican songbook. The songs run the gamut of reactions to heartbreak. There is the stereotypical despondent man drowning his sorrows in the cantina. Or trying to shore up his wounded pride by feigning indifference. Or waiting for his ultimate revenge when the tables turn and the woman who once rejected him comes begging to be taken back.

No song crystallizes the image of drunken despondency better than "Ella," one of the most famous songs by José Alfredo Jiménez, the preeminent ranchera composer of the twentieth century (figs. 31, 32). Frontera has at least nineteen versions of the song, in styles from guitar duet to traditional mariachi and swinging Tex-Mex. Among them is a version by Jiménez himself on Columbia 78 rpm, one of the legendary composer's earliest recordings.

> Yo sentí que mi vida
> se perdía en un abismo, profundo y negro
> como mi suerte.
> Quise hallar el olvido
> al estilo Jalisco,
> pero aquellos mariachis
> y aquel tequila
> me hicieron llorar . . .

Figure 31. The songs of José Alfredo Jiménez, the foremost composer of rancheras, defined the genre and embodied what it meant to be Mexican. He is seen here in a studio portrait from the 1950s. His songs of heartache and lost love expressed a range of sentiments, from machismo to magnanimity, that resonated with millions of Mexican fans. Photograph courtesy of José Alfredo Jiménez Jr.

> Los mariachis callaron,
> de mis manos sin fuerza
> cayó mi copa sin darme cuenta.
> Ella quiso quedarse
> cuando vio mi tristeza,
> pero ya estaba escrito
> que aquella noche perdiera su amor.

In this case, the man's despair is so deep and dark that not even the normal palliatives of tequila and sentimental mariachi songs—"al estilo Jalisco"—could bring relief. His hopelessness is underscored by this memorable image of a defeated man who can't even hold his own cocktail glass: "The mariachis went quiet. Without my realizing it, my cup fell from

Figure 32. This early recording of "Ella" is by José Alfredo Jiménez, Mexico's premiere ranchera songwriter, who captures the despondency of rejection in this prototypical cantina song. The 78-rpm Columbia release from Mexico credits the conjunto of Gilberto Parra as the accompaniment, though a mariachi is actually heard on the recording. Photograph courtesy of the Arhoolie Foundation.

my hands that had no strength left." This is the polar opposite of the man so driven by anger that he lashes out violently. One ends up in prison, the other as a vagabond with no purpose or direction in life. Either way, they are lives wasted by lost love.

I Heard It through the Grapevine

Short of its ultimate drastic expressions, *despecho* can be a coping mechanism, a way for men to manage the passions aroused by an unrequited love, or worse, a two-timing woman. They can laugh it off. They can act as if they don't care. And, most satisfying of all, they can take the woman off her pedestal and cut her down to size.

A prime example is "Por Despecho," a song written by Alvino García and performed by Los Fronterizos for the Falcon label, based in the border town of McAllen, Texas (fig. 33). As in many songs of this type, the lyric is addressed directly to the woman who betrayed or abandoned the relationship, serving as a vicarious monologue for all those wounded men who didn't get a chance to tell off their tormentors, or who didn't find the right words to wrap up their resentments with face-saving panache. In this case, there's a complex interaction, as the man tries to get the upper hand in the aftermath of the breakup. He first accuses the woman of feigning love for him and breaking his heart. Then he insists on setting the record straight: "Now you go around saying that I'm talking out of spite [*despecho*], and that you never did care for my affections." In no uncertain terms, he pronounces his love dead, then twists the metaphoric knife with these devilish lines:

> Ya puedes conquistar
> un diablo en el infierno.
> Ya a mi nada me importa.
> Pa' siempre te he olvidado.

Figure 33. "Por Despecho" is a breakup song whose title refers to spite or vengeance. This recording by Los Fronterizos was released on the legendary Falcón label, founded in 1948 by Arnaldo Ramírez in McAllen, Texas. Photograph courtesy of the Arhoolie Foundation.

(You can go ahead now
and seduce a devil in hell.
It doesn't matter to me anymore.
I've forgotten you forever.)

That song stops just short of saying "You can go to hell." The strong reaction is fueled by a double offense: the woman's original rejection and her subsequent gossip, in which she rewrites the relationship in order to belittle him. Herein lies another recurring theme in Mexican music: the importance of what people say after the relationship is over. It hearkens to an era before Facebook and Twitter, when word got around through the talk of the town. Often, it's the gossip—*chisme*—that inspires the song to begin with. In a final attempt to salvage what's left of his pride, the man comes looking for the woman to set the record straight out in the open.

The mariachi tune "Te Volaste la Barda" illustrates how a song gives the man the final word in the gossip war. (The title literally translates as "you jumped the fence," but in this context means "you crossed the line.") Though performed by a female act, Las Alondras, the song was written by a male songwriter, Cecilio Ortiz.

> Ahora si te volaste la barda
> con lo que anda diciendo la gente:
> que me paso las noches llorando,
> que me muero tan solo por verte.
>
> Para mí solo fuiste un capricho,
> de los muchos que tengo en la vida.
> Anda, busca otro amor que te quiera.
> Como siempre, gané la partida.

(Now you've really crossed the line,
with what people are going around saying:
that I spend my nights crying,
that I'm dying just to see you.

For me, you were just a whim,
like the many that I have in life.
Go find yourself someone who will love you.
As always, I won the game.)

In this case, the man returns to dispute the worst thing that can be said about him: that he still pines for her and wants her back. No macho—at least no sober one—wants to be publicly cast in the pitiful position of having to beg for love from the woman who doesn't want him. Thus, he lets it be known that he never really cared to begin with. She was just a whim, one of many. So who needs her? Here again, he bids her farewell with a contemptuous kick in the pants. He doesn't send her to hell, but to some place like it—the loser's box.

The importance of what people think is also underscored by the final line in the song "De Mañana en Adelante" (From Now On), written by bandleader and producer Manuel S. Acuña. Here there's no doubt the betrayed man still feels hurt because the woman was unfaithful. In fact, that's the reason he's leaving her, because he won't let her make a fool of him ("De mi no te has de burlar"). There are no insults nor pretense of indifference. He asks only one favor of her at the end: "When you talk to your girlfriends, never tell them that I begged you." ("Cuando platiques con tus amigas, nunca les digas que te rogué.") Whether he begged her or not, he doesn't say. What matters to the man is avoiding the appearance of humiliation, being on his knees, begging his love to stay.

Another song in this vein telegraphs the theme in the title: "Andas Diciendo" (You Go Around Saying), by the duo of Miguel y Laurita on the Los Angeles–based Colonial label (fig. 34). The man in this case is incensed because his ex has been speaking ill of their relationship. And he wants her to know that he's heard all the bad things she's been saying about him: that he is her plaything ("papalote"), that his love is cheap, that he's only deserving of her pity, that he's still crazy about her, and that she's already found a new love who now owns her heart. On that last point, the maligned man makes sure to pop his former lover's boastful bubble: "No seas farsante, mujer, no seas

Figure 34. "Andas Diciendo" (You Go Around Saying), by the duo Miguel y Laurita, is typical of songs about bitter gossip after a breakup. The recording was released on the Los Angeles–based Colonial label owned by bandleader, composer, and producer Manuel S. Acuña. Photograph courtesy of the Arhoolie Foundation.

farsante. No me presumas ni te hagas la ilusión." (Don't be a phony, woman, don't be a phony. Don't come bragging to me, and don't kid yourself.)

The upbeat norteño arrangement with its playful clarinet helps make a mockery of her gossip. This sort of musical ridicule is characteristic of what might be called the delicious kiss-off category of love song. Often in this style, the song's dismissive message is highlighted by a happy-go-lucky arrangement. The playful music reinforces the point that the man doesn't care anymore about the former relationship. A case in point is the giddy-up tempo and plucky guitar-picking in "No Tengo Tiempo" (I Don't Have Time), written by Andrés Cortez Castillo and performed by Trío Tariácuri on a 78-rpm Decca recording. In this song, the no-nonsense man comes to tell his ex-lover that he's tired of her games and her gossip. He's too busy for such things, and only has time for work.

Andas diciendo
que lloro por que me quieras.
Hmmmm, hmmmm
Estas torcida.
Ni me he vuelto a ocupar.

(You go around saying
that I cry for you to want me.
Hmmmm, hmmmm
You're twisted.
I haven't given it a second thought.)

The teasing tsk-tsk between the lines—
hmmmm, hmmmm—is delivered with a softly
sarcastic tone. In contemporary slang, it's
equivalent to the skeptical expression, "Yeah,
right." It conveys disdain and disapproval with
a harmonious hum.

You're So Vain, I'll Bet You Think This Song Is about You

Despecho is not a state of mind, but a process. The anger, the spite, the put-downs, and
the desire to get even are just emotions along
the road to leaving it all behind. Humor is one
more weapon in the male's defense armor, another way of establishing distance between
himself and the woman who hurt him. One
of the sharpest humorists in the field was the
late Lalo Guerrero, a native of Tucson, Arizona,
known as the father of Chicano music (fig. 35).
In his biting composition "La Vampiresa" (The
Female Vampire), he begins by telling his
blood-sucking ex that he knows the lies she's
been spreading about him.

No tienes que estar hablando,
ni a todo el mundo contando,
que por pobre me dejaste,
y otras cosas que yo sé.
¡Pero cuenta realidades!
Sé que no tienes vergüenza.
Diles a tus amistades,
cómo y con quién te encontré.

Si esto es lo que tú querías,
el que todos lo supieran,

Figure 35. Lalo Guerrero, considered the father
of Chicano music, was known for his humorous
and satirical songs, such as the biting composition
"La Vampiresa" on Colonial, which depicts a former lover as a blood-sucking vampire. The versatile
singer-songwriter was the first Chicano to receive
the National Medal of Arts, the nation's highest arts
award, for a career that spanned more than half a
century. He is shown here as a classic crooner in a
studio portrait from the 1950s. Photograph courtesy
of Mark and Dan Guerrero.

sé que vas a sufrir mucho;
te arrepentirás después.
Porque a mí no me hacen mella
tus aires de vampiresa.
Si antes no me dominaste,
menos hoy que te dejé.

Sé que estás muy mal parada;
ya no eres mujer deseada.
Se acabaron esos tiempos,
ahora ni te quieren ver.
Solamente se te acercan
los que son de tu calaña.
Pero que Dios te socorra,
y que te vaya muy bien.

(You shouldn't go around talking
and telling everyone
that you left me because I'm poor,
and other things I've heard.
But tell the truth!
I know you have no shame.
Tell your friends how you were
when I found you, and who you were with!

If this is what you wanted,
for the whole world to know what happened,
I know you're going to suffer a lot;
you'll regret it later.
Because I'm not impressed
by your vampire airs,
if you didn't dominate me before,
much less now that I've left you.

I know you've really hit the skids;
you're no longer a desired woman.
Those days are over;
now people don't even want to look at you.
Only people of your own ilk
will come close to you.
But may God help you,
and have a good life.)

In these three verses, Guerrero manages to pile on several layers of *despecho*: the pity, the put-down, the shame, and the fare-thee-well. He starts by demanding that the woman tell the truth: admit that she used to be beneath him and that he raised her social status. In the second verse, to counteract her gossip he calls her bluff: she'll regret it if the real truth comes out. The implication is that he's not about to let her put him down and get the upper hand. Finally, the kiss-off comes in the third verse. He tells her he knows that she's not doing well, that she's no longer desirable, and that people don't even want to look at her, other than her own low-class crowd.

The use of "calaña" to describe her "kind" or her "ilk" is just dripping with disdain. In a country obsessed with social classes, love songs often play on these sorts of status or peer distinctions. Often, the woman is accused of being a social climber or gold digger who leaves because she thinks she can find somebody better than her current partner, whom she rejects for his poverty or low station in life. In those cases, the songs serve to puncture the pretense and put the woman back in her place, thereby reclaiming the man's self-respect.

Of course, a scorned woman also needs to reassert her self-worth following a romantic rejection. In "El Cheque en Blanco" (The Blank Check), female composer Ema Elena Valdelamar explicitly puts a price on the bankrupt affairs of the heart. It's a cynical yet heart-wrenching goodbye, handled pitch-perfectly by torch singer Chelo Silva (fig. 36), who was born in Brownville, Texas, and who, coincidentally, was once married to border scholar Américo Paredes.[8] In this aching lyric filled with financial metaphors, the so-called Queen of the Bolero tells a former flame that she's not for sale, though he thinks the world is all about business. In her final kiss-off verse, she plays on the word "desprecio," which means contempt or rejection but which literally translates as "de-pricing," that is, devaluing.

Ay, me decepcionaste tanto,
que allí te dejo un cheque en blanco,
a tu nombre para ti.

Ven, pon la cantidad que quieras.
En donde dice desprecio,
ese debe ser tu precio.
Y va firmado por mi.

(Oh, you disappointed me so much,
that I'm leaving you a blank check
written out for you, in your name.

Come, put whatever amount you want.
Where it says "desprecio" [scorn]
that must be your price.
And it's signed by me.)

In "Abandonado y Despreciado" (Abandoned and Scorned), a 78-rpm recording on the Ideal label, Jesús Maya and Raúl Martínez continue

Figure 36. Chelo Silva, a native of the border town of Brownsville, Texas, achieved international fame as "La Reina del Bolero," queen of the quintessential Latin love song. Her husky, emotional voice was well suited for songs of heartbreak and rejection such as "El Cheque en Blanco" (The Blank Check), a bitter but heart-wrenching tune that literally puts the concept of *desprecio* (contempt) into monetary terms. Photograph courtesy of the Arhoolie Foundation.

the theme of reclaiming self-worth following a rejection. Here, the scorned man is still stinging from the woman's betrayal, "still wandering the earth sad and alone in search of a love that isn't false." But he still manages to fire off a zinger—and save his wounded pride—in the final verse:

> No te ilusiones ni te creas tan grandota,
> ni estés pensando que en el mundo estoy
>   de sobra.
> A ti te sobran tus pachucos enmañados.
> Ya me despido para no hacerte mal obra.

Again, the man takes the social climber down a notch and tries to pump up his own damaged self-esteem, described with "despreciado" in the title, which means scorned or rejected.

Peppered with slang, the verse warns the woman not to get such a big head ("no te hagas tan grandota"), using a superlative form of the Spanish word for big that adds to the ridicule. The phrase also has a class connotation since it can also be translated as "don't act like such a big shot." In the second line, he makes sure to establish his self-worth ("Don't go thinking that I'm dispensable in this world"), using a term ("estar de sobra") that suggests someone is extraneous, useless, or insignificant. He finishes her off by degrading her current circle of friends as "your vice-ridden gang-bangers" ("tus pachucos enmañados"). Finally, as if restraining his basest macho instincts, he bids farewell in his last line, corrido-style: "I'll say goodbye now, so I don't do you any harm."

On the subject of love and violence, one of the most fascinating lyrics is from the unidentified composer of "De Mañana en Ocho Días" (A Week from Tomorrow), which turns machismo into an internal struggle of opposing impulses. In the version by La Veracruzana con Sus Jarochos (fig. 37), the spurned man battles the desire to hurt the ex-lover who betrayed a promise to love until "the stars fell to the ground."[9] The feelings are obviously tearing him apart and he's being pulled in two directions: "I'd like to give you death, but not take your life." In the end, he poetically turns the negative reactions into positive intentions:

> Quisiera verte y no verte,
> quisiera hablarte y no hablarte.
> Quisiera darte la muerte,
> y la vida no quitarte.
> Guerra quisiera tener,
> pero una guerra de abrazos,
> con una bomba de besos,
> y fusil en tus brazos.
>
> (I'd like to see you and not see you,
> talk to you and not talk to you.
> I'd like to give you death,
> but not take your life.

Figure 37. "De Mañana en Ocho Días" (A Week from Tomorrow), a somewhat twisted torch song by La Veracruzana con sus Jarochos, turns machismo into an internal struggle of opposing impulses. The label for Discos Taxco, another Los Angeles-based recording company, features an etched drawing of the company's namesake colonial town. Photograph courtesy of the Arhoolie Foundation.

> War I'd like to have,
> but a war of embraces,
> with a bomb of kisses
> and a rifle resting in your arms.)

That final struggle between possessing and letting go, between violence and tenderness, is a big step toward defusing the macho mentality. The song shows signs of self-reflection and self-control. By restraining the impulse to do harm, the man shows the desire to rise above what he knows to be his baser instincts. It's the macho's first step toward redemption.

Hey You, Get Off of My Cloud

Obviously, the Mexican male is just as capable of moving on and shaking off a bad relationship as his Anglo counterpart. In Mexican folk songs, however, the kiss-off tends to come with an artful or particularly piercing put-down.

In "Adiós Canoa," a 45-rpm released in 1979 by Los Hermanos Záizar with the Mariachi Vargas, the man takes pleasure in putting the woman in her place:

> Ni te odio, ni te amo,
> ni de ti me ando acordando.
> Ni las copas yo derramo
> cuando ando emborrachando.
> Como tu no vales nada,
> me alegro si al fin te largas.
> Que te cuida la manada
> de borregos que te cargas.

> (I don't hate you or love you
> or even think about you.
> I don't even spill my drink
> when I'm out getting drunk.
> Since you are worthless,
> I'll be happy when you finally leave.
> Let that herd of sheep you hang around with
> take care of you.)

The line about not spilling his drink is especially pointed in light of other typical Mexican songs where the macho drowns his sorrows in liquor. Compare this song to the aforementioned "Ella," by José Alfredo Jiménez, in which the man can't even keep his glass from falling out of his hand in the cantina. Here, the jilted lover cares so little about the woman that he can keep his cool even when he's drunk. The line about the "herd of sheep" is another slap at the new company she keeps, a wicked expression of *desprecio* or disdain that also suggests that he has too much self-respect to be among the herd of men she leads around blindly with her charms.

In the upbeat norteña "Ni Con Dinero" by Los Hermanos Prado, the wronged man restores his pride by relishing the fate of the woman who failed to value his affections (fig. 38). She now "wanders the world" with the kind of love she deserves, or literally, "with your class of love" ("con amor de tu clase"). She put on airs and now they've knocked her off her high horse ("nomás por lo que presumes . . . te

Figure 38. The classic conjunto norteño Los Hermanos Prado, with its playful accordion, high-pitched harmonies, and derisive reeds, conveys the mocking tone of the upbeat "Ni Con Dinero" (Not Even with Money), a tune that revels in the turned tables of a soured romance. The Del Valle recording is one of over sixty 45-rpm singles by the band on Texas labels in the Frontera Collection. Photograph courtesy of the Arhoolie Foundation.

bajaron de las cumbres"). The shoe is now on the other foot: he is happy and wouldn't have her back even, as the title suggests, if she paid him: "Ni con dinero te consigues mi cariño."

In another song, "Las Pollas Voladoras," the man uses the sarcastic kiss-off to reassert his macho dominion over women in general. And what better way for a macho to rein in these undomesticated two-timers than to compare them to farm animals. In this defiant number, written by Tío Lencho, the betrayed man says he doesn't want any more stray chickens who will fly the coop, because he's already got plenty of good hens to lay a surplus of eggs for him.

Yo no quiero mas pollas voladoras,
que se salgan del corral por los portillos.
Y es que tengo ya bastantes ponedoras,
y me sobran por ahora los blanquillos.

No song captures the bravado and sheer cathartic joy of a good dressing-down better than "Ya Estarás Jabón de Olor" (You Must Think You're Scented Soap), written by Jesús Silvestre Tejada. Unlike other songs of *despecho* where indifference is either feigned or used as a weapon, this spirited tune really conveys the feeling that the man is totally over it, citing traditional folk wisdom about the surplus of fish in the sea. Frontera has four 78-rpm versions of the song, including one norteño rendition on the Tico label by Dueto Río Bravo with Los Alegres de Terán. The rousing ranchera version by the male-female duet Águila y Sol was recorded in Mexico by RCA Victor, with the backing of the great Mariachi Vargas de Tecalitlán.

> Pos que te crees que vales tanto,
> que te estás engrandeciendo
> con tan bajo despotismo.
> Pos no te vengo a rogar.
> Si me quieres olvidar,
> para mi me da lo mismo.
>
> ¿Cómo la ves?
> Después de todo, si vas a seguir creyendo
> que eres una joya de oro,
> buscaré otra en tu lugar,
> y a tí te mando a volar,
> pa' que veas que no te lloro.
>
> Pos que te crees que por tu amor,
> ya voy a soltar el llanto.
> Ya estarás jabón de olor,
> ni que perfumaras tanto.
>
> Puedes andar con quien tú quieras,
> dándole vuelo a la hilacha,
> gozando de mil amores.
> Pues ya no se va a poder,
> que me vas a convencer,
> porque en el mundo hay mejores.

> (Well, you think you're worth so much,
> you're getting such a big head,
> with such low-class arrogance?
> Hey, I'm not here to beg.
> If you want to forget me,
> it's all the same to me.
>
> So what do you say?
> After all this, if you're still thinking
> that you're a golden jewel,
> I'll look for someone to replace you,
> and I'll send you packing,
> so you see I don't cry for you.
>
> Well, don't tell me you think that for your love
> I'll now be shedding tears?
> You must think you're scented soap,
> but it's not like you smell so good.

> You can go with whomever you choose,
> spreading your wings,
> enjoying a thousand loves.
> 'Cuz it won't be possible anymore
> to talk me into it,
> 'cuz hey, in the world there's much better.)

El Destino: What Goes Around Comes Around

No composer captures the spirit, attitudes, and values of Mexican popular culture better than José Alfredo Jiménez, the premier ranchera composer of the classic era in Mexican mariachi music, from the 1940s through the 1970s. In this tune, "Cuando el Destino," sung by superstar Pedro Infante, Jiménez describes how sweet revenge can be "when God grants it to us."

> Me contaron tus amigos
> que te encuentras muy solita,
> que maldices a tu suerte,
> por que piensas mucho en mí.
> Es por eso que he venido
> a reírme de tu pena,
> yo que a Dios le he pedido
> que te hundiera más que a mí.
>
> Dios me ha dado ese capricho,
> y te vengo a ver hundida,
> para hacerte yo en la vida,
> como tú me hiciste a mi.
> Ay, que bonita es la venganza
> cuando Dios nos la concede.
>
> Yo sabía que en la revancha
> te tenía que hacer perder.
> Ahi te dejo mi desprecio,
> yo que tanto te adoraba,
> pa' que veas cual es el precio
> de las leyes del querer.

This poor, embittered man has obviously been licking his wounds for quite a while. Then he hears gossip about the sad state of his ex-lover that gives him a wicked sense of satisfaction. Her friends have come to tell him that she's all alone and crying about her cruel fate because she can't stop thinking about him, the man she hurt. "And that's why I've come to laugh at your pain," he says. "I who had asked God to make you sink lower than me." So now that God has granted his whim ("capricho"), he is anxious for the chance to pay her back with an equal measure of pain, "to do to you in life what you have done to me." He departs with this line, suggesting that his desire to exact revenge follows some sort of romantic moral code: "I adored you so much and now I leave you my disdain, so you'll know what price there is to pay, per the laws of love."

The last line begs the question, as in the old doo-wop song: who wrote the book of love? In Mexican music, the laws of love—"las leyes del querer"—are spelled out virtually chapter by chapter, as in that golden oldie. In chapter one, the woman breaks the man's heart. In chapter two, she feels regret and wants him back. That leads to the final chapter, in which the man can exact his emotional revenge: now that she wants him again, he can reject her and make her feel how much it hurts. That is, the victimizer must feel what the victim has felt in order for the cosmic laws of love to be fulfilled. This Mexican version of the book of love could be titled Destiny's Payback, as succinctly expressed in the chorus of the song: "Ya lo vez como el destino todo cobra y nada olvida." (You see how Destiny forgets nothing and claims everything.)

Compared to José Alfredo's straightforward expression of *despecho,* the lesser-known composer Jesús Coronado has a more colorful, folkloric way of getting wounds off his chest in his song "Desquite," or revenge. (Again, the roots of the word illustrate the meaning; from the word *quitar,* or take away, *des-quite* suggests recovering what has been taken, or reversing the loss.) In this version, by the great Mexican folk ensemble Trío Tariácuri, the rejected lover predicts the pain that awaits the woman who is

leaving him. She can leave if she chooses, and he makes no effort to stop her.

> Qué culpa tengo que por tu mala cabeza, vas
>   a sufrir.
> No te detengo; si es tu gusto, ese camino lo has
>   de seguir.
> Tarde o temprano, yo te he de ver lamentando
>   tu proceder,
> ya cuando en vano tú quieras arrepentida
>   retroceder.

> (Don't blame me if you suffer because of your
>   wrong-headedness.
> I won't hold you back; if it pleases you, that's
>   the path you must follow.
> Sooner or later, I'll see you lamenting your
>   course of action,
> when finally, repentant, you want in vain to
>   come back.)

This vengeful verse is reminiscent of that segment in the classic Anglo-American musical *My Fair Lady* when Eliza Doolittle decides to leave the spurned Professor Higgins, who then bellows: "She'll regret it!" The cross-cultural comparison is quite apt, since both Higgins and Eliza express in song the same desire for revenge that courses through many Mexican love songs. At one point Eliza tires of being treated like a lab rat in the professor's Pygmalion experiment, and she imagines the tables turning in "Just You Wait." She envisions her tormentor sick, poor, drowning, and even executed at her command, while she flaunts her newfound wealth and her cold indifference to his suffering. Higgins expresses similar sentiments in the finale, after Eliza leaves to marry a younger suitor. The rejected professor imagines her married and penniless, only to be abandoned herself when she's "prematurely gray and the blossom in her cheeks has turned to chalk," and her husband runs off with a "social climbing heiress from New York." Higgins doesn't disguise the fact that he'll enjoy the reversal of fortunes: "Poor Eliza. How simply frightening.

How humiliating. How *delightful*!" When she finally returns "in tears and rags, miserable and lonely," begging him to take her back, the haughty Higgins exacts his revenge: "Let her promise to atone, let her shiver, let her moan. I'll slam the door and let the hellcat freeze!"

Paredes might argue that, just like machismo, revenge is a universal human emotion. We see the same elements of Mexican songs in the 1950s Broadway musical: the desire for the tables to turn, the hope of repaying the rejection, and the idea of delighting in the other's eventual suffering. The one thing that remains unique to the Mexican worldview is the faith that Destiny will really make it happen. In *My Fair Lady,* the principals are just musing about their partners getting their comeuppance. In Mexican songs, there's a certainty that the day of reckoning will come.

In song after song, couplets capture the concept of destiny as the ultimate avenger, as the following selection shows.

"Tú Amas a Otro Hombre"
Performer: Pantaleón Ramos y Manuel Treviño
Label: Okeh 16789

Yo soy el hombre
pobre y sin fortuna.
Tal vez con otro
tú tendrás que disfrutar.
Pero te advierto mujer,
que se ha de llegar el día,
en que llorando,
tú de mí te has de recordar.

(I am a poor
and unfortunate man.
Perhaps you'll have to find pleasure
with someone else.
But I warn you, woman,
that the day is bound to come,
when weeping,
you will no doubt remember me.)

"Ni el Oro ni las Piedras de Colores"
Performer: Johnny Canales
Label: Eréndira 178-B

No te reprocho, que me echaras al olvido.
En esta vida, solo da lo que sembramos.
Mas no te asombras que te miren para abajo.
En esta vida lo que hacemos lo pagamos.

(I don't blame you for forgetting me.
In this life, we only reap what we sow.
But don't be shocked that people now look
    down on you.
In this life, we pay a price for everything we do.)

"Mujer Vanidosa"
Performer: Las Norteñitas con el Conjunto Los Huracanes
Label: Del Valle 78-DE-117

Coqueteaste con toditos los ricos
para ver si se te podía ser,
sin pensar que el dinero no te quita
lo que has sido ni lo que vas a ser.

El desprecio que en un tiempo me hiciste,
con los ricos que no has de merecer,
hoy lo pagas con una pobrecita
pero honrada, no de tu proceder.

(You flirted with every last rich guy
to see if you could make it with them,
without thinking that money won't take away
what you've been and what you always will be.

The scorn which you once showed me
with the rich men whom you could not deserve,
is now being repaid with some poor little girl,
but one who's honest, not one who acts like you.)

The rules of love are like a ledger that requires balance. A wound in love needs to be repaid in kind. A wrong needs to be righted. There's almost a metaphysical aspect to the principle, as if the original rejection or heartbreak threw some cosmic equation off balance. Until the parties meet their fates, for better or worse, that balance cannot be restored (fig. 39).

That principle can be gleaned from the lyrics of another song called "El Desquite" (one of five with that word in the title in the Frontera Collection), this one by Hermanos San Miguel. Here, the singer is dumped by Lupita, who bluntly announces that she has another man. When they meet again by chance after a long time, Lupita is sad and offers her hand to her ex. But the man lets her down softly, regretfully breaking the news that he's getting married: "Siento causarte esta pena, pues yo me voy a casar." The man says he's sorry about hurting her, but the consequences are beyond his control. Destiny has set in motion the repercussions of her actions:

Te quise mas no pretendas
que yo te vuelva a querer.

Ya tú puedes darte cuenta
cómo se siente el perder.

Qué bonito es el desquite
cuando se sabe pagar.
Ya ven que yo mis pendientes,
pues ya logré desquitar.

(I loved you but don't pretend
that I should love you again.
Now you can realize
how it feels to lose.

How sweet is revenge,
when one knows how to lose.
Now you all can see that for my worries
I was able to get even.)

Figure 39. The music of Las Norteñitas (The Little Northern Girls), Sofia and Panchita, often featured sax and accordion, a style popular in the Monterrey, Mexico, region. They appear here with the conjunto of Lalo García: (*from left*) Alfonso Villagomez, bajo sexto; Rogelio Gutierrez, saxophone; García, accordion; and Canuto Perez, tololoche. The photograph was taken circa 1956 for Cristobal García, owner of Del Valle Records, for an LP that was not issued. Photograph courtesy of Billy Roy Morales and the Arhoolie Foundation.

Interestingly enough, "pendientes" also means pending matters. In this case, that could be taken to mean the pending unpaid debt in the relationship. Thus, returning the rejection settled those "pendientes." In other words, the act of betrayal remained pending as a debt until it was repaid years later through the act of rejecting the original offender. Life can go on, but until the score is settled, in this case by a chance encounter years later, the old relationship remains unresolved. The same concept, seen from the other side, is expressed in the song "Lo Pasado Pasado" (The Past Is Past, or What's Done Is Done), written by Lorenzo Elisea and performed by Luis Pérez Meza, nicknamed El Trovador del Campo, or the Country Troubadour.

In this case, there's a touch of compassion in the man's position, despite his wounds. Still, the laws of love exact their harsh justice. There is no peace until balance is restored. And there is no faster way to settle the scores of a lost love than to find a new one to replace it.

> Alza los ojos, no hagas recuerdo de lo pasado.
> Tuviste el gusto de abandonarme,
> tal vez por otro más desgraciado.
>
> Esa aflicción que traes en tu alma es tu desgracia.
> No tienes calma, no tienes calma.
> Andas mareada del corazón.
>
> (Lift up your eyes and forget about the past.
> You had the pleasure of leaving me,
> perhaps for somebody who's even more
>   unfortunate.
>
> That anguish you carry in your soul is
>   your disgrace.
> You have no peace, you have no peace.
> Your heart is making you dizzy.)

I've Got a Woman

In Mexico, there's a popular saying that sums up the concept that a new love heals old wounds: "Un clavo saca otro clavo." Literally, one nail drives out the other. Which is to say, one love can replace another.

Finding true love after heartbreak is one of the most common themes in Mexican music. However, it often comes with a spiteful twist. Just finding a new love is not enough. Showing off the new partner is an integral part of the *despecho* process. Many Mexican songs are driven by the desire for such face-to-face encounters, so the former unfaithful partner can witness the man she rejected with a new partner who offers true love. It's even better if the cheating ex has not fared so well in romance and the encounter serves to rub the disparate destinies in her face.

For the most wicked, in-your-face example of this strategy, nothing beats the old song "Falsa y Mancornadora" (Liar and a Cheat), by Emilio Martínez with Conjunto Los Caminantes, a 78-rpm recording on another San Antonio label, Corona. In the song, the jilted man goes out of his way to bring his newfound love to the home of the woman who has been cheating on him. In a deliciously vengeful twist on the traditional serenade, he asks her to come to her window to meet the woman who replaced her.

> Ya te voy abandonar,
> por falsa y mancornadora.
> Nomás te vengo a decir,
> que ya tengo a quién querer.
> Asómate a tu ventana,
> si la quieres conocer.
>
> (I'm going to leave you now,
> for being a liar and a cheat.
> I've just come to tell you that
> I already have someone to love.
> Come and look out your window
> if you want to meet her.)

A similar message is delivered in another norteño song by the duo Tomás y Juanita with the Conjunto Los Arrieros, also on a 78-rpm recording from a Texas border label, Del Valle, based in McAllen. The title in this case gives away the motivation behind having the two women meet: "Para Que Sufras" (Just So You'll Suffer). Once again, the happy runs on the accordion underscore the pleasures of sweet revenge.

> Para que sufras, mujer, para que sufras,
> mi nueva novia te traigo a presentar.
> Que no presuma como a ti tanto te gusta,
> ni se me raja, ni se sale del huacal.
>
> Para que sufras, mujer, pa' que te admires,
> hoy he querido venirte a noticiar.
> Para que sufras, nomás para que te piques,
> pues ya mañana, yo te voy a abandonar.
>
> (Just so you'll suffer, woman, just so you'll
>   suffer,
> my new girlfriend I bring for you to meet.
> She doesn't put on any airs, as you like to do,
> and she doesn't give up, nor try to run around.
>
> Just so you'll suffer, woman, so you can be
>   amazed,
> I've wanted to come to put you on notice.
> Just so you'll suffer, just so you'll be piqued,
> because tomorrow I'll be leaving you.)

In most cases, however, the man doesn't go looking for his old flame to break the news that he's found somebody new. Often he gets the opportunity when the repentant former lover comes begging for him to take her back and he can be the one to walk away; this is yet another take on turning the tables. In the aptly titled "Las Consecuencias" (The Consequences), a 45-rpm on the CBS Mexico label from 1976, the legendary norteño duo Los Alegres de Terán settles scores with a former lover and delivers a blistering I-told-you-so speech. It's a bitter goodbye, punctuated by a cold, and very final, last line:

> Sin medir las consecuencias me dejaste.
> Ahora vienes implorando mi perdón.
> Pa' que sepas que te tardaste,
> ya en mi pecho esta viviendo un nuevo amor.
>
> Te lo dije aquella tarde que te fuiste,
> "No te vayas que me vas a hacer llorar."

> Pero al verme la tristeza te reíste,
> y ya vez que hasta la risa hay que pagar.
>
> Te perdoné una vez y lo volviste hacer
> como juguete tomaste mi querer.
> Tú te reías de mi, y ahora me río de ti.
> Para que sepas, ya no te quiero ver.
>
> (Without weighing the consequences, you left
>   me,
> And now you come begging for my forgiveness.
> You should know that you're too late,
> A new love already lives in my chest.
>
> I told you that afternoon when you left,
> "Don't go because you're going to make me cry."
> But upon seeing my sadness you laughed,
> And now you see that even laughter has its cost.
>
> I forgave you once and you did it again.
> You took my love to be a toy.
> You laughed at me and now I laugh at you,
> Just so you know, I don't want to see you again.)

Finally, we come to a song that makes a total break with the macho worldview of wallowing in pain, resentment, anger, and revenge. The title, "Mi Vida Vale Más" (My Life Is Worth More), signals a self-confident, life-affirming attitude that stands as a counterpoint to the psychological insecurities at the root of machismo. In this song, written by M. C. Valdéz, the man doesn't need a new love to break free of a bad relationship. Just knowing there are many other women to choose from provides a sense of optimism. Here, the back-up band is the top-notch Tex-Mex Conjunto Bernal (fig. 40), with vocals by Vidal y Valdéz. Celebrated composer M. C. Valdéz also performed with other duos in San Antonio. Note the delightful accordion which, once again, does more than provide accents between verses. It makes its runs up and down every line of lyric, weaving and skipping though the stanzas. There could be no more joyful musical accompaniment—for a man who has just been dumped. Incidentally, when the singers mention the old standbys of the achy-breaky heart—mariachis and liquor—the request is for a love song ("una canción de amor") because the guy is so happy he wants to enjoy himself. No more crying in his beer, and certainly no thoughts of killing himself.

Ayer se fue mi prieta,
quién sabe a donde irá.
Nomás me dejó dicho
que ya no volverá
porque se fue con otro,
por allí a vacilar.
A poco esta creyendo
que yo me he de matar.

Qué va si no estoy loco,
mi vida vale más.
Al cabo las mujeres,
jamás se acabaran.
Si son como las olas
que vienen y se van,
si ayer se fue mi prieta,
mañana otra vendrá.

Que sirvan más cervezas,
y traigan más licor,
que canten los mariachis
una canción de amor,
porque me siento alegre,
me quiero divertir.
Que por una traidora,
ni quién piense morir.

(My dark-skinned girl left me yesterday;
who knows where she's headed.
She only left me word
that she wasn't coming back.
Because she left with some other guy,
to fool around somewhere,
I hope she's not thinking
that I ought to kill myself.

No way, I'm not crazy.
My life is worth more than that.
In any case, we'll never
run out of women.
Since they are like the waves
that come and go,
if my dark-skinned girl left yesterday,
another one will come tomorrow.

Serve some more beer

Figure 40. Conjunto Bernal, founded in 1954 by teenage brothers Eloy (*left*) and Paulino Bernal of Kingsville, Texas, gained a reputation for musical expertise and innovation within the conjunto format. They served as the backup band on many recordings for the Ideal label, where they got their start. Their skills are evident on the Ideal track "Mi Vida Vale Más" (My Life Is Worth More), where the irrepressible accordion matches the optimistic message of life after a breakup. Photograph courtesy of the Arhoolie Foundation.

and bring more liquor,
and have the mariachis
sing a song of love,
because I feel happy
and I want to enjoy myself.
Since for a two-timing woman,
nobody should think of dying.)

There's another school of thought in Mexican love songs in which destiny and revenge don't play a role in the end of a relationship, and neither does the settling of accounts. These songs take a more dispassionate, philosophical attitude toward heartbreak. The partner realizes there's no point in going forward, for either side. The core message here echoes that Bob

Dylan line from the 1960s: "You go your way and I'll go mine."

> Caminos que ya anduvimos,
> volver andarlos es por demás.
> Amor como el que juramos
> ya no te tengo, ni tú me das.
> Pensabas que tus traiciones,
> toda la vida te iba a aguantar.
> Hoy quedamos a mano;
> si a tu corazón le sobra,
> al mío no le ha de faltar.
> Si sufres como tú dices,
> yo te aconsejo, no sufras más.
> Ya no somos lo que fuimos;
> ya no me importa si tú te vas.

> (It's useless to try to travel again
> down the roads we once traveled.
> Love like the one we vowed,
> I no longer have, and you no longer give.
> You thought that I would put up
> with your cheating ways all my life.
> Now we're even;
> if your heart is overflowing,
> mine will not be empty.
> If you suffer as you say,
> I counsel you to suffer no more.
> We are no longer what we were;
> I don't care anymore if you leave.)

In English, when accounts are settled people often use the colloquial expression "We're even." The Spanish counterpart is the title of a song by Cornelio Reyna, "Estamos a Mano," released in 1972 as a 45-rpm single on Reyna's own label, CR Records, based in McAllen. The song was written by Pedro Puente and performed with a mariachi accompaniment by Reyna, who is one half, along with Ramon Ayala, of the legendary norteño conjunto Los Relámpagos del Norte. In his husky, soulful voice, Reyna sadly laments the end of a relationship, without rancor, bitterness, or desire for retribution. With unsentimental frankness, he marks the death of romance, without looking back and without false hopes for the future

Clearly, Cornelio leaves the relationship with a cold, cold heart, which is a lot better than rage and revenge. But in the final step of romantic macho evolution, wounded partners are capable of magnanimity, even a certain emotional largesse, in their parting statements. In the song "Más Vale Que No" (Better Not), by composer Lorenzo Hernández, the man tells his former love to forget him and move on with her life. It is a stark and blunt example of "letting go," Mexican style.

> Yo ya no quiero que me andes molestando,
> y ni tampoco que me vengas a llorar.
> Ya te lo he dicho, que estoy feliz con otra,
> tú búscate otro que al fin todo es igual.

> Cuando te quise, despreciabas mi cariño,
> cuando te amaba, te burlabas de mi amor.
> Pero los tiempos de ayer ya se acabaron,
> ya ni siquiera me acuerdo de tu amor.

> De qué te sirve seguir buscando
> este cariño que ya no es para ti.
> Es preferible que busques otro
> porque conmigo ya no se va a poder.

> Si acaso piensas que todavía te quiero,
> pues de ilusiones te vas a mantener.
> Yo te aconsejo que sigas tu camino.
> Vive tu vida y olvida mi querer.

> No pierdas tiempo buscando mi cariño,
> no sacrifiques tu vida por mi amor.
> La vida es corta y tenemos que vivirla,
> aunque tengamos que sufrir una traición.

> (I don't want you to keep on bothering me,
> nor to come to me crying.
> I've told you, I'm happy with someone else.
> Go find another; in the end, it's all the same.

> When I wanted you, you rejected my affections.
> When I loved you, you mocked my love.
> But those past times are over.
> Now, I don't even remember your love.

> What good does it do for you to keep looking for
> this love that is no longer there for you.
> It's better for you to find someone else,
> because with me, it's no longer possible.

If you should think that I still want you,
well, you'll have to live off illusions.
I advise you to continue down your path.
Live your life and forget my love.

Don't waste time looking for my affections.
Don't sacrifice your life for my love.
Life is short and we must live it,
though we may have to suffer a betrayal.)

Who says Mexicans can't move on? These verses reflect the aforementioned sentiments that Acosta-Alzuru attributed to US culture—that is, "moving on" and "shaking off" a heartbreak. The song's carefree attitude is embodied in the light-stepping norteño arrangement of the 78-rpm version by the Dueto Río Bravo with Los Alegres de Terán (Tico 78-3811) (fig. 41). The playful accordion runs conjure the image of someone skipping down the road, leaving his suffering behind. Another version of the same song in the Frontera Collection, this one by Dueto Monterrey, features the precise vocal harmonies of Lydia and María Mendoza. It replaces the accordion with guitars, adding a bright, clanging accompaniment. Both of these upbeat musical backgrounds underscore the message: the man is really moving on and wishes her well.

Still, there is a lingering touch of hurt feelings in "Más Vale Que No," reflected in the fact that the singer repeats the complaint about what she did and how much it hurt. The positive sign, from a macho perspective, is that he's able to rise above the hurt and give her constructive, selfless advice: find somebody new and live your life.

There is one song that totally transcends the negative reactions of the brokenhearted macho—all the pain, regret, recrimination, rage, violence, drunkenness, and despair. It's a timeless, tender tune written, once again, by the great José Alfredo Jiménez. Titled "Que Te Vaya Bonito," it is the quintessential sweet so-long song in the Mexican music repertoire. The

Frontera Collection lists eleven versions of the song on 45s, LP, and CD, including one RCA recording by the composer himself. (As of this writing, none of these versions had been added to the UCLA database.) The song's opening verse is constructed as a series of good wishes for the ex-partner, presumably the woman who is leaving the relationship. They start with the unique Spanish term "Ojalá," a word with Moorish roots that can mean "I wish" or "I hope" or "God willing." It connotes a desire for good fortune and wish fulfillment.

Ojalá que te vaya bonito.
Ojalá que se acaben tus penas,
que te digan que yo ya no existo,
que conozcas personas más buenas.
Que te den lo que no pude darte,
aunque yo te haya dado de todo.

Figure 41. "Más Vale Que No" (Better Not), a Tico 78-rpm release by Dueto Río Bravo with Los Alegres de Terán, is a song about letting go after a breakup. New York–based Latin music labels such as Tico and Seeco, which specialized in tropical dance music, released recordings by Mexican acts under license from labels based in Mexico, such as Columbia. The source is indicated by a matrix number (Mex 78 4289) etched into the vinyl near the label. Photograph courtesy of the Arhoolie Foundation.

Nunca más volveré a molestarte;
te adore, te perdí, ya ni modo.

Here, the man says to his departing love: "I hope things go well for you. I hope that your sorrows will end, that you meet better people who can give you what I could not give, though I gave everything I had. I'll never bother you again. I adored you. I lost you. That's all."

That final colloquial phrase, "ya ni modo," is a very Mexican expression. There is no direct English translation, but it suggests that there is no use in trying, there's nothing left to do—*ni modo*. In other words, the situation cannot be fixed and it's time to let go, to surrender. That, of course, is the opposite of the macho impulse to control the outcome, by either demanding a woman's love or destroying her to avenge her offense.

The third line in the stanza—"que te digan que yo ya no existo"—stands out because it adds what seems at first to be a dark element to a song of good intentions. He hopes that that people will tell her "I no longer exist." He doesn't threaten to kill himself, so it lacks the emotional blackmail of many macho songs. But he wants her to think he's disappeared, erasing any memory of himself *for her sake*. This stands in direct contrast to the vicious or vindictive side of gossip we've seen in so many other breakup songs, in which ex-lovers continue to wage war through what they say to others, or what others say about them. In this case, the man specifically wants the talk to be a relief, a way to clear the path for her happiness.

In the end, we have come full circle. Instead of thinking only of himself and his needs, the man thinks only of her, to the point of denying his own existence. Yet, we are left to wonder. Is this sort of self-sacrifice the polar opposite of machismo—or its ultimate expression?

Gringos, Chinos, and Pochos
The Roots of Intercultural Conflict in Mexican Music

As a mirror on Mexican American and Latin American pop culture, the Frontera Collection provides a unique and unvarnished reflection of the beliefs and values of people throughout the Americas, spanning four generations. The songs in this historic archive document how people felt about everything from social justice to true love, from revolution to assimilation. Many artists also touched on one of the thorniest issues faced by any society: racial and ethnic group relations. On this score, the Frontera Collection does not discriminate. Through its thousands of tracks, it shows Latinos as both the victims and the perpetrators of cultural stereotypes memorialized in music. Because the older 78-rpm collection is so extensive, it gives us a panoramic snapshot of racial attitudes from the first half of the twentieth century, before the civil rights movement set social limits on the most offensive ethnic expressions. In the case of working-class Mexicans who immigrated to the United States in large numbers, music was often the only vehicle of expression for political, social, and cultural thought. So these songs are among the only surviving testaments to the cultural mores and attitudes they held toward other ethnic groups they encountered along the way. The archive also shows, through its massive collection of more recent 45-rpm singles, that similar attitudes persist to the present day.

In the Caribbean, where slavery was entrenched during the colonial era, the stereotype of the lazy, shiftless black man has been enshrined in danceable tunes of the modern era. An example is "El Negrito del Batey," a hugely popular merengue written by Medardo Guzmán. There are currently three versions in the Frontera Collection, including one Seeco 78 by Cuba's legendary Sonora Matancera, which curiously credits a different composer. On another Seeco disc featuring Ramón Marquez, the title is incorrectly translated as "The Boy in the Backyard" (fig. 42). The song opens with the black man of the title boasting that he hates work as much as he loves women:

A mí me llaman el Negrito del Batey,
porque el trabajo para mí es un enemigo.
El trabajar se lo dejo todo al buey,
porque ese asunto lo hizo dios como castigo.

(They call me the Little Black Man from the Batey,
because for me work is an enemy.
I leave the work to the ox
because God created labor as a punishment.)

A batey is a labor camp for sugar workers, with conditions reminiscent of plantation slavery. The lazy "negrito" goes on to say that he much prefers to dance merengue with a tasty black woman ("una negra muy sabrosa"). Despite its overt stereotypes, the song is still considered a standard of Afro-Caribbean dance music and

Figure 42. This recording of "El Negrito del Batey," a popular Dominican tune about an indolent black worker on a sugar plantation, was released by Ramón Marquez on Seeco, a label known for its extensive Latin music catalog by major stars of the 1940s and '50s. The title, which literally means "Little Black Man of the Batey," or labor camp, is incorrectly translated as "Boy in the Backyard." Photograph courtesy of the Arhoolie Foundation.

continues to be played in salsa nightclubs in newer renditions.

In 2009 the song became part of an international incident when a Honduran official used its title to insult President Barack Obama. Stung by US opposition to a coup in his country, Honduras's interim foreign minister, Enrique Ortez Colindres, lashed out sarcastically and condescendingly at the first black president of the United States. "I have negotiated with queers, prostitutes, leftists, blacks, whites. . . . I am not racially prejudiced," Ortez said. "I like the little black sugar plantation worker who is president of the United States." ("He negociado con maricones, prostitutas, con ñángaras [izquierdistas], negros, blancos. . . . No tengo prejuicios raciales. Me gusta el negrito del batey que está presidiendo los Estados Unidos.") English-speakers back in Washington

might have scratched their heads, wondering what he meant. But the song's racial meaning is so deeply entrenched in Latin American culture that the title alone served as a code to smear Obama with centuries of racial stereotypes contained in those three words, "negrito del batey."[1]

Under pressure, the bigoted politico sent a letter of apology to the White House. But he never apologized for using the offensive term "maricón" to refer to homosexuals, another group that has been the target of bias in Latin American popular music. The Frontera Collection, for example, contains a song that uses a gay slur as its title. "Joto," written by Alfredo Marín and performed by the popular female duo Las Hermanas Padilla, is dripping with contempt for homosexuals ("eres joto y rete joto") and their effeminate mannerisms, high voices, and swishy walk. The female singer lashes out at one gay man who pretended to be straight and who almost became her husband: "Me decían que eras casado. No lo puedo comprender, pues el hombre afeminado aborrece a la mujer." (They told me you were married. I just can't understand, because effeminate men abhor women.) She says it would have been a huge embarrassment for her to think she had gotten married only to find out she was living with another woman, instead of a good husband. And she urges him to find other "jotos" to help with his housework. The composer never resolves the song's glaring internal contradiction: if the guy was so obviously gay, how was she almost fooled into marrying him?

Many other examples of overt prejudice can be found in the archives. "El Negro José," a 1978 single by Lalo Treviño on the Texas-based Cara label, recycled black stereotypes to a tropical beat a decade after the civil rights movement had peaked. It's about a happy, footloose, and carefree man named José who is so black he can't be seen in the dark: "Allí viene el Negro

José. Prendan las luces que no lo pueden ver." (Here comes José, the black man. Turn on the lights so you can see him.)

In the remainder of this chapter, we examine more closely how three very different ethnic groups are depicted in Mexican songs: the Chinese immigrant in Latin America, the white Anglo majority in the United States, and the assimilated Mexican immigrant known disparagingly as pocho. For each group, we look at a set of songs that reflect how they were perceived in popular music. These examples are not meant to be exhaustive, but they serve as an indication of the possibilities for further research into a relatively overlooked field, the racial attitudes of Mexicans toward "the other." The topic is especially relevant now. At a time when Mexican Americans are again subjected to harsh stereotypes in the course of a heated immigration debate, it is useful to look at how they view and treat other groups when the shoe is on the other foot.

Los Gringos

The history of the borderlands between Mexico and the United States is one forged in ethnic conflict and warfare. The US-Mexican War of 1846–48 was motivated by imperialist dreams of territorial expansion and was rationalized, at least in part, by racist theories about the inferiority and savagery of the Mexican people. Thus, the conflict that established the current border between the two nations also delineated the social divide between neighboring peoples, with one side destined to be dominant, the other subservient.[2] Even the newspapers of the day fanned the flames of racial conflict in the run-up to the war. James Gordon Bennett, a Scottish immigrant who was the founder and editor of the *New York Herald*, predicted a swift victory for the United States, citing the "imbecility and degradation of

the Mexican people" due to the "amalgamation of the races" in that country, a blend of bloodlines he considered "abhorrent to the Anglo-Saxon race on this continent."[3] Bennett's use of the media to fan racial discord remained a tradition in the United States. It was carried on a century later by the *Los Angeles Times* when it incited violence against Mexican American youths during World War II, resulting in what became known as the Zoot Suit Riots—a reference to the flamboyant style of clothing sported by the Mexican American men who were stripped and beaten by US servicemen during these attacks.

From the mid-1800s through the last half of the twentieth century, Mexicans and Mexican Americans had no comparable voice to defend their interests or to represent their viewpoints in the mainstream media. They were not entirely voiceless: a network of Spanish-language newspapers often mounted a vigorous defense of the rights of immigrant minorities. But for the masses of working-class, poorly educated Mexicans and Mexican Americans living on both sides of the border, the strongest and most authentic expressions of their intercultural experience came in the form of songs. The love-hate relationship between the two countries is expressed with almost snarky satire in one early song, "La Pasadita," which dates to the US-Mexico war itself. The lyrics, cited in the 1905 memoirs of Mexican geographer and historian Antonio García Cubas, mock the Mexican women who sought to strike up relationships with the invading Yankee soldiers. In one sarcastic verse, the women ("las margaritas") are quoted as speaking a bastardized Spanish that they try to pass off as English.

> Ya las margaritas
> hablan el inglés.
> Les dicen: "¿Me quieres?"
> Y responden: "Yes.
> "Mi entende de monis;
> mucho güeno está."

The song and the geographer's memoirs are cited by Guillermo E. Hernández in his Spanish-language essay titled "The Comic Characteristics of the Pocho and the Pachuco: Literary and Popular Antecedents."[4] The UCLA scholar highlights the contempt that the verse heaps on these "harlots of infamous character" ("meretrices de ínfima calidad"), as García Cubas called them. The way they speak, Hernández notes, is meant to signal their low station in life, most likely indigenous and rural. And their crass, comical reference to money ("Mi entende de monis") brands their pursuit of Americans as purely materialistic. This caricature of the treacherous native female has roots in La Malinche, the Indian woman who became the symbol of betrayal when she became the ally and concubine of Hernán Cortés, the conquering Spaniard.[5] Four centuries later, the same opprobrium would apply to the figure of La Pocha, the assimilated Mexican immigrant scorned by Mexican society for trying to act American. "The pocha will inherit this stigma and it will become common to refer to her intentions by alluding to her materialism and lack of sincerity," writes Hernández. "Later, in their full maturity, the pocho and pocha would be transformed into negative and denigrating examples of Mexican culture, and to their comical character would be added the hostility of considering them disloyal."

However, the culture clash led not only to venting. It also served as the crucible for the creation of certain forms of music along the border between Mexico and the United States, according to Manuel Peña, an anthropologist specializing in Mexican American folklore and music. Essential to this symbiotic border culture is the love-hate relationship between the two groups, in which both sides simultaneously oppose and emulate each other in a dialectical push-pull. On the one hand, Peña notes, there is the "Anglos' romantic fascination with things Mexican," including the lifestyle of the grand haciendas, the fandangos, the chili and fajitas, and the macho pride and bravado reflected in the *vaquero*, a model for the western cowboy. And on the other, subordinated Mexican Americans have so internalized elements of Anglo culture that they even adopt a belief in the superiority of "the American way of doing things," especially compared to the ways of Mexicans themselves. "At times, in assimilating Anglo customs, the border Mexicans have reinterpreted them in their own fashion, as in the case of the low-rider car and the zoot-suit cultures," Peña writes. "A musical example of this kind of assimilation/reinterpretation is that of the 'kikker' music-culture of South Texas, so popular for many years among Texas-Mexicans. It is permeated through and through with a country-western, cowboy style, yet is also quintessentially a border Mexican expression."[6]

Peña pinpoints three musical styles unique to the Southwest border region, each of which "played a powerful role in defining and mediating the interethnic relationship in all of its complexities." They are the Mexican American orquesta, the Texas-Mexican conjunto, and the corrido of interethnic conflict. The first two are defined by the makeup of specific musical ensembles. The latter is a folk genre that can be played with a wide variety of accompaniments in many styles. The Frontera Collection contains many examples of all three.

As we've seen in a previous chapter, the Mexican corrido, or narrative ballad, provided an especially powerful outlet for the racial reactions of Mexicans toward the dominant Anglo culture. Border scholar Américo Paredes defined a special subcategory he called the corrido of intercultural conflict, which emerged during the early period of Anglo-Mexican relations, an era marked by "open hostility" in Mexican American folklore.[7] Mexican singers and songwriters used the genre as a vehicle for voicing their reactions to the disdain and discrimination they faced in their daily dealings with the Anglo population, which considered itself culturally superior in every way. The corrido, therefore, emerges as an affirmation of culture in the face of a hostile antagonist—pop music as self-defense. It is a historical irony that these biting and sometimes bitter expressions of racial animosity toward the Anglo majority were recorded and preserved by major American record companies that were an integral part of the dominant white culture. In many instances, representatives of labels such as Victor, Brunswick, and Columbia would travel from New York to cities such as San Antonio and Los Angeles to supervise the recordings of songs that were harshly critical of the way Mexicans were being treated by whites.

On those recording trips, the New York executives relied on the locals to tell them which songs would be popular, especially local music shop dealers who knew the talent in town. The executives didn't much care what the lyrics said as long as the song was a hit. "Some of the songs were outright hateful to certain groups, how evil the Germans were to Mexicans in South Texas, and so on," notes Chris Strachwitz. "I'm sure they didn't understand. They were just looking for what sold."[8]

"Pregúntale a los Presentes"
Performers: Alejandro Luna and Regino Delgado
Label: Bluebird B-3007-A
This track, recorded in 1936, represents an angry, frontal assault on the United States and on what the composer, unidentified on this recording, perceives as US imperial arrogance. The title, which translates literally as "Ask Those Present," is a call to arms, beseeching

Mexicans to defend their country and not allow it to be humiliated by invaders. The first three lines express confidence that the nation will answer the call; even women will drop their chores to respond. But the last line of that verse makes clear that valor and manhood will be the first line of defense against "los patones," the big-footed neighbors to the north: "Que vengan esos patones. Que habiendo hombres se morirán." (Let the "big foots" come. As long as there are men [here], they will die.)

In the second verse, after identifying Mexico as the "land of gold," a reference to the colonial plundering of the Aztec nation, the song issues this rallying cry: "Don't let those avaricious people send their troops to rob us."

México hermoso, tierra del oro,
¿por qué te dejas así humillar?
No permitieras a esos golosos
que manden tropas para robar.

In the final verse, the song alludes once again to the wealth of the enemy and vows that Mexicans will die rather than live under their boot:

Si porque tienen sus capitales
quieren tenernos bajo sus pies.
Pues eso nunca permitiremos
nos moriremos mando a sus pies.

The macho message of the song contrasts sharply with the slowly strummed guitar accompaniment and the warbling, harmonized vocals of Luna and Delgado, a duet that recorded many nonpolitical, romantic songs. All of their recordings in the Frontera Collection appear on Bluebird, Victor's Depression-era budget label.

"El Gringo y el Mexicano"
Performer: Los Populares del Norte
Label: AGO Records AGO-3223-A
As corridos go, the narrative of this number is rather generic. Two men fight over a two-timing woman and both end up dead. However, in this case the romantic rivals are the "gringo"

and the "Mexicano" of the title, thus setting up a culture clash as subtext within the melodrama. After setting up the love triangle, the song describes in the third and fourth verses exactly what this "very lovely woman" saw in each of her men. The gringo won her first with his money. The Mexicano later woos her heart, but he doesn't steal her away. She wants to keep them both:

> Ella estaba contenta,
> porque vivía con los dos.
> El gringo daba el dinero,
> y el mexicano el amor.

> (She was happy
> because she had both of them in her life.
> The gringo offered money,
> and the Mexican offered love.)

The gringo's character is further established in the fifth verse, when he discovers that the lovely "rosa" has been cheating on him: he forgives her "because he was in love." He goes on to challenge his rival to a duel, and by sunrise they have shot each other to death. Although the song does not say how the Mexicano feels about her betrayal, one might assume from other such situations in Mexican folklore that he would want to kill them both.

In this concise story, the qualities of these two rivals, and by extension the nations they represent, are revealed by what the woman wants from each of them. The gringo is attractive because he's wealthy, and she is portrayed as not shy about using him. The Mexicano may not have money, but he has strong feelings and knows how to give love. It is a classic dichotomy seen time and again when Mexicans draw comparisons between themselves and their Anglo neighbors. And once again, the Mexican woman's attraction to the gringo is seen as completely self-serving and therefore lacking in emotional fulfillment. Her needs—to be cared for monetarily and emotionally—are only fulfilled by having two men. This duplicity sets up the song's deadly denouement.

"Humorismos Yankees"
    Performers: D. Herrera and J. Rachini
    Label: Victor 30571-A
Like the offensive faux-Asian lingo that uses "ching-chong" sounds to make fun of the Chinese, this song derides Americans by using Anglo-sounding vocalizing to capture how Mexicans hear the English language as spoken by their US neighbors. It is simply two and a half minutes of mushy gibberish that makes Americans sound either dense or pompous, or both. Though the song has few intelligible lyrics, the composing credit is given to the performing duo of D. Herrera and J. Rachini. At about the fifty-second mark, the duo breaks into song, doing what sounds like scatting over a fast-tempo, jazzy rhythm with guitar accompaniment. This section is really quite funny, as the singers sprinkle recognizable English phrases into their Anglo-sounding banter. At the right rhythmic moments, they drop phrases such as "Oh, yes . . . that's all right . . . Hollywood . . . my boy . . . no? yes? Oh, my golly . . . I kill no dog . . . I come now." This musical portion is obviously tightly arranged, with vocal parts assigned to each member of the duo, demonstrating a certain level of satirical talent that goes beyond the normal frat-house stereotyping of other songs. Listen for a break in the tempo where they repeatedly squeeze in the line from a popular English-language novelty song, "Ice cream sundae, I scream, you scream."

"El Mosco Americano"
    Label: Columbia 4371-X
    Performer: Cancioneros Picarescos
    "El Mosquito Americano"
    Labels and Performers: Corona 1095, Daniel Garzés y Su Conjunto Los Tres Reyes; Falcon

*A989, Los Tres Reyes; Ideal 851-A, Carmen
y Laura*

Composers: Daniel Garzés and Paulo Alonzo

This satirical, anti-American song is based on a popular broadside of the same title dating to the prerevolutionary years between 1900 and 1910. The broadside features an illustration by famed artist José Guadalupe Posada (1852–1913), known for his biting political artwork that satirized conditions under the dictatorship of Porfirio Díaz. In this case, his drawing depicts five Mexicans of diverse social standing all being attacked by a swarm of large mosquitoes. The allegorical drawing and the accompanying text suggest that the mosquitoes represent various evils that descended on Mexico from the border during the corrupt Díaz regime. Observers over the years have said the insects could represent American tourists who entered the country at the border, or the waves of American technical advisers imported by Díaz to help develop mines and railroads. Others suggest the plague could be the US dollar itself, which was seen as corrupting the Mexican economy. In any case, it's clear that the "American mosquito" represented a pestilence inflicted on Mexico.

The first version of the song, as listed above, is the only one from the Frontera Collection that does not use the diminutive form of the Spanish, "mosquito," in the title. Instead, the label text uses the word "mosco." However, the comic duet on this track is heard singing the title as used in the broadside and on the other recordings. Despite the apparent error, this version is more faithful to the original text of the broadside. In between the short musical chorus, one of the members of the duet recites several verses with no musical background. These spoken verses follow the concept of the original text by tracing the travels of the "mosquito Americano" as it makes its way through

Mexico, leaving a trail of trouble from Laredo through Zacatecas and Veracruz. The other versions are more loosely based on the text of Posada's broadside, with pared-down lyrics put to a tropical beat and no recited dialog. The song's catchy, childish chorus bluntly reinforces the original message:

> Pero mira, mira, mira.
> ¡Ay, qué maldito animal!
> Pero mira, mira, mira,
> ¡comó les vino a picar!"
>
> (But look, look, look.
> What a cursed creature!
> But look, look, look,
> how he came to bite them!)

Of these three versions, the earliest is most likely the 78-rpm recording on the San Antonio–based Corona label by the composer, Daniel Garzés and his conjunto Los Tres Reyes (fig. 43). In this rendition, the song's satirical spirit is spiked by a Tex-Mex accordion that tickles its way through the song. In a subsequent recording on the Falcon label, the artist credit is reversed, with the trio getting top billing and Garzés listed in small type as singer. The third copy, by Carmen y Laura (fig. 44) with the conjunto of Chuy Compeán, sticks to the lyrics but replaces the accordion-based conjunto with the brass-and-reed sound of a dance orchestra.

"El Turismo"

Performer: Netty Rodríguez

Label: Bluebird 2328-B

With its mocking tone, this satirical song, which makes fun of Mexicans who copy American ways, echoes other songs that explicitly mock pochos. Here, singer Netty Rodríguez laments the many bad habits her countrymen are adopting as a result of their contact with American tourists. The first verse starts by noting that "we Mexicans, we're all becoming gringos." Everybody is "chewing gum," and some even chew tobacco. Instead of saying "frijoles," they say "beans." As usual, the song reserves special contempt for Americanized women: "Now, all the girls are blond and have their hair bobbed. And even the Chinas Poblanas say they are Chicagonas." ("Ya toditas la muchachas andan güeras y pelonas. Y hasta las chinas poblanas dicen que son chicagonas.") The play on words, and on place names, in the second line adds to the mockery by suggesting a profanity related to bodily functions. It turns the "china poblana," the ultra-feminine indigenous woman from Puebla—one of the most iconic and revered traditional symbols, whose almost mythical persona can be traced back to

seventeenth-century Mexican folklore—into something filthy. These revered and dignified women from Puebla start claiming instead that they are from Chicago, or "Chicagonas." This invented, Mexicanized term for Chicagoans—a more grammatical Spanish term might be "Chicaguenses"—mischievously contains the word "chica," or young woman, and "cagonas," a crude term for someone who has lost control of a certain toilet function.

The final verse sums up the impact of this cultural dyspepsia in stark terms: "El turismo esta de moda, pero arruina la nación." (Tourism is fashionable, but it's ruining the country.)

Figure 43. Daniel Garzés (*center*) led Los Tres Reyes, one of the most popular Texas conjuntos of the post-war era. Garzés (sometimes spelled Garcés) was also one of the most prolific songwriters in the genre (see appendix D). He is credited with writing the satirical, anti-American tune "El Mosquito Americano," of which there are several versions in The Frontera Collection, including one by Garzés and his conjunto. Photograph courtesy of the Arhoolie Foundation.

Figure 44. Two sisters from Kingsville, Carmen Hernández Marroquín (*left*) and Laura Hernández Cantú, formed one of the most popular female duets of the 1940s and '50s. Carmen y Laura launched their recording career in 1943 and later became one of the top acts on the legendary Ideal record label, founded by Carmen's husband, Armando Marroquín. The duet was one of the first to add blues and swing to the Tejano repertoire, performing with major acts that included Narciso Martínez and Beto Villa. On the satirical "El Mosquito Americano," they are backed with a tropical beat by the conjunto of bandleader and arranger Chuy Compeán. Photograph courtesy of the Arhoolie Foundation.

Los Chinitos

In the United States, the stereotypical snippet of music known as the "Oriental riff" is so common it even has its own page on Wikipedia. Every schoolchild could recognize the supposedly Chinese-sounding melody, often embellished by the reverberating clang of a gong, which is meant to represent all things Asian in Western culture. In Latin American music, the riff is equally ubiquitous. Many of the songs from the Frontera Collection cited in this section contain the riff as convenient musical shorthand to convey "orientalism," to borrow Wikipedia's term.

In Spanish, stereotypes can also be conveyed through distinct language usage, especially the diminutive forms of nouns, which can express fondness but also a patronizing attitude. Thus, blacks are often referred to as "negritos," no matter how big they may be, and Asians as "chinitos," no matter what country they actually come from. Defenders of the diminutive argue that the terms are used affectionately. And indeed, some of the songs in the Frontera archives use the terms "chino" or "china" in a hyper-romantic way. For example, the Trío Los Panchos, a popular singing act during the 1940s and '50s, bring their sweet harmonies to the love-at-first-sight lyrics of "Chon-Chon-Chon" (Columbia 6212-X):

> Soñando siempre con el Asia estaba yo,
> y pronto una china linda vino a mí,
> pidiendo que yo le cantara el Chon-Chon-Chon.
> Me dio un beso y me robó el corazón.
>
> (I was always dreaming of Asia,
> when suddenly a lovely Chinese woman came to me,
> asking that I sing for her "Chon-Chon-Chon."
> She gave me a kiss and stole my heart.)

In another tune by Cuban composer Osvaldo Farrés, the "Oriental riff" serves as background for the cooing of two lovers who affectionately call each other, as the title indicates, "Chinito . . . Chinita." Curiously, the title on the version by Mexico's Dueto Azteca (Columbia 2466) has the gender of the terms reversed—"Chinita Chinito." The song "China Poblana," written by Pepe Guízar and recorded on the Decca label by the duo of Margarita Cueto and Perla Violeta Amado, is a lyrical, sentimental ode to the Chinese woman's graceful style and idealized character. The track, a 78-rpm recording, was taken from a film with a fittingly romanticized title, *La India Bonita*, or the Pretty Indian Woman.

Still, the negative aspect of the Chinese stereotype persists in contemporary Latin culture. In 2005, for example, an Asian reader asked about the issue in a letter to author Gustavo Arellano, who writes a widely read Q&A column for the *OC Weekly* titled "Ask a Mexican!" The reader, a resident of Orange County, California, which has a large Vietnamese population, asked whether Latinos would consider him a "chinito" even though he is not Chinese. The reader signed his query as "OC Asian," but Arellano addressed him as "Dear Chino," as if to provide the answer by underscoring the insult. In his response, the columnist writes:

> Like Americans assume all Latinos are Mexican, Mexicans think all Asians are *chinos—Chinese.* . . . "Chino," like so many of our swear words, has multiple negative meanings. In the colonial days, a *chino* was the offspring of a half-Indian/half-black and an Indian. This association with race also transformed *chino* into a synonym for "servant" and "curly." The term "barrio chino" (Chinatown) also became a euphemism for a town's red-light district.[9]

One of the largest, most established Chinatowns in Mexico is located in Mexicali, on the border with California, east of Tijuana. Until recently, the border city's Barrio Chino boasted one of Mexico's oldest Chinese restaurants, Restaurant 19, named after an alley that was one of the early Chinese corridors in the city. The restaurant, which operated from its founding in 1928 until it closed in 2001, became a meeting place for diplomats and celebrities from both sides of the border, representing the affluence of Mexicali's Chinese minority. Ironically, Mexicali's ethnic enclave was created by Chinese immigrants seeking refuge from racism in the United States.[10] They came to find, as the following songs suggest, that stereotypes know no boundaries.

"El Chinito Vacilador"
 Performer: Carmen y Emilio Cabrera
 Label: Victor 46550-A

In this 78-rpm recording on the RCA Victor label, the duet of Carmen y Emilio Cabrera performs a comedy skit, or *diálogo cómico*, replete with Chinese stereotypes. In the dialog, a woman mockingly questions a man who speaks with an exaggerated Chinese accent, pronouncing the letter *r* as an *l*, and so forth. In the following snippet, the contemptuous woman makes fun of the man's slanted and narrow eyes.

> Mexican Woman: Pos, si creo que ustedes los chinos no tienen ni corazón. Yo he oído decir por ahí que es que lo tienen atravesado.
>
> Chinese Man: Mentira! A mi no se me atalaviesa nada.
>
> Mexican Woman: ¿Cómo no tienes atravesado nada? Y esos ojos que parecen puñaladas metidas en jitomate.
>
> (Mexican Woman: Well, I think that you Chinese people don't even have a heart. And I've heard it said somewhere that you even have it sideways.
>
> Chinese Man: That's a lie. I don't have anything sideways.
>
> Mexican Woman: What do you mean you don't have anything sideways? And what about those eyes that look like stab wounds stuck in a tomato.)

The man tries to defend himself by listing all the services he provides: "I wash clothes, I do the ironing, and for you I make your coffee with milk." ("Lavo la ropa, la pa-lancho, a ti te hago tu café con leche.") But her retort is again demeaning: "Those are tasks for old ladies!" ("¡Esos son quehaceres de viejas!") Hold on a minute, the Chinese man protests. He is about to launch his candidacy, which is mangled in faux Chinese accent as "mi candalatuna," instead of "mi candidatura." This time, her retort stoops to a religious insult: "What are you thinking, that any son of Sir Confucius can be a Congressman? You're twisted."

And once again, the Chinese man's attempt to defend himself backfires. He asserts that he was with revolutionary leader Pancho Villa, but instead of proving his bravery, he confesses cowardice. Whatever Villa did, the Chinese man asserts, he was always behind ("siempre detlas"). Behind what, the woman asks. "Behind the door," says the cowardly Chino.

The increasingly annoyed woman then calls him a "disgraceful chino," and in her final insult she threatens to call her husband to administer a beating: "Oye, chino desgraciado. Ya me estas cansado y le voy a llamar a mi marido pa' que te meta tus trancazos."

"Conflicto Galaico-Chino"
 Performer: Zabala, Otero, y Sevilla
 Label: Victor 46870-B
 Composer: Adolfo Otero

This is another comical skit from the 78 era, recorded on the RCA Victor label. Identified as a "terceto cómico," it was composed by Adolfo Otero and performed by the trio of Zabala, Otero, and Sevilla. The gist of the "conflict" referred to in the title involves two knife sharpeners, a Spaniard from Galicia and a Chinese man, again speaking Spanish with an "Asian" accent. The two tradesmen compete for the business of a female customer who is bargaining for the best price. At the end of the haggling, the Chinese worker brings his price down to zero in order to undercut the Spaniard, proving that Chinese labor is so cheap it puts everybody else out of business.

"El Chino Camarero"
  Label: Victor 23-1218-A
  Performer: Daniel Santos

Daniel Santos is one of the foremost tropical music vocalists from Puerto Rico. His career spanned more than half a century. For a time in the 1940s, he lived in Havana, where he performed with the seminal salsa band La Sonora Matancera, which later would feature singer Celia Cruz. Santos wrote this upbeat danceable number about a "Chinese waiter" who works at a "fonda," or small, cheap restaurant, where he calls out his dishes with that stereotypical Chinese accent. The food is great, says Santos in the song, but the best thing about the place is the "chino camarero" who calls out, "Labo con alo! Labo con alo!" Of course, once again, the Spanish *r* has been replaced with an *l*, making his phrase sound meaningless. What he meant to say is "rabo con arroz," or oxtails and rice. The accented punch line is repeated over and over as the chorus of the song, in the traditional Caribbean style of call-and-response vocals. So the song uses the traditional salsa format to repeatedly rub in the mockery. As the notes in the Frontera database indicate, "This song parodies the way an Asian waiter speaks. This would be considered very offensive by today's standards." Indeed.

"El Chinito"
  Performer: Cancionero Solitario
  Label: Bluebird B-3497-B
  Performer: Aarón González
  Label: Decca 10256A
  Performer: Quinteto Yucatán
  Label: Vocalion 8444

This song has no purpose other than to engage in the most extreme form of Chinese accent mockery. The fact that there are three versions of the tune, in three entirely different styles, is an indication of the popularity of this type of belittling ethnic humor in the first half of the twentieth century.

The number is built around the following refrain, which serves simply to set up the segments of fake Chinese-speak: "But Chinese Man, what are you selling that I want to buy from you? Oh, tell me what you're selling so I can hear you shout your pitch." ("Pero chino, ¿qué vendes tú, que yo te quiero comprar? Ay dime lo que tu vendes, para oírte pregonar.") The Chinese merchant then launches into a rhythmic recital of his goods, which amounts to stanzas of Chinese-sounding Spanish gibberish. Remarkably, the three Frontera versions are so similar they suggest that the "ching-chong" nonsense verses have actually been written out. However, the only recording that credits an author is the Decca 78-rpm by Aarón González and his Orquesta de Tango. It's described as a rumba (ballroom, not Afro-Cuban folklore) written by Sergio M. Pérez, with the chorus, or *estribillo*, written by Pérez with Bobby Ramos. This dance version ends with the obligatory clang of a gong at the end.

The version by the Quinteto Yucatán, on Brunswick's Vocalion imprint, brings trio-style harmonies and romantic Spanish guitars to the arrangement. But the lyrics, and the mockery, remain the same. The rendition by El Cancionero Solitario wastes no time getting into the accent shtick. Apparently, the Lonely Troubadour fancies himself such a master of the Chinese accent that he opens with a monologue of Asian gibberish and later riffs on more spontaneous Sino-sounds in the middle of the song. Otherwise, he also sticks to the script.

"Chino Soy"
> *Performer: Xavier Cugat and his Waldorf-Astoria Orchestra*
> *Composers: Xavier Cugat and Pedro Berrios*
> *Label: Victor 25184-A*

Spanish-born bandleader Xavier Cugat was at the peak of his popularity in the United States with his Waldorf-Astoria Orchestra, named after the chic hotel where his band had a standing gig in the 1940s. The classically trained musician elevates the Chinese stereotype with a sophisticated arrangement and stylish performance of the tune "Chino Soy," which he wrote with singer Pedro Berrios. Cugat even gives the ethnic shtick its own genre, "Chinese rumba," although this seems to be the only song in that category. Still, the underlying stereotype remains the same, complete with the opening gong cliché. The lyrics are a romantic appeal by a Chinese man from Shanghai seeking a Cuban woman who can dance "lumba," with no *r*, of course. However, it's hard to imagine a woman who would respond to the man's mating call, since the record ends with some spoken Chinese-accented talk that goes beyond gibberish and sounds like the whine of a wounded dog. It's notable that so much musical thought can go into a subject so inane.

Los Pochos

Permit me to introduce this section with a personal anecdote. In the mid-1980s, when my older son Miguel was about five years old, we took him on a trip to visit Guanajuato, the marvelous colonial city in central Mexico. One evening as we sat on a park bench in the lively central plaza facing the iconic Teatro Juárez, Miguel started playing with some Mexican children nearby. He was naturally friendly and seemed to blend in with the kids from the country of my birth, even though he himself was born and raised in the United States. After a short while, however, he came back with a sad look on his face and said, on the verge of tears, "Me dijeron ocho." I could not figure out why the kids would tag him as the number eight, but I thought it might be a game. "Entonces tu diles 'siete'" (Then you call them "seven"), I advised playfully, still oblivious to the cultural insult that had just been hurled at my boy.

It suddenly dawned on me that they had not called him "ocho" at all. They had called him "pocho," but my son had misunderstood the term because he had never heard it before. I, on the other hand, was well aware of what it meant and how it must have been delivered, with a sneering, or at least dismissive, schoolyard contempt. *Pocho*, as many Mexican Americans are painfully aware, is a pejorative term used by Mexican nationals to describe other Mexicans who have either lost or deliberately shed their language and homeland traditions after migrating to the United States. In short, it's a derogatory term for an Americanized Mexican, complicated by thorny connotations of class distinctions. Even without understanding the term, my son would have instinctively felt the offensive sting behind it, and its instantly distancing impact.

In his above-cited essay on pochos and pachucos, Guillermo Hernández attributes the earliest use of the term "pocho" to the devilishly named column "Crónicas Diabólicas" (The Diabolical Chronicles), written between 1916 and 1926 by author Julio G. Arce under the pen name Jorge Ulica.[11] Published in *Hispano América*, a newspaper based in San Francisco, the columnist uses the term pocho to satirize those Mexican immigrants whose language and customs betray a marked Anglo-American influence. But Hernández traces the prejudicial and demeaning attitudes toward pochos to the early 1800s. He quotes from the diary of a Mexican military official, Lt. José María Sánchez, who travelled to the border region adjoining Texas in 1828–29. "Accustomed to continuous commerce with Americans," the lieutenant writes about his countrymen in the United States, "they have imitated their customs, and thus it can be said truthfully that they are Mexicans by birth only, since they speak the Castilian language with very little knowledge of it." More than one hundred years later, with World War II raging, the same disdain would be aimed at the "pachucos," especially their flashy style of dress which drew heavily on American fashion sensibilities.

"The pocho and the pachuco alike," writes Hernández, "are figures who break the established norms within their social and cultural environment. This violation provokes, on the one hand, the censure of those who attack their behavior as unacceptable and disparaging and, on the other hand, the defense of critics and writers who consider it socio-historically unavoidable and justifiable."

The ridicule of Mexicans who act Anglo was commonly found in both the theater productions and popular music of San Antonio during the first half of the twentieth century, according to Peter Clair Haney in his 2004 doctoral dissertation for the University of Texas at Austin.[12] Citing studies by José Eduardo Limón and Américo Paredes, he notes that songs often "satirized the linguistic habits of *pochos* or *agringados*" as part of the effort by Mexican nationals in South Texas to "police the boundaries of their identity through jokes about those who adopt Anglo-American ways." Some of the songs reserve special contempt for the *agringada*, the archetypal pocha "who puts on airs and refuses to speak Spanish." This female character, Haney notes, is frequently found in the comic dialogs recorded between 1928 and

1937 by Netty and Jesús Rodríguez (fig. 45), "two Mexican immigrant vaudevillians who enjoyed considerable success on San Antonio's ethnic Mexican stage." More than four dozen of the duo's recordings can be found in the Frontera Collection. (Their song, "El Turismo," is cited above in the section on Los Gringos.) These recordings, Haney contends, are imbued with a "a nostalgic aesthetic of *costumbrismo* . . . which re-interprets the dislocations of exile in gendered terms." The couple's songs grow progressively more pessimistic as they delve into the corrosive effects of the cultural dislocation caused by immigration. "For Netty and Jesús Rodríguez," Haney concludes, "this anomie was a symptom of the deep social pathology of life in the United States."

"El Charro y la Pocha"
Performer: Contreras – Carrillo
Label: Victor 80585

On the label, the title of this song is translated in parentheses as "The Cowboy and His Girl," but that rendering is completely inaccurate, both literally and figuratively (fig. 46). In this spoken dialog, El Charro, or Mexican Cowboy, is engaged in a conversation with a woman, La Pocha, who is a total stranger he meets on the street. The humor of the skit is built around the man's confusion during a visit to an American city because he doesn't understand English. He miscommunicates and misinterprets everything. He sees a dark-skinned Mexican woman pass by, but his hopes of finally speaking to somebody in Spanish are dashed when he discovers that she is Americanized and doesn't speak his language, or doesn't want to. "What you say?" she responds, with a heavy Spanish accent. That inability to communicate opens the door to the age-old conflict between Mexicans, represented by the emblematic charro figure, and Mexican Americans, represented by the pocha who sounds clueless from the start. In

Figure 45. La Bella Netty y Jesús Rodríguez was a vaudeville-style musical comedy act that was extremely popular in the San Antonio area during the 1930s and '40s. The duo's satirical skits—*diálogos cómicos*—relied heavily on vernacular accents and expressions leading to humorous misunderstandings or double entendres. The Frontera Collection contains many of their recordings, including "El Turismo" on Bluebird, which mocks Mexicans who copy American ways. Photograph courtesy of the Arhoolie Foundation.

this classic confrontation, the Mexican always assumes that his uprooted counterpart is simply pretending not to know Spanish, a strategy used by pochos not only to fit in but to feel superior to the people left behind in Mexico. The charro unmasks the pocha's pretensions by craftily smoking out her true identity. After she pretends not to understand his request for directions, he mutters an insult as an aside, in Spanish of course: "Diablo de vieja tan meca. Es purita zapoteca y presume de sajón." The insult itself reveals the calcified class and race

divisions that, as Hernández points out, underpin much of the Mexican's resentment against the pocho. He skewers her by pointing out that she looks completely Indian but is acting white: "She is all Zapotec but she fancies herself a Saxon."

As soon as the woman hears the man's critique, she suddenly "remembers" her Spanish and responds through her hurt pride. "Usted será un pelado," she says, calling him a Spanish slang term for lowlife. And the charro quickly leaps on the opportunity: "¡Mira como ahora

Figure 46. "El Charro y la Pocha" is a comedic skit, or *diálogo cómico,* performed by a male-female duet known as Contreras y Carrillo. A 78-rpm release on the Victor label, it is a stinging satirical exchange between a traditional Mexican man, the "charro," who encounters an Americanized Mexican American woman, derogatively called the "pocha," during a US visit. The incorrect translation of the title on the label, "The Cowboy and His Girl," fails to capture the cultural conflict the skit is meant to convey. Photograph courtesy of the Arhoolie Foundation.

entendió!" (See how now you understand!) This is the turning point in the dialog. The Mexican realizes he has forced an opening. But instead of rubbing it in, his tone becomes sweet and intimate, asking her to come closer and listen carefully to what he has to say: "Vengase acá chatita y óigame con atención." He even uses the affectionate term "chatita" to address her, instantly establishing the Mexican trait of acting friendly toward strangers. That natural warmth foreshadows the speech he is about to deliver on the greatness of Mexico, glorifying its culture and its people: "¿Por qué niega a su patria si es la tierra del Señor? Mi México querido fue donde nació Dios." (Why do you deny your homeland if it is the Lord's land? My beloved Mexico is where God was born.) He

argues that denying her country is tantamount to denying her own mother. That leads to her conversion with quasi-religious overtones as she embraces once again her Mexican identity and, miraculously, loses her gringo accent in Spanish. The song ends with the two strangers, now reconciled in their common patriotism, singing an exultant duet praising the land of their mutual origin. El Charro is victorious. La Pocha is redeemed. And Mexico is reconciled.

"El Alambrista y La Pocha"
> *Performer: Hermanas Mosqueda*
> *Composer: E. Navarrete*
> *Label: Imperial 647*

In this song, La Pocha of the title has no redeeming moment. It tells the sad tale of a hapless *alambrista* (undocumented Mexican immigrant) and the pocha he falls in love with in the United States. Just as he's about to get married—"when I was the happiest I've ever been"—he's caught by immigration authorities and deported. The rest of the song recounts the harrowing experiences endured during multiple border crossings by the *alambrista*, which literally means tightrope walker but which is used as slang to refer to Mexicans who stage a dangerous balancing act when they try to jump the line to get into the United States. On one occasion, he's held in a detention center where he loses his hair and a lot of weight. His stubborn efforts to return to the United States are all aimed at reuniting with "la pochita who had all my love."

But when he finally does make it back, he finds that she has two children, "and neither of them look like me." He's so angry he's ready to kill her. But just at that moment, in keeping with the song's theme, La Migra grabs him and sends him back to Mexico again. He is sadly "disillusioned" that his pocha "turned out to be such a live wire." In fact, in the time that it took for him to tell the story, the song says, she had twins.

Performed by the female duo of Las Hermanas Mosqueda with the Mariachi Chapala, the song invites the listener to sympathize with the poor Mexican victim of the fickle pocha who stole his heart. Yet it is the pocha, as a symbol for assimilated immigrants, who is victimized by such extreme stereotyping. In suggesting the woman might be promiscuous, the song confirms the assertion by Hernández that pochas are portrayed as self-interested, materialistic, unfaithful, and untrustworthy.[13] In this case, the inference is that becoming Americanized turned her into a libertine. When she abandoned her traditional Mexican morals, she lost her conscience and her self-respect.

"El Pocho"
Performer: Conjunto Hnos. Rojo
Composer: Eligio Aguayo
Label: Ema's Records

This song provides a rousing rationale for being, or at least acting like, a pocho. It is not exactly a defense of the Mexican American identity, but rather a practical justification for why an immigrant would want to assume that identity.

In the first verse, the pocho of the title sets the stage for his argument, delivered to a spirited polka tempo and a sprightly accordion:

"Allí viene el pocho," me grita la gente
cuando en mi moto me miran pasar.
Pues nadie sabe que yo ando de alambre
porque español no me oyen hablar.
Hoy yo no quiero tener el problema
que La Migra me llegue a agarrar,
y por falta del inglés,
a los coyotes les tenga que pagar.

(Everybody cries out, "Here comes the pocho,"
when they see me pass by on my motorcycle.
Well, no one knows I'm here as a line jumper,
because they don't hear me speak Spanish.
I don't want to have the problem
that La Migra might come and catch me,
and for lack of speaking English,
I'd have to pay the coyotes.

The song, written by Eligio Aguayo and recorded on the Los Angeles–based Ema's label, is certainly told from the immigrant's point of view. But it's not a pocho viewpoint per se. Here, the immigrant admits that he consciously assumes the pocho persona as an act of self-preservation. "It's not that I don't want to speak English," he sings, "it's that I want to throw off La Migra." He then recommends this strategy to his countrymen, advising them to learn English ("Aprendan inglés, mis paisanos"). Then, he confronts the heart of the pocho controversy head on, advising others to hide their essential Mexicanness in case the Migra should catch them some day too ("Por si La Migra los encuentra, traigan bien escondido el nopal"). The phrase he uses—"make sure your cactus [nopal] is well hidden"—resonates deeply with the concept of Mexican identity. In fact, when someone is unmistakably Mexican, with dark skin and distinctly indigenous features, he is said to wear the cactus on his forehead ("trae el nopal en la frente"). That very group of Mexicans, the ones who look indigenous, are the ones targeted for greatest contempt and animosity when they try to deny their roots and act American. A Mexican might say that the Americanized immigrant person is acting white but he has the cactus on his forehead. In other words, try as he might, he does not pass.

El Mariachi
From Rustic Roots to Golden Era

by Jonathan Clark

Recorded mariachi music dates back to the first decade of the twentieth century, and an abundance of important mariachi recordings were made during the 1920s and 1930s. Yet, in contrast to American jazz and pop music of the same era, virtually none of these early mariachi discs were reissued on vinyl after the LP was introduced in the 1950s. When I first became interested in mariachi music in the mid-1970s, the earliest commercially available mariachi recordings were the LP reissues of Lucha Reyes on the RCA label, featuring material that dated mainly from the early 1940s. There was a dearth of print material as well, and I was able to find very little information on mariachi music in my local libraries in and around San Jose, California. I used to say to myself, "Someday I'll get to Mexico, and there I'll find all the information I've been looking for!"

As it turned out, toward the end of the decade I found myself in Mexico City, working as a mariachi guitarrón player. One of the first things I did was to visit all the major record stores and libraries. In the record stores, I found virtually no mariachi music predating the 1940s. In the libraries, I was repeatedly informed that no book on this subject existed. To my dismay, I also discovered that most books on Mexican music didn't even include the word *mariachi* in their indexes. At that point I turned my attention primarily to conducting oral history interviews with elderly mariachi musicians, and to scouring flea markets and secondhand stores in search of 78-rpm discs of mariachi music.

Although 78s of popular singers with mariachi accompaniment abounded, trying to find records by the mariachi groups themselves, particularly of sones, was far more difficult. Nonetheless, I did manage to find a handful of fragile shellac discs by early mariachi groups. I had one of the early Sony Walkman cassette players, and at night, when I performed outdoors in Mexico City's Plaza Garibaldi, I would often bring a cassette of this music to share with my compañeros. Elderly musicians would put on the headphones and smile, making remarks like "That's what mariachi music used to sound like when I was a boy!" Younger musicians were also fascinated, although many found the music quaint, or even bizarre. At that point it dawned on me that several generations of musicians had virtually no access to any early recorded examples of the music they devoted their lives to interpreting. In that respect, they had been cut off from their roots.

"This is almost the opposite of the situation with American vernacular music," I thought.

I continued to live in Mexico through the 1980s. On a trip to California in 1985, I was fortunate enough to meet Chris Strachwitz at a mariachi festival held at Universal Studios. Chris invited me to visit his archives, where he played many mariachi 78s from his magnificent collection for me. He had almost no information on any of these discs, and he asked if I could help him identify some of them. Upon my return to Mexico, I began this research. In some cases I was actually able to meet musicians who had performed on these early recordings. In other cases I met the musicians' descendants, who generously shared their archives and anecdotes with me. Fruits of this effort include two early mariachi LPs released in the late 1980s and the CD series *Mexico's Pioneer Mariachis*, released in the 1990s, all on the Arhoolie label. These re-releases marked the first time in over half a century that any of those seminal recordings had been available to the public for purchase, other than on the used market.

Eventually, Chris Strachwitz and the Arhoolie Foundation formed a partnership with UCLA, which now offers access to the Strachwitz Frontera Collection online. At the time of this writing, this collection contains the largest publicly accessible repository of early mariachi music available anywhere.

What Is a Mariachi?

Of all Mexico's regional musical ensembles, the mariachi is undoubtedly the most emblematic of Mexican culture, as well as the most popular internationally (fig. 47). Exactly what constitutes a mariachi is not always clear, however, particularly to non-Mexicans. To the uninformed, *mariachi* may mean simply any Mexican music or, in an extreme case,

Latin American music in general. Not surprisingly, the word is frequently misused and misattributed.

When Hernán Cortés landed on Mexico's gulf coast in 1519, his entourage included musicians who brought instruments to the New World that would come to constitute the basic ingredients of the mariachi ensemble—members of the harp, violin, and guitar families. These instruments were almost immediately adopted by an indigenous population that quickly mastered European musical practices and techniques of instrument construction, creating new musical genres and unique variations of European instruments. Subsequently, large numbers of Africans brought to New Spain as slaves during the colonial era added a third element to this mixture. The mariachi emerged from this epic cultural fusion.

Unfortunately, few particulars of the mariachi's early evolution are known with any degree of certainty. We do know that by the nineteenth century evidence of the ensemble and the term *mariachi* begin to appear in a region of western Mexico whose epicenter is the present-day state of Jalisco and that can easily be expanded to include at least ten other Mexican states. Although there have been attempts to attribute the mariachi to a specific town or micro-region, these are controversial and inconclusive.

Scholars are still debating whether *mariachi* is an indigenous or a mestizo word, and from which indigenous language or tribe it originated. Contrary to popular belief, no connection between the word *mariachi* and the French word *mariage* has ever been successfully demonstrated.

Historically speaking, the makeup of a mariachi ensemble varies depending on the era and the geographic region to which it pertains. A century ago, two of the most prominent mariachi regions were central Jalisco, where the

Figure 47. An unidentified mariachi group at the landmark restaurant El Sombrero Charro, which opened in the early 1940s outside Monterrey, Mexico. The roof is shaped like the iconic charro hat, a symbol of the mariachi ensemble and of Mexican culture. Photograph courtesy of the Arhoolie Foundation.

typical ensemble featured two violins, vihuela (a small guitarlike instrument with a convex back and five strings), and guitarrón (a large, bass version of the vihuela); and southern Jalisco and Michoacán, where the typical ensemble featured two violins, harp, and guitarra de golpe (the original mariachi guitar). Different variants of the mariachi have existed and still exist in different parts of Mexico, and many of these are represented in the Frontera Collection (see appendix K, "Forty Notable Mariachi Recordings").

The contemporary mariachi typically includes at least twice as many musicians as the common mariachi of a century ago, although the size of an ensemble is often reduced for economic reasons. The standard instrumentation for a full mariachi today includes two trumpets,

three or more violins, a vihuela, a nylon-string guitar, and a guitarrón. A harp and an additional guitar or trumpet are sometimes added. All mariachi members typically sing as well.

Origin of the Mariachi Trumpet

Although today's listeners consider the trumpet an indispensable element of any mariachi, this instrument is a relative latecomer to the ensemble's ranks. Numerous wind instruments, including the cornet, clarinet, soprano saxophone, flute, and even the trombone, appeared sporadically in late nineteenth- and early-twentieth-century mariachi groups. Over the decades, the cornet became the most accepted of these. By the 1930s, the cornet had been supplanted by the more modern trumpet, which by the 1940s had evolved into a mariachi institution (although not without controversy).[1]

As I have noted, mariachi music has always been a difficult subject to research. While printed reference materials are scarce, there exists an abundance of assumptions that lack clear supporting evidence—a case in point being the ubiquitous myth regarding the alleged French origin of the word *mariachi*. Thanks in part to the Internet, many more sources exist on mariachi-related topics today than a few decades ago, but the number of dubious and contradictory statements concerning this genre has increased as a consequence. The great majority of these are essentially reiterations of previously published assertions, and only in rare cases is the validity of the earlier assumption questioned or challenged.

One of the most pervasive and problematic of these assertions attributes the introduction of the mariachi trumpet to radio pioneer Emilio Azcárraga Vidaurreta, who founded Mexico City station XEW in 1930. According to this legend, broadcast technology of the 1930s was unable to capture and reproduce the sound of violins adequately, so Azcárraga came up with the idea of adding a trumpet to the mariachi to allow its instrumental melodic line to be heard prominently over the radio, allegedly for the first time. As the story goes, this is how the mariachi trumpet was born.

Numerous testimonies and photographs of mariachis from before 1930 with cornet and trumpet players clearly contradict this contention, which is also contravened by basic sound reproduction principles.[2] The earliest "acoustic" mariachi recordings, made at the turn of the twentieth century, capture the violins quite well, and the first "electric" mariachi recordings of 1926 do so even more successfully. Subsequent commercial recordings of mariachis and of other musical genres, made with microphones and amplifiers similar or identical to those used by radio stations of the day, reveal few problems in adequately capturing and reproducing the sound of this high-pitched, bowed string instrument. With or without a trumpet, mariachi music would surely have been transmitted effectively over the airwaves of the 1930s, the main difference being that the trumpet added a new timbre to the traditional string ensemble's palette of sound colors.

While most particulars of the Azcárraga trumpet myth are clearly without merit, that visionary magnate of the Mexican telecommunications industry must indeed be credited for playing a vital role in popularizing the emergent mariachi trumpet tradition by featuring frequent broadcasts of Mariachi Tapatío de José Marmolejo (and later, other mariachi groups that included this instrument) over the powerful and prestigious radio station he owned and managed.

Early Mariachi Recordings

The earliest mariachi recordings were of mariachi groups themselves, without the intervention of any vocalists who were not members of those groups. The same appears to be true in early radio and cinema. At some point in the 1930s, however, mariachi accompaniment for ranchera vocalists came into vogue. Today, of the total number of extant mariachi recordings, probably less than 1 percent feature a mariachi as the primary artist; in the vast majority, the mariachi plays an accompanying role. As a result, original early recordings of pure mariachi music are quite difficult to find. Fortunately, the Strachwitz Frontera Collection contains an abundance of these rare, historic 78-rpm discs.

Cuarteto Coculense

The first known mariachi recordings are those of the Cuarteto Coculense (Cocula Quartet). According to historian Rafael Méndez Moreno, the group was brought to Mexico City from the village of Cocula, Jalisco, for the celebration of Independence Day and the birthday of president Porfirio Díaz in 1905.[3] The musicians were Justo Villa (vihuela), Cristóbal Figueroa (guitarrón), Crescencio "el Tirilingue" (first violin), and Hilario Chanverino (second violin).

Three American record companies (Columbia, Edison, and Victor) had branches and studios in Mexico City at that time, and all three recorded this ensemble using the primitive, mechanical "acoustic" process of the day, which rendered bass frequencies almost inaudible. The Columbia discs were by far the most popular and most widely distributed, and almost all the twenty Cuarteto Coculense recordings in the Frontera Collection are on this label.[4]

Although Méndez Moreno identifies this turn-of-the-century rural quartet as the Mariachi de Justo Villa, the word *mariachi* does not appear anywhere on the record labels, nor does it appear in any documentation associated with these recordings. The Victor discs designate the ensemble as a "Spanish Quartet." The word *mariachi* was certainly in use at this time, but perhaps it wasn't deemed common or commercial enough for marketing purposes. Notwithstanding, this is pure mariachi music. The "son jalisciense" is the musical genre most exclusive to the mariachi, and all of the twenty-three song titles recorded by the Cuarteto Coculense fall in this category. Many are designated as "sones abajeños" (sones from the lowlands of Jalisco, the geographic region corresponding to Cocula). A number of these sones—like "El Carretero," "El Ausente," "Las Abajeñas," "Las Olas," "El Cuervo," and "El Cihualteco"—remain popular today, while others have been largely forgotten.

In 1910 the Mexican Revolution broke out. Due to the prevailing risk and political instability, all three American record companies pulled up stakes and abandoned their agencies in Mexico. No further recordings of mariachi music would be made until the Revolution had subsided.

Mariachi Coculense de Cirilo Marmolejo

By late 1925, the "electric" recording process was being used commercially. Instead of a primitive acoustic recording horn, sound waves were now captured by a microphone and sent to a vacuum tube amplifier that in turn drove an electromagnetic cutting head that scribed the amplified sound into a master disc. The improved fidelity and increased frequency response was a spectacular improvement over the previous "acoustic" recording system. By 1926, the Victor company had brought this new technology to Mexico City.

The 1926 Victor session by Mariachi Coculense "Rodríguez" yielded the first phonograph recordings of mariachi music to be made since the outbreak of the Mexican Revolution. As would be expected, their fidelity represents an immense improvement over the records made by the Cuarteto Coculense almost two decades earlier. The ensemble's name, as it appears on the original discs, is misleading. Luis I. Rodríguez, a physician from Cocula who lived in Mexico City and was responsible for bringing Cirilo Marmolejo's mariachi there, apparently secured this recording session with the Victor Mexicana company and renamed Cirilo's group in his own honor for the purpose of these releases (fig. 48).

The most unusual recording from this session is the son "La Ensalada." In this piece, the guitarrón player fingers a full chord with the left

Figure 48. Mariachi Coculense de Cirilo Marmolejo is shown here in a publicity shot with the group's patron, Luis I. Rodríguez, head of Mexico City's Red Cross. Dr. Rodríguez is in the center, wearing riding boots. To his left, with the guitarrón, is leader Cirilo Marmolejo. In the rear, on far right, is Cirilo's nephew José Marmolejo. Standing in front on the far right is Cirilo's son Juan Marmolejo (see also figure 64). The photo was taken in Mexico City in about 1926. Photograph courtesy of the Arhoolie Foundation.

hand while the right hand rakes all the strings in a circular motion, producing a low-pitched drone reminiscent of a bass drum. Behind the peculiar vocal and violin melodies, one of the musicians lets out animal-like howls and bird-calls. This is probably the most unusual and the most indigenous-sounding commercial mariachi recording ever made.

While the son originally constituted the major part of the mariachi repertory, it was eventually eclipsed in popularity by what became known as the canción ranchera (literally "ranch song," a genre that parallels American country music). Mariachi Coculense's version of "Las Cuatro Milpas" is perhaps the first recorded example of a canción ranchera performed by a mariachi.

In 1933, Cirilo Marmolejo and his group traveled to Chicago, where they performed at the World's Fair. While there, they made their first recordings that feature a trumpet. (Two of their later recordings, "La Cantinera" and "El Becerro," feature a flute.) These Chicago sessions for the Columbia label are sonically superior to any of the Mexico City recordings by this group, and they capture Cirilo's energetic guitarrón playing particularly well.

Arhoolie Productions re-released twenty-one tracks by Mariachi Coculense de Cirilo Marmolejo on Arhoolie/Folklyric CD 7011. Many more interesting recordings by this group that were not reissued—such as "El Ausente" and "El Camino Real" (Camino Real de Colima)—may be found in the Frontera Collection.

Mariachi Tapatío de José Marmolejo

By the mid-1930s, vihuela player José Marmolejo had left his uncle Cirilo's ensemble and had become leader of his own group, Mariachi Tapatío de José Marmolejo, which became the first stellar mariachi in history. It was the dominant mariachi on radio, records, and cinema from approximately the mid-1930s to the mid-1940s. Representing the ultimate in modernity within its genre, Tapatío was the mariachi that initially popularized the trumpet in mariachi music through the artistry of its original trumpet player, Jesús Salazar.

Mariachi Tapatío recorded for the Victor label from the mid-1930s until 1942, then for the Peerless label from 1942 until at least 1953. Arhoolie Productions re-released twenty-four songs by this seminal group on Arhoolie/Folklyric CD 7012. At least forty additional recordings by Mariachi Tapatío de José Marmolejo that have not been reissued can be found in the Frontera Collection.

Mariachi Vargas de Tecalitlán

The earliest mariachis to make sound recordings were from the region of Cocula, in the central part of Jalisco. In the mid-1930s, however, a group from the village of Tecalitlán, in the southernmost part of Jalisco, made its debut on the Mexico City musical scene (fig. 49).

This mariachi, led by a young violinist named Silvestre Vargas, made its first recordings in 1937 for the Peerless label (Mexico's first national record company). Its style was noticeably different from that of the Cocula mariachis— above all, in the rhythmic accompaniment. At the time of these Peerless recordings, of which "El Perico Loro" is exemplary, the Vargas group did not yet use a trumpet. Mariachi Vargas recorded only four songs for Peerless before signing with the Victor label, where the group remained an exclusive artist for four decades, even though they moonlighted extensively for other companies under numerous recording pseudonyms.

Silvestre Vargas was quite reluctant to add a trumpet to his all-string mariachi. Nonetheless, by the 1940s the trumpet had become so popular in mariachi music that public demand forced Vargas to add one to his group. His first permanent trumpet player was Miguel Martínez, who entered Mariachi Vargas in 1942. While it was Jesús Salazar who initially popularized the trumpet in a mariachi context, it was unquestionably Martínez who defined its role and set the standard to which all future mariachi trumpet performances would be compared. The Frontera Collection contains a large number of recordings featuring the magnificent Miguel Martínez, including romantic and tropical trio recordings.[5] One of his earliest mariachi trumpet showpieces is the un-reissued polka "La Pelusa," dating from the mid-1940s.

In 1944, Rubén Fuentes, widely considered the most important musical figure in the history of mariachi music, joined Mariachi Vargas as a violinist, soon becoming the group's arranger and musical director. Fuentes cut his teeth as an assistant to pioneer mariachi arranger Manuel Esperón and went on to become the most influential mariachi arranger-composer-director-producer of all time. Similarly,

Figure 49. Mariachi Vargas de Tecalitlán is considered the genre's emblematic ensemble. This incarnation of the group included three of the most influential figures in mariachi music of the twentieth century: leader Silvestre Vargas (*back row, third from right*), flanked by arranger Rubén Fuentes, with violin, and Miguel Martínez, with trumpet. The photograph was taken at Chapultepec Park in Mexico City in the mid-1950s. Photograph courtesy of the Arhoolie Foundation.

in great part thanks to Fuentes, Mariachi Vargas went on to become the most influential mariachi group of all time. A large number of arrangements by Fuentes are included in the Frontera Collection, showcasing numerous singers and almost always featuring his mariachi of preference—Vargas de Tecalitlán (albeit sometimes under pseudonyms).

The Golden Era of Mariachi Music

One often hears the term "golden era" in reference to Mexican cinema and to mariachi music. Although their historical trajectories are largely parallel, the mariachi seems to have come of age a little later than the cinema, perhaps because

Mexico's cinematic boom played such an essential role in the mariachi's rise to popularity. The mariachi's glory days also seem to have endured long after Mexican cinema began to wane.

Mexico's first sound motion picture, *Santa* (1931), featured Cirilo Marmolejo's Mariachi Coculense, albeit in an incidental role. The launching of the so-called *comedia ranchera* craze is usually attributed to *Allá en el Rancho Grande* (1936). In that film, however, singer Tito Guízar is accompanied only by guitars. Many consider the participation of José Marmolejo's Mariachi Tapatío in *¡Ay Jalisco, No Te Rajes!* (1941), and Jorge Negrete's subsequent rise to fame, to mark the start of mariachi music's golden era.

In his *Breve historia del cine mexicano*, film historian Emilio García Riera describes the state of Mexican cinema of the late 1950s as "tired, routine and vulgar, lacking in creation and imagination."[6] Mariachi music, on the other hand, remained vibrant and vital for at least another decade. Some consider the death of Javier Solís in 1966 as a cutoff point for mariachi music's golden era; others date it to the death of singer-songwriter José Alfredo Jiménez in 1973. Other interpretations are also plausible.

Mariachi Pulido

Twin brothers Francisco and David Pulido were natives of San José de Gracia, Michoacán, a village on the border with Jalisco, and they had frequently entertained General Lázaro Cárdenas in his nearby hometown of Jiquilpan. When Cárdenas ran for the presidency in 1934, he used the Pulido brothers' mariachi on his campaign tour. After he won the election, Cárdenas secured a position for Mariachi Pulido as an official musical ensemble of the government agency Acción Cívica, in Mexico City.

Mariachi Pulido became a formidable group, and by the 1940s it was popular on radio, records, and film (fig. 50). It attracted some of the finest musicians in mariachi music, including violinist-arranger-composer Bonifacio Collazo, best known for his polka "Las Coronelas." Collazo became the band's musical director and was primarily responsible for creating Mariachi Pulido's trademark style, which later became the legendary Mariachi México style.

Thanks to Cárdenas, both Pulido brothers also held patronage positions as police officials in Mexico City. This job occupied most of their time, and they consequently neglected their mariachi, delegating its leadership to Pepe Villa, who in due course ended up taking most of the group with him to form Mariachi

Figure 50. Mariachi Pulido was the forerunner of Mariachi México de Pepe Villa. On the far left is leader Francisco Pulido. On far right is Pepe Villa, who later took over the group. Front and center is Bonifacio Collazo, creator of the Mariachi México style. This promotional photo, from about 1950, announces the group is available at "reasonable prices" for "birthdays, serenades, rodeos, and any kind of festivity." Photograph courtesy of the Arhoolie Foundation.

México. Although Mariachi Pulido regrouped after Villa's defection and continued to exist for another decade or so, it never regained its former glory and eventually disbanded.

Mariachi México de Pepe Villa

Vihuela player Pepe Villa was a member of Mariachi Vargas de Tecalitlán during that group's early years in Mexico City. In the early 1940s he joined the popular Mariachi Pulido, where several of his fellow musicians were also ex-Vargas members. Although it was officially Francisco Pulido's group, Pepe soon became its de facto leader. When trumpet player Miguel Martínez had a falling out with leader Silvestre Vargas and quit Mariachi Vargas in 1952, Pepe invited Miguel to the group he was in the process of reorganizing. The most striking feature of this new ensemble was that it had two trumpets, something virtually unheard of in a mariachi of the early 1950s.

The two-trumpet instrumentation was immediately rejected by mariachi musicians and fans alike. Most were still getting used to the idea of one trumpet in a mariachi, and they considered two a sacrilege. The newly organized group's initial radio broadcasts were met by torrents of criticism in the form of phone calls and letters to the station, criticizing this abnormal instrumentation. Not ready to concede defeat, trumpeters Miguel Martínez and Jesús Córdoba rehearsed long hours daily to perfect their duet work. As they developed more rapport, the criticism subsided, and public response slowly turned favorable.

Pepe Villa soon broke away from Mariachi Pulido and started his own group, which in the beginning was basically Mariachi Pulido under a new name. On February 2, 1953, Mariachi México de Pepe Villa made its official debut on radio station XEX. The band soon became a sensation with its trademark instrumental pieces, particularly polkas. In 1954, Discos Peerless presented Mariachi México with an award for being one of the top-selling recording artists of 1953–54. To date, no other mariachi has received a similar distinction or achieved such a high percentage of record sales.

After its popularization by Mariachi México de Pepe Villa, mariachi groups almost universally adopted the trumpet duet. Since that time, the standard instrumentation of the mariachi has remained unchanged. Although nonstandard instruments are sometimes used to supplement the basic mariachi ensemble, particularly in recordings, none of these has endured or been universally adopted.

Mariachi México de Pepe Villa's recorded legacy begins with 78s made under the name of Mariachi Pulido for Discos Peerless, and continues on that label under the name Mariachi México. The Frontera Collection contains an impressive number of these rare and largely un-reissued discs. In 1954 Mariachi México moved to the Musart label, where the group made most of the hit recordings for which it is recognized today.

Mariachi Perla de Occidente

Originally called Mariachi Los Diablos Rojos, this group was founded in the 1930s by valve trombone player Marcelino Ortega Sr., who had earlier played that instrument as a member of Cirilo Marmolejo's mariachi. After the senior Ortega's death in 1941, his son, guitarist Marcelino Ortega Jr., took over the group's leadership and changed its name to Mariachi Perla de Occidente. From the late 1940s through the 1950s, Perla de Occidente was considered one of Mexico City's finest mariachis, appearing extensively in films and on radio and records. Silvestre Vargas often used Perla de Occidente as a substitute group for his mariachi, and numerous Perla de Occidente members went on to be members of mariachis Vargas and México, as well as other top ensembles.

Mariachi de Miguel Díaz

Violinist Miguel Díaz (1924–2009) and his father, clarinet player Teodoro "el Cócono" Díaz, played together inside the Tenampa bar in Mexico City as members of Concho Andrade's legendary mariachi which, ironically, is alleged never to have made a recording. In the early 1940s, young Miguel joined Mariachi Pulido. In 1944 he joined Mariachi Vargas de Tecalitlán. After a year, he joined Mariachi Perla de Occidente, where he remained for the rest of the decade.

In the early 1950s, Miguel organized his own Mariachi de Miguel Díaz, where he served as leader, violinist, arranger, and musical director. In spite of the fact that this group had frequent personnel changes and broke up and regrouped numerous times, it had considerable success, making many recordings and performing on radio programs. Incarnations of the group existed until 1971, when trumpeter Arcadio Elías took over its leadership. The Mariachi de Miguel Díaz's best-known recordings are three LPs made for the Audio Fidelity label in the late 1950s, which were widely distributed internationally and continue to turn up daily on the used record market.

Mariachi Chapala

Brothers Leopoldo, José, and Miguel Sosa were born in the mountains above Lake Chapala, where, as adolescents, they began playing together in the early 1930s. The brothers eventually joined with other musicians to form Mariachi Chapala, which worked mainly in the tourist village of Chapala until 1949, when it moved its base to Mexicali, Baja California. After the group's musical director, Rafael Arredondo, left in 1951, the Sosa brothers brought young violinist Nati Cano from Guadalajara to take his place. Shortly afterward, singer-violinist Heriberto Molina and, later, singer-guitarist Ricardo González joined the group. Molina and González performed frequently as the duet Los Dos Palomos. In 1952 Molina left Mariachi Chapala to join Mariachi Vargas, where he had an illustrious career for three decades. Another distinguished member of Mariachi Chapala was Esteban Hernández, whose talented sons would later form Mariachi Los Galleros and Mariachi Sol de México in the Los Angeles area.

In the early 1950s, Mariachi Chapala was extremely popular in Mexicali. Between stations XED, XECL, XEAO, and XEAA, they could be heard on live radio broadcasts almost every day. Arranger, director, composer, and bandleader Manuel S. Acuña would travel from Los Angeles to Mexicali once a month to produce recordings with the group. As a result, large numbers of records featuring Mariachi Chapala, accompanying a wide variety of soloists and duets, were released on Azteca, Colonial, Colony, Columbia, Imperial, and other labels.

By 1956, Mariachi Chapala had immigrated to Los Angeles, where it became the house band at the downtown hotspot Jeanette's Place (later Granada Lounge). In 1961 Nati Cano left to join Mariachi Los Camperos, a group led by José García Frías. After Frías's death in a car accident, Cano took over the ensemble's leadership. Under his direction, Los Camperos became the most important US group in popularizing mariachi music among non-Hispanics. From 1969 to 2007, they had their own trendsetting restaurant, La Fonda de Los Camperos, in Los Angeles. Ricardo González, a member of all three previously mentioned groups, went on to a successful career as a solo singer. After an extended engagement at the Seattle World's Fair in 1962, Mariachi Chapala disbanded permanently.

Lesser Known but Notable Mariachis

While much of the Strachwitz Frontera mariachi material features well-known mariachi groups, recordings by lesser-known mariachis represent some of the most fascinating tracks in this collection. Though their musical quality varies, some of the recorded works of these minor groups are truly exceptional. Although the performances are sometimes less than outstanding, these discs frequently offer rare material or interesting alternate versions of better-known repertory. Additionally, they often document seldom-heard regional styles that have fallen into obscurity or even disappeared, since dominant recorded models have tended to homogenize performance practice throughout the mariachi world.

Many of these obscure records were released on tiny regional labels about which little is known, and in many cases our knowledge of these ensembles and featured vocalists is limited to what is printed on the record labels. Hopefully, future research will unearth more information on these discographical enigmas.

Although an exhaustive listing of the lesser-known mariachi groups found in the collection is beyond the scope of this book, the following is a representative sampling taken from the 78-rpm era, which ended roughly in the mid-1950s.

Mariachi Los Abajeños

In 1939, a group called Mariachi Los Abajeños, presumably from the lowlands of Jalisco, recorded half a dozen sides for the Peerless label. No company documentation regarding the identity of this mariachi survives, and no one seems to know anything about it today. The Frontera Collection has only one rare 78 by this group.

Mariachi Los Charros de Atotonilco

In mid-1939, after a heated discussion over the division of tip money and other grievances, Silvestre Vargas's entire mariachi, with the exception of his father, Gaspar, quit the group. The members who left appointed singer-guitarist Pepe Gutiérrez as their leader, and a few days later they found work accompanying singer-songwriter Pepe Guízar, who baptized the group Los Charros de Atotonilco (fig. 51). Pepe Gutiérrez used his extensive artistic connections to get the group radio and recording work, but within a short time they made peace with Silvestre and returned to Mariachi Vargas. A year or two later, however, a similar mutiny occurred and Los Charros de Atotonilco was reborn. The group accompanied Jorge Negrete on a tour of the United States in the early 1940s. Until the late 1940s, when he retired from the music scene, Gutiérrez revived the group periodically when work opportunities arose.

Mariachi Coculense "El Costeño"

Presumably unrelated to Cirilo Marmolejo's similarly named ensemble, Mariachi Coculense "El Costeño" recorded for the Vocalion label in Los Angeles. Details about this group remain a mystery. Another similarly named group, Mariachi Los Costeños, is basically a reinforced version of the prolific Los Angeles–based Los Costeños, a conjunto created by arranger Manuel S. Acuña.

Mariachi Los Coyotes

When this group from Zapotiltic, Jalisco, arrived in Mexico City in the late 1940s, it caused a sensation among mariachi fans and musicians for its extraordinary interpretation of sones. Los Coyotes recorded fourteen sides for the Peerless label between 1951 and 1954, six of them sones. The Frontera Collection has half of these discs, as well as one of their subsequent singles on the Musart label. (Unfortunately, there were no sones by this group in the collection at the time of this writing.) The group's heyday was short, and by the 1960s Los Coyotes had disappeared from the artistic scene.

Mariachi Guadalajara

Numerous groups, in many places and eras, have called themselves "Mariachi Guadalajara" or some variant of that name, and many will undoubtedly continue to do so. The most famous of these is Mariachi Guadalajara de Silvestre Vargas, of the late 1950s. Originally Silvestre Vargas's second-string group, it eventually became Mariachi América de Alfredo Serna. One of the most interesting mystery ensembles known by this name is the Mariachi Guadalajara that made 78s for the Discos Mexicanos label based in Fresno, California. This appears to be

Figure 51. Los Charros de Atotonilco, with leader Pepe Gutiérrez (*far left*) and his singing partner Marita Muñoz. The two formed the duet Pepe y Marita. Los Charros de Atotonilco was originally formed in 1939 by members who defected from Mariachi Vargas. In the back row, third from the right, is Jesús Salazar, the first famous mariachi trumpet player. Fourth from the right is composer-arranger Bonifacio Collazo. The photograph was taken in Mexico City in the early 1940s. Photograph courtesy of the Arhoolie Foundation.

a different group than the Mariachi Guadalajara that recorded sones for the Los Angeles–based Master label. Also worthy of note is Diego Villanueva and his Guadalajara Charros, a mariachi that recorded for the Trilón label based in Hollywood and San Francisco.

Mariachi Güitrón

Juan Güitrón was a violinist with Mariachi Tapatío de José Marmolejo who was widely respected for his musical abilities, including his directing and arranging skills. In the mid-1940s he established a strong relationship with the Peerless company, which for a number of years gave him the concession on mariachi recordings for that label. Although Juan Güitrón occasionally organized public performances using this ensemble name, Mariachi Güitrón was basically a phantom studio conglomerate assembled from musicians of many different mariachi groups for the purpose of recording.

Mariachi de Mendoza

No information seems to have survived regarding the field recordings of this mystery mariachi and other groups that John H. Green recorded in Mexico. These 78s were issued by the New York City–based General record label. Nothing seems to be known about them today, other than what appears on the disc labels.

Mariachi Reyes de Chapala

Although this group bears the name of Mexico's largest freshwater lake and its adjoining town in the state of Jalisco, it's believed that few, if any, of its members were actually from that area. Reyes de Chapala was apparently one of the earliest mariachis to emigrate to Southern California. They recorded extensively on numerous Southern California labels and at one point were featured weekly on a Los Angeles television show. By the mid-1950s, however, the group had disbanded.

Rafúl y Sus Jumileros

A Taxco, Guerrero, native of Lebanese descent, Rafúl Krayem (1909–39) led this regional variant of a mariachi that recorded for the Victor and Anfión labels. His best-known song is "Camioncito Flecha Roja." The group's name refers to an edible insect native to that region, the *jumil*, which the Aztecs considered a delicacy and which remains a symbol of local Taxco culture.

As in the case of the Cuarteto Coculense, the word *mariachi* is absent on the labels of all recordings made by this group. Nonetheless, upon hearing their music, one will immediately note a connection between it and that of the mariachi—notwithstanding the inclusion of a güiro!

The Singers

Unlike many of the long-forgotten mariachi groups previously mentioned, the names of certain ranchera singers remain household words throughout the Spanish-speaking world. While these singers' greatest hits have been reissued countless times, many of their lesser-known works are quite difficult to obtain today. Fortunately, the Strachwitz Frontera Collection contains an abundance of such gems. The following highlights some of the more important ranchera vocalists found on 78-rpm discs in this collection.

Lucha Reyes

The mother of all female ranchera singers is undoubtedly Lucha Reyes (1906–44). Though she was originally a lyric soprano who sang operetta and zarzuela, legend has it that she became aphonic during an aborted tour of Germany. When she finally regained her voice a year later, the story goes, it was so damaged that she was forced to resort to singing ranchera music for a living.

In the early 1930s, Reyes teamed up with singer Pepe Gutiérrez and formed the duet Los Trovadores Tapatíos (fig. 52). Pepe introduced her to his friend Silvestre Vargas when Vargas arrived in Mexico City with his mariachi in 1934. Soon thereafter, Lucha left the duet and became a ranchera soloist. Her career rose to great heights but faded prematurely due to excessive drinking, ending with her tragic death in 1944. Her numerous recordings with Mariachi Vargas and Mariachi Tapatío constitute the archetypal early ranchera recordings by a female singer. The Frontera Collection contains several hard-to-find recordings by Reyes.

Figure 52. Los Trovadores Tapatíos—Lucha Reyes and Pepe Gutiérrez—in a photograph taken in Mexico City in the early 1930s. Reyes is considered the mother of all female ranchera singers, and her recordings continue to exert a major stylistic influence today. Photograph courtesy of the Arhoolie Foundation.

Popular Duets

Vocal duets have always been an important part of Mexico's música ranchera tradition. Some of the earliest duets that sang with mariachi accompaniment—all represented in the collection—were Ray y Laurita, Angelina y Toño, Las Soldaderas, and Las Cantadoras del Bajío.

Likewise worthy of mention are the multiple duets associated with two important male singers: Pepe Gutiérrez and Martín Becerra. Each man was the stable member of his own duet, while the female counterparts changed frequently. After Lucha Reyes left Gutiérrez to pursue a career as soloist, he formed a series of duets with different partners, including Pepe y Chabela, Pepe y Elvira, Pepe y Juanita, Pepe y Laura, Pepe y Rosita, Pepe y Marita, and Pepe y Dora. Martín Becerra, lead voice of Trío Guayacán, was half of the famous duet Martín y Malena. Magdalena Pérez Tejada was the original Malena. She had several successors in the duet, but it continued to be billed as Martín y Malena for many years after she left. Martín Becerra also made recordings under the duet names Martín y Eloisa, Martín y Lily, and Martín y Catita.

Hermanas Padilla

Originally from Tanhuato, Michoacán, sisters María and Margarita Padilla arrived in Los Angeles with their family in 1927. From an early age, both girls sang superbly and the duet became popular at local fiestas, fairs, and talent shows. They made their first commercial recordings in 1937. Their career spanned over four decades, making them among the most successful and prolific artists of the early Los Angeles–area Hispanic recording scene.

According to María Padilla, the Hermanas Padilla duet made some of the very first recordings of mariachi music featuring trumpet, frequently teaming up with virtuoso classical trumpeter Rafael Méndez. Since no local mariachis of sufficient caliber for recording existed during the early part of their career, they were often accompanied by a pseudo-mariachi comprised mainly of non-mariachi studio musicians and directed by Manuel S. Acuña or Francisco Camacho Vega. In 1946 María Padilla married Mariachi Vargas member Memo Quintero, and the two formed the famous Dueto Azteca.

Jorge Negrete

Jorge Negrete (1911–1953) was one of the early idols of ranchera music and of Mexican cinema. Originally an operatic vocalist, he reluctantly accepted a role as a ranchera singer alongside Lucha Reyes in the 1941 film ¡Ay

Jalisco, No Te Rajes!, never imagining this genre would bring him enduring fame as both a singer and an actor. Manuel Esperón was Negrete's musical arranger throughout his career, and Mariachi Vargas was the group that most often accompanied him. His imposing figure, prodigious voice, and lyrical expressiveness make Jorge Negrete the quintessential male ranchera singer.

Pedro Infante

Perhaps no other figure in popular culture is as deeply etched into the Mexican consciousness as Pedro Infante (1917–57) (fig. 53). In contrast to Jorge Negrete, who came from a well-to-do military family and had extensive vocal training, Pedro Infante was of humble origin, a champion of the proletariat, and a natural crooner. Endowed with extraordinary charisma, he tugged at the heartstrings of the Mexican people in a manner that remains unsurpassed, and his recordings and films continue to be broadcast daily.

Pedro Infante made his first ranchera recordings in 1943 with Mariachi Tapatío de José Marmolejo. He subsequently recorded with Mariachi Güitrón, and in 1950 he began recording with Mariachi Vargas de Tecalitlán. (For contractual reasons, the Vargas recordings credit the group as Mariachi Los Mamertos or Mariachi Guadalajara.) Infante's mariachi repertory consisted mainly of rancheras, corridos, and huapangos until 1952, when he launched a series of what were promoted as boleros rancheros. This new subgenre was created by Mariachi Vargas's musical director, Rubén Fuentes, in conjunction with lyricist Alberto Cervantes. Loosely based on the Cuban danzón rhythm, it started a craze that lasted through the 1950s. But the style was eventually superseded by the type of bolero made famous by Javier Solís, which had less rhythmic

Figure 53. Pedro Infante, the most popular Mexican singer-actor of all time, made his first ranchera recordings in 1943. The Frontera Collection contains more than 300 of his works, making him one of the top performers in the archive (see appendix E). Photograph courtesy of the Arhoolie Foundation.

syncopation. Today, the term *bolero ranchero* has become ambiguous and generally refers to any bolero interpreted by a mariachi.

After a falling out with Mariachi Vargas in mid-1956, Pedro Infante recorded ten songs with Mariachi Perla de Occidente, but that December he went back into the studio with Vargas and cut what would be the final four songs of his recording career. On April 15, 1957, a tragic plane crash took the artist's life.

With the exception of soundtracks from the nearly sixty films he appeared in and four demo recordings that were rejected by RCA Victor, all of Pedro Infante's commercial recordings were made for the Peerless label. Although the entire Infante Peerless catalog is available in Mexico, browsing through the Frontera Collection's discs by this artist is fascinating, as these were issued in different countries, with different label designs, and in different formats. As is the case with many other 78- and 45-rpm discs in the collection, certain credits and tidbits of information found on these labels have never appeared on subsequent LP and CD reissues.

Miguel Aceves Mejía

One of the most prodigious voices in the history of ranchera music is that of Miguel Aceves Mejía (1915–2006), also known as "El Rey del Falsete" (The King of Falsetto). Aceves made his first recordings in 1938 for the Decca label, interpreting boleros as a member of the trio Los Porteños, and twenty of these sides can be found in the Frontera Collection. Between 1940 and 1945 he worked for the Peerless label, where he recorded thirty-six songs as a soloist, mainly boleros and Afro-Antillean "música tropical." In 1946 he moved to the RCA Victor label, where he continued to record tropical music until artistic director Mariano Rivera Conde came up with the idea of converting him into a ranchera singer. In 1947 Aceves began this new phase of his career with recordings of "Oh Gran Dios," "La Embarcación," "Hay Unos Ojos," and "Carabina 30-30," initiating a long relationship with Mariachi Vargas de Tecalitlán and that group's musical director, Rubén Fuentes. These were some of twenty-year-old Fuentes's first recorded arrangements.

Miguel Aceves Mejía became an immediate sensation as a ranchera singer, releasing at least eighty rancheras and corridos between 1947 and 1953. When his first huapango, "El Jinete," was released in 1953, it became obvious that this genre was exceedingly well suited to the singer's powerful voice and extraordinary falsetto. In an unheard-of gesture, RCA's Rivera Conde gave Rubén Fuentes free reign to use as many additional instruments as he

wanted in Aceves Mejía's recordings. This allowed Fuentes to create a new modality in huapangos, using novel orchestrations in combination with Mariachi Vargas de Tecalitlán. The series of over twenty huapangos that followed created a revolution in mariachi music and transformed what had previously been a minor mariachi genre into one of its mainstays. Without doubt, huapangos form the most important and interesting part of Miguel Aceves Mejía's prolific recorded repertory.

José Alfredo Jiménez

No other singer-songwriter of the golden era made a greater contribution to ranchera music than José Alfredo Jiménez (1926–73). His straight-to-the-heart lyrics, devoid of any literary pretensions, penetrate the deepest recesses of the Mexican psyche. His unconventional, highly emotive vocal delivery of his original songs, combined with the arrangements of Rubén Fuentes and his collaborators and the accompaniment of Mariachi Vargas de Tecalitlán, created some of the most beloved mariachi recordings of all time.

José Alfredo Jiménez's discography can be divided into two main periods. The first is on Discos Columbia (CBS), where he recorded 121 of his own songs between 1949 and 1960, accompanied mainly by Mariachi Vargas. The second period is on RCA Victor, where from 1960 until his death in 1973 he recorded 170 of his own songs, fifty-three of which he had recorded previously for CBS. On his RCA recordings, José Alfredo was accompanied almost exclusively by Mariachi Vargas. In addition, soundtrack recordings from many of his forty-odd films are available on the Orfeón label, and some demo recordings by him are available on the Continental label. Of all José Alfredo's recordings, those on RCA have the highest production values and are the best known today.

Lola Beltrán

One of the most popular female ranchera singers of all time, Lola Beltrán (1932–96) began her career as a secretary at the powerful radio station XEW, where she soon became a central figure in that station's impressive roster of artists. In 1951 Peerless signed her as an exclusive artist, and it was on this label that she made the majority of her classic mariachi recordings. In 1969 she moved to RCA Victor, but stayed for only two years. From 1971 on, she recorded for Discos GAS. Beltrán remained active and popular until the end of her career, even hosting her own television show, *El Estudio de Lola Beltrán*, in the mid-1980s.

Conclusion

Although the mariachi has long been symbolic of Mexican culture, and mariachi groups have long been ubiquitous in Mexico and the southwestern United States, the history of this musical tradition remains largely undocumented.[7] Given the lack of customary sources, perhaps the most useful documentary material for studying how this music evolved from a rural to an urban genre is the large body of commercial phonograph recordings of mariachi music made during the first part of the twentieth century. Until now, however, most extant early discs of this music have been in private collections and archives to which the public had little or no access. To everyone but a small handful of collectors and archivists, it was as if these recordings had never existed. Fortunately, this is no longer the case.

The Strachwitz Frontera Collection is the most important publicly accessible archive of early recorded mariachi music in the world today. This recent availability of such a large repository of early mariachi recordings promises to enhance our understanding and appreciation of this music, particularly in light of UNESCO's recent designation of the mariachi as an international cultural heritage.

Scholars and researchers can use this collection as primary source material for books, articles, theses, and dissertations, while educators can use it for didactic material. Filmmakers can use it for documentaries. Musicians can use it to discover the roots of their music and to reintroduce forgotten material into the contemporary repertory. Composers, arrangers, and songwriters can use it as a source of inspiration for new creations. Others can simply enjoy listening to this music for its own merit. The possibilities are endless.

Los Tigres del Norte
From Hit Makers to Historians

The four brothers who make up Los Tigres del Norte, the world's premier Mexican norteño band, have been playing corridos since they were boys growing up in Mexico (fig. 54). In keeping with the music's oral tradition, they learned their first songs from older musicians in their hometown, a remote hamlet in the northwest state of Sinaloa. The Hernández boys had no sheet music, no songbooks, no albums or tapes to guide their instruction in this rustic folk genre. In fact, they didn't even have access to a radio in their rancho in those days.

It was the 1960s, when the rest of the world was exploding with new pop sounds, from Liverpool to Lima. This global music phenomenon was largely informed by local forms of what would come to be called roots music, from hillbilly and blues to bossa nova, mambo, and the plaintive indigenous music of the Andes. Throughout Latin America, the movement sparked an interest in native musical styles and genres, rediscovered and revived by a young generation. It was dubbed the New Song Movement, and it energized music capitals from Havana to Buenos Aires, Santiago to Mexico City.

The brothers Hernández, however, may as well have been living on another planet. Not only were they cut off from these global musical currents, but they were isolated even from major artists working in the same genre in other parts of Mexico. As kids in a village with no radio or record player, they had never heard of many norteño recording stars popular in their day. Much less could they have imagined that, more than 1,000 miles to the north, a German immigrant in California was busy collecting and documenting the recorded music they were learning through the oral tradition. During the 1960s, while the Hernández boys were starting to perform informally as a local group, record producer and collector Chris Strachwitz had started his quest to collect all forms of roots music, including the music popular along the border between Mexico and the United States.

Four decades later, fate would bring together these two important musical figures: Strachwitz, who had become an influential music producer, and Los Tigres del Norte, who had emerged as the most successful Mexican regional artists ever. Their alliance would lead to the creation of the Frontera Collection at UCLA, launched with an unprecedented community-to-academia donation from the band. What Los Tigres received in return was priceless: information about the history of their music, which they had been seeking all their lives.

"We had always wanted to know exactly where the songs came from, where these stories originated," says Jorge Hernández, the elder brother, lead singer, and spokesman for the band. "Because we did not have any of that history, or at least we were not aware of it. Where

Figure 54. Los Tigres del Norte, the leading norteño band for four decades, is composed of four brothers and a cousin: (*left to right*) Luis Hernández, Hernán Hernández, Jorge Hernández, Oscar Lara, and Eduardo Hernández. Photograph courtesy of Fonovisa.

does the music come from? Who were the first singers? Who started this style that we had been working for so many years? We wanted to know more."[1]

By chance, both Strachwitz and the Hernández brothers, immigrants from different continents, wound up living within fifty miles of each other in the San Francisco Bay Area.

And they settled there at roughly the same time. Los Tigres have been based in San Jose since 1968. Eight years earlier, Strachwitz launched Arhoolie Records from his small rented house while he taught at Los Gatos High School. But it would be some thirty years before they joined forces for the Frontera archives. The story of Los Tigres in those intervening years is one of struggle, family devotion, charmed choices, and an unwavering commitment to a musical vision.

The Band with No Name

Los Tigres hail from a tiny rural hamlet with a poetic name, Rosa Morada, the Purple Rose. In Mexico, such small country settlements are known as ranchos. Rosa Morada, which belongs to the larger nearby municipality of Mocorito, is no more than a cluster of homes surrounded by farmlands, a speck on the map of Sinaloa. Its fame today is due entirely to its most successful native sons—the Hernández brothers, Jorge, Raul, Eduardo, and Hernán—who left over forty years ago. Many other residents of the region have followed the band on the immigrant trail to the United States, leading to a dwindling census count in recent decades. The population of Rosa Morada today is 397 and falling.

Their parents, Eduardo Hernández and Consuelo Angulo de Hernández, were small farmers who raised an assortment of crops in the hilly terrain. Hernández still recites by memory a litany in Spanish of the produce they grew—*maíz, ajonjolí, cártamo, sandia, chile, melón, cebolla, rábanos, cilantro, lechuga.* "We were campesinos—peasants," he says, "and we worked the land with ox-drawn ploughs."

Today, Sinaloa is a state known primarily for its violent drug cartels and its loud, brassy banda music. Historically, however, it has also been a powerful agricultural and fishing center, with three important coastal cities: the capital of Culiacán, the resort of Mazatlán, and the modern port of Los Mochis, the western terminus of the Chihuahua-Pacific Railroad, which crosses the Copper Canyon and was originally conceived as a trade route between the cattle markets of Kansas City and the Pacific Ocean.

Despite the state's commerce and industry, modern life seemed to bypass Rosa Morada, southeast of Los Mochis. Jorge, the eldest son, born in 1954, recalls one of the biggest events in the life of his little town—the day his grandmother, Petronila Flores Hernández, brought home a Philco radio.

It was the only electronic contraption of its kind in town, and nobody was sure it would even work, considering the hilly terrain. Amid the static, it managed to pull in just one radio signal, and it wasn't even a station inside Mexico. It was a 150,000-watt powerhouse from Harlingen, Texas, which played pure norteño music, "música de acordeón." It was a style not nearly as popular in this region of Mexico as banda, the brash and brassy genre synonymous with Sinaloa, featuring tubas and tamboras, or big bass drums, but normally no accordions. That's when Hernández recalls hearing the music of major norteño artists for the first time, groups like Freddie Gómez, Los Donneños, and Los Dos Gilbertos, who were already making waves across the border. "They were known only in the United States because they had no presence or projection in Mexico," he recalls. "Nobody ever bothered to promote them."

During fiestas in his home town, people set up an old Victrola, the kind with a crank and a bullhorn for a speaker that they'd hang from a post and turn up full blast. That's how he first heard Los Alegres, as well as such big-name stars as Pedro Infante.

There were only a few men back home who performed norteño music when the Hernández brothers were little, and most were relatives. They listened to their maternal grandfather Ascensión Angulo sing on his ranch. One of the old man's cousins, named Marcelino, played the accordion. The men had a local group that people would call upon to play at family functions and the like, but they didn't have a name.

People just knew them by the place where they lived: "los músicos de Limón."

The older men taught the boys all the old corridos about bandits and rebels, horses and heroes. They memorized verse after verse about figures such as Gabino Barrera, Lucio Vasquez, Rosita Alvirez, and Pancho Villa.

"They knew them all, start to finish, and they knew them by heart," recalls Hernández. "We would just sing them that way and we didn't know if we were right or wrong, because we had no record or documentation to say this is the original. Later, when I came to read the lyrics of these corridos, they coincided with the lyrics they had taught us."

Jorge always thought of being a professional singer. But he wanted to take his music beyond his little rancho, beyond even Mocorito, Los Mochis, and Mazatlán. He aspired to communicate through his music, "to convey to people our history, our way of life, how we act and who we are." He yearned to let the world know that what they played was more than just cheap beer-joint music—"música de cantina"—that people with good taste looked down on. The more people put the music down, the more he felt committed to be its champion. "When we started to sing this kind of music, everybody said we were crazy," recalls the band's leader. "They said we were going to starve to death, and whatever. So I wanted to prove to myself that those people were wrong. The more they stubbornly stuck to the negative belief that what we believed in wasn't possible, the more I was determined to show just the opposite, with deeds."

When the elder Hernández was not yet twelve, a tragic accident in the family would, paradoxically, put him and his brothers on the road to accomplish that dream. In 1966 his father suffered a serious back injury in a work-related accident that left him unable to walk. To raise money for his medical care,

Jorge and his brothers decided to take their act on the road. As a band, they still didn't have a name. They were known around town simply as the Hernández boys—"los hijos de Lalo y Consuelo." People came calling for them at home, sometimes in the middle of the night, when they needed live music for a party or family gathering. With the family in a bind, they decided to go out and look for regular work every night, in addition to their day jobs. "So we made a kind of pact among brothers to support our father," says Jorge.

Although they never discouraged his interest in music, Jorge's parents always wanted him to be a teacher. Thus, after secondary school, he moved to Los Mochis to continue his studies. But the plan was quickly derailed. "Music would not let me rest in peace. From the moment I opened my eyes in the morning, I thought about music. I was obsessed."

His brothers joined him and they continued to perform as a group, still raising money for their father's recovery. They were in demand and started getting more engagements and making more money. They played a regular gig at a restaurant that sold chicken *gorditas*, Jorge remembers, and they sang at the tables for tips. But still they were the band with no name. "People sort of called us whatever they wanted," says Hernández. "Los Norteñitos de Chihuahua. Los Alegres de Rosa Morada. Wherever they wanted us to be from, that's what they called us."

Pressed to earn even more money for their father's medical bills, they decided to move to the border town of Mexicali, where they were told there would be more opportunities. And so it was. Lodged with an aunt, their father's sister, Tía Teresa, the boys hit the city's busy bar and restaurant circuit. Here, to their amazement, they could draw a dollar a song. They got so busy they even took on a manager and acquired a van so they could hit venues all across town, from noon to dawn.

It was here in Mexicali that they caught the break that would change their lives, and the future of norteño music forever. Once again, their good fortunes would be defined by their personal devotion to their father's cause and their family's need.

In order to send money home, Jorge made regular visits to the telegraph office in Mexicali. By chance, the telegraph worker who handled his business also happened to book acts for state-sponsored fairs all across Baja California. One day the man told Hernández of an opportunity for his band to perform in the United States. A promoter in San Jose had put the word out that California state authorities were looking for Spanish-language acts to perform for Mexican inmates at the prison in Soledad. The gig did not pay, but it would give the boys exposure. And with a ninety-day visa, they could stay and look for additional paid gigs in the area. It was a great opportunity, the telegraph man said.

The Hernández brothers were hired as part of a caravan of artists brought in for the prison show. And in a most unexpected way, this band of brothers finally got the stage name that would make history. While filling out their visa papers, a US immigration agent asked what the group called itself. But the boys said they didn't have a name. "Put down whatever you want," Hernández told him. So the border bureaucrat, needing to fill the space on the form, came up with one on the spot. The agent showed a creative streak, musing about what to call them. In America, he reasoned, boys who exhibit a go-get-'em spunk are often affectionately nicknamed "little tigers." And since they were headed north, the agent dubbed them the Little Tigers of the North. But on second thought, he eliminated the diminutive, so they wouldn't outgrow the name when they grew up—if they were still a band, that is. "He was the one who christened us," says Hernández. "That's what he wrote on our papers. So when we arrived at Soledad and had to introduce ourselves, I said, 'Tell them that we are Los Tigres del Norte.'"

After the prison performance, the promoter of the show, a businessman named Manuel Morales, took the group to San Jose. The city had a growing Mexican American community at the time, and it planned to celebrate its very first official Mexican Independence Day the following month, on September 16, 1967. The band was hired for the event and the plan seemed to be working fine. But soon, says Hernández, they discovered that the other artists from their prison caravan had vanished, presumably back to Mexico. Also missing: Los Tigres' passports.

Being stranded turned out to be another lucky break. People offered to lend them a hand. Promoter Morales began booking them every Sunday at a spot on the east side of town called Paseo de las Flores. It was a popular open-air venue that people nicknamed "El Hoyo," The Hole, because it was sunken between railroad tracks and the creek, keeping it cool in hot weather. Morales put them up in a home behind his Mexican store, La Internacional, on Alum Rock Avenue, where they shared living quarters with the promoter's mother.

The group started garnering more attention. They made the rounds of bars and restaurants, still passing the hat. But they also did live radio shows on KOFY (referred to as Radio Coffee), the only Mexican station at the time. They also performed during popular live radio remote broadcasts at the Pink Elephant on King Road, another business serving the growing Mexican consumer market.

At one of their early shows, a photographer named Richard Díaz approached them with word about a British-born record distributor who wanted to meet them. His name was Art Walker, and he would become the first person to put the music of Los Tigres on record. At first, remembers Hernández, they couldn't even communicate, because Walker didn't speak Spanish and the Tigres hadn't yet learned English. But Walker's wife was bilingual and served as an interpreter, thus laying the groundwork for what turned out to be one of the most successful recording careers in the history of Mexican music. Walker (later nicknamed Arturo Caminante in Spanish) took the group to Fresno that fall to make their inaugural recording, a single titled "De un Rancho a Otro."

The band was far from an overnight success. It took three years before they had their first big hit, "Contrabando y Traición," which launched their career and, somewhat to their dismay, helped create the controversial subgenre known today as narcocorridos. The song, about a drug-smuggling couple whose exploits end in betrayal and murder, was followed in 1973 by "La Banda del Carro Rojo," another narcocorrido about a drug-smuggling gang in a red car.

Soon, Hernández would realize his goal of bringing his music to an international audience. The breakthrough came when Los Tigres were invited to star in Mexican films, alongside top stars of the day, such as David Reynoso and Lucha Villa. "And that's the moment when it all changed for us," says Hernández. "When people saw us on the screen with accomplished and revered artists, they started looking at us with different eyes. The whole panorama changed."

Over Four Decades of Recordings

In all, Los Tigres recorded eight albums over sixteen years for Walker's San Jose company, Fama Records (fig. 55), helping make

it one of the most important Mexican labels on the West Coast in the 1970s. Yet, unbelievably, Hernández says the band was never paid a penny for those records. They made their money from the live concerts, but the label never paid royalties. "Out of gratitude to Arturo, there were never any payments or any of that," recalls Hernández. "Instead, I recorded with him because we were friends. We became very good friends and Arturo always behaved like a gentleman with me."

Hernández can't say the same for an Italian businessman who became Walker's partner. The introduction of a third party led to conflicts, and Los Tigres finally asked to be released from their contract with La Fama. Eventually, the case wound up in court when Los Tigres sued the company. Yet again, the charmed band's problems would become their good fortune. The judge, says Hernández, ruled in the band's favor and, as compensation for past inequities, gave the group all rights to their songs and ownership of their recorded masters, which in those days were usually kept by record companies even after artists left their rosters. That old catalog became like a musical 401K for the band, which retains the rights to this day. Los Tigres went on to record for Fonovisa, part of the Televisa empire, and broadened its popularity internationally. They have toured Latin America, Europe, and Asia, making them the first global norteño band in history.

By the time Los Tigres celebrated their fortieth anniversary as a band in 2008, they had recorded more than 500 songs on sixty albums, starred in more than fourteen films, scored multiple Grammys, and sold over 35 million units worldwide (see appendix L, "Recordings by Los Tigres del Norte in the Frontera Collection"). In 2003 the group performed at the Kennedy Center in Washington, DC and four years later won the Latin Recording Academy's Lifetime

Figure 55. Los Tigres del Norte issued their first recordings on Fama Records, based in San Jose, California. Shown on the cover of their third Fama LP, *Si Si Si/Chayo Chaires* (circa 1971), are (*from left*) Jorge Hernández, accordion; Hernán Hernández, torroloche; Oscar Lara, redoba; and Raul Hernández, bajo sexto.

Achievement Award. In 2011 Los Tigres broke another barrier by becoming the first regional Mexican act to be featured in the popular recorded concert series MTV Unplugged. For the filmed acoustic concert, the band brought together top stars representing diverse countries and styles, including Juanes, Residente of Calle 13, Paulina Rubio, Andres Calamaro, and Zack de la Rocha of Rage Against the Machine in his first-ever Spanish language performance.

"For more than thirty years they have lifted up a music once looked down on for its lower-class roots, making norteño a commercially viable pop music," wrote music critic Chuy Varela in a 2005 feature story for the *San Francisco Chronicle*.[2] "Yet there is a higher sense of purpose to what they do. Los Tigres give strength to people who feel marginalized and under attack in these days of widespread anti-immigrant sentiment."

Perhaps the band's most enduring accomplishment has been its support for the Frontera Collection at UCLA, starting with a $500,000 donation made to the Chicano Studies Research Center on April 19, 2000. The Los Tigres del Norte Fund at UCLA supports research, acquisition, documentation, dissemination, and presentation of authentic traditional and folk musical traditions in Spanish.

It was the band's own thirst for knowledge about the music that led to the massive UCLA project. They had been looking for an authoritative source to provide the musical history that the genre had always been missing. "We read books, but every author had his own version of the story, and they were all different," says Hernández. "We wanted to know more and we wanted the real history of the corrido."

The controversy over narcocorridos, which intensified during the 1990s, made them even more anxious for the truth behind the music. They had always considered themselves story tellers, like travelling troubadours of old whose songs simply recounted the daily lives and struggles of common people. The corridos they sang were in the best tradition of the genre as journalism put to music, going back to the villains and heroes who predated the Mexican Revolution. They never intended to take sides in any drug war, and so they were eager to put their work in its proper context.

That quest led them to Guillermo Hernández, a corrido expert and professor at UCLA. Through their label, they made contact with Hernández, a longtime associate of Strachwitz, who had been looking for ways to preserve his friend's Mexican record collection for posterity. The group's grant to the university was the first of its kind from a community-based source. This humble band of brothers from Rosa Morada, Sinaloa, helped establish the largest library archive of Mexican and Mexican American music in the world.

"Getting their music recognized by the state's biggest university as literature of the masses, that was to them the epitome of making it, of getting verification of who they are," says Strachwitz.[3]

Through this academic collaboration, the band started discovering the history of corridos they had been singing for decades. "Apparently they were really knocked out when they found that some of these songs had been recorded fifty years ago. They were just amazed that there were so many more verses than they had heard," Strachwitz continues. "Nobody had ever seen these old records, and they finally began to realize that all this music had been documented since the beginning of the last century. So they were really impressed."

Hernández hopes that future generations will also use the Frontera Collection to learn about their cultural history and traditions. Today, students and researchers have access to that information instantly through Frontera's painstaking digital transfer of a century of recorded music. The archives provide in an instant what Los Tigres took a lifetime to discover.

"Ours is a group which, like the music itself, came here and has had to work hard to be recognized and acknowledged," says Hernández. "We didn't have the technology that exists today. We had to go from *rancho* to *rancho*, village to village, city to city, country to country. In other words, we did it all by hand."

The Frontera 400
A World of Genres from Chicano Rock to Cha Cha Chá

While amassing his collection of Mexican and Mexican American music, Chris Strachwitz also came to compile, albeit incidentally, a much broader archive of the most beloved and recognizable tunes from the global repertoire of Latin American pop music. The Frontera 400 is a list of such tunes representing standards from several countries and a variety of genres. These recordings are like dolphins caught in tuna nets: they were acquired by chance as part of larger acquisitions consistent with the archive's main focus on the music of the US-Mexico border. Yet they represent a remarkable range of songs popular throughout the Latin American continent and Iberian peninsula during the twentieth century.

The Frontera 400 could be considered a Latin American songbook in its own right. It features some of Latin music's most revered songwriters and includes tangos, mambos, boleros, paso dobles, sambas, congas, rancheras, and cha cha chás (figs. 56, 57).

This list was assembled through a systematic review of every title within the UCLA database, which as of this writing includes almost 27,000 songs. The selection was made by the author based on subjective judgment regarding a song's popularity and stature, especially over time. Many are tunes encoded in the pop music DNA of Spanish-speaking people, who would instantly recognize the melody or lyric as a "golden oldie" or a cherished "chestnut," to use pop music terms. Some songs echo bygone eras while others remain in cultural currency, continually covered by contemporary artists or dusted off annually for special occasions, such as Christmas or birthday celebrations.

Because this is a song list, composers are listed for every title. This task was much more challenging than it may seem at first blush. In most cases it was not a matter of just using the names of songwriters printed on the labels of the recordings in the collection. For many reasons, those credits are often unreliable. In fact, where multiple recordings of the same song exist, labels sometimes give contradictory credits, citing completely different composers for the same song. Traditional songs such as "Cielito Lindo"—the folk song that is emblematic of Mexico, with its chorus of "Ay, ay, ay, ay / Canta y no llores"—go through so many permutations over the decades that some composers may take credit for their revisions and new verses on specific recordings. At least five different composers are credited on various versions of the song in the collection.

Finally, label credits can often be sloppy and inaccurate, misspelling a composer's name

Figure 56. Pianist and composer Agustín Lara (*seated*) remains one of the most beloved figures in Mexican pop music from the twentieth century. He collaborated with some of the most glamorous stars of his era, including sultry actress María Felix, whom he married in 1946. The marriage lasted only a year, but it inspired such timeless songs as "María Bonita," one of twenty Lara compositions on the list of 400 Latin music standards in the Frontera Collection. In this early photo, from the 1920s, Lara strikes a sophisticated pose with tenor Juan Arvizu (*left*) and his fellow tango singer Maruca Pérez. Photograph courtesy of the Arhoolie Foundation.

or omitting co-composers for certain tunes. Thus, care was taken to give the most accurate credit for each title. In most cases, in particular where the credit was clouded or contradictory, multiple sources were consulted to verify the legitimate songwriters and their countries of origin. The country listed is the one associated with the composer, not the genre. So, for example, the famous composition "Nereidas" is a danzón, which is typically Cuban, but the composer hails from Mexico, where the style also took root.

The main sources used were the websites for two major song royalty and licensing agencies in the United States, BMI (Broadcast Music, Inc.) and ASCAP (American Society of Composers, Authors and Publishers), as well as songwriter organizations in Mexico, SACM (Sociedad de Autores y Compositores de México), and in Spain, SGAE (Sociedad General de Autores y Editores). All four have excellent song and author search engines, often providing full names instead of just initials for first names as is customary in the record industry. The SACM site also has very useful biographies of many songwriters, including their major works. However, credit conflicts still arose even within these searches. In those cases, other music and

A la orilla de un palmar

A la orilla de un palmar
yo vide una joven bella,
su boquita de coral,
sus ojitos una estrella.
Al pasar le pregunté
que quién estaba con ella
y me contestó llorando:
sola 'oy en el palmar.
Soy huerfanita,
no tengo padre ni madre
ni un amigo
que me venga a consolar.
Solita paso la vida
a la orilla del palmar
y solita voy y vengo
como las olas del mar.

Figure 57. This *carta cancionera*, an illustrated postcard with song lyrics, features "A La Orilla de un Palmar" (At the Edge of a Palm Grove), a traditional Mexican love song that is among 400 Latin American standards found in the Frontera Collection. Photograph courtesy of the Arhoolie Foundation.

culture websites were consulted (see the full list, which follows the table). For most songs where credits were even marginally in question, composers were confirmed on at least two of the fifty resource sites. In the few cases where conflicts could not be resolved, the designation D. R. (Spanish initials for "rights reserved") was used to indicate that the composer's name could not be immediately determined. For songs that were clearly part of cultural tradition where no author can be credited, the designation "traditional" was used.

One final note: Most versions of these songs are of excellent musical quality and enduring interest; a few are even performed by their original authors. However, some renditions found in the collection are covers by lesser-known artists on small labels, which in a few cases fail to do aesthetic justice to the original compositions. From a critical standpoint, the performances could be considered second-rate, and the recordings would merit no special attention beyond being the only version of certain standards in this collection. For example, "El Reloj," the famous bolero by Mexico's Roberto Cantoral, has been recorded probably hundreds of times, but the Frontera Collection has only one unexceptional version on a regional Texas label, Falcon A652, by the unknown group Los Chafas. These are the exceptions, however, and do not reflect on the overall value of the collection itself, since its central mission did not include the acquisition of this type of song.

Nevertheless, the inclusion of so many ancillary styles of music is a measure of how vast the collection truly is. Even by accident, the Frontera Collection managed to amass a treasure trove of classic songs that should delight music lovers and intrigue researchers for some time to come.

The Frontera 400

Title	Composer	Country
A la Orilla de un Palmar	Manuel M. Ponce	Mexico
A los Muchachos de Belén	Adolfo O'Reilly – Félix Chappotín	Cuba
A Pesar de Todo	Nelson Ned	Brazil
Abril en Portugal	José Galhardo – R. Ferrao	Cuba
Acércate Más	Osvaldo Farrés	Cuba
Acuyuye	Johnny Pacheco	Dominican Republic
Adiós Mariquita Linda	Marco A. Jiménez	Mexico
Adiós Mi Chaparrita	Ignacio Fernández Esperón "Tata Nacho"	Mexico
Adiós Palma Soriano	Ramón Cabrera	Cuba
Adiós, Muchachos	Julio Sanders – César F. Vedani	Argentina
Ahora Seremos Felices	Rafael Hernández	Puerto Rico
Aires del Mayab	Guty Cárdenas	Mexico
Al Vaivén de Mi Carreta	Ñico Saquito (Benito Antonio Fernández Ortíz)	Cuba
Albur de Amor	Alfonso Esparza Oteo	Mexico
Allá en el Rancho Grande	S. Ramos – J. del Moral – E. D. Uranga	Mexico
Alma con Alma	Juan Rafael (Juanito) Márquez	Cuba
Alma Llanera	Pedro Elías Gutiérrez	Venezuela
Almendra	Abelardo Valdés de la Cantera	Cuba
Alto Songo	Luis Martínez Griñan	Cuba
Amada Amante	E. Carlos – R. Carlos	Brazil
Amanecí en Tus Brazos	José Alfredo Jiménez	Mexico
Amar y Vivir	Consuelo Velázquez	Mexico
Amarga Navidad	José Alfredo Jiménez	Mexico
Amigo	Rafael Hernández	Puerto Rico
Amor con Amor Se Paga	Manuel Esperón González	Mexico
Amor de la Calle	Fernando Z. Maldonado	Mexico
Amorcito Corazón	M. Esperón González – P. de Urdemalas	Mexico
Anabacoa	J. Ramírez	Cuba
Angelito	Rene Herrera – Rene Ornelas	United States
Angelitos Negros	Álvarez Maciste – Eloy Blanco	Venezuela
Anillo de Compromiso	Cuco Sánchez	Mexico
Animas Que No Amanezca	Guadalupe Ramos	Mexico
Anoche Estuve Llorando	Cuco Sánchez	Mexico
Aquellos Ojos Verdes	Nilo Menéndez – Adolfo Utrera	Cuba
Arráncame la Vida	Agustín Lara	Mexico
Arrieros Somos	Cuco Sánchez	Mexico
Aunque Me Cueste la Vida	Luis Kalaff	Dominican Republic
Aventurera	Agustín Lara	Mexico
Ay! Jalisco No Te Rajes	Manuel Esperón González – Ernesto Cortázar	Mexico

Title	Composer	Country
Ay! Mamá Inés	Eliseo Grenet	Cuba
Babalú	Margarita Lecuona	Cuba
Babarabatiri	Antar Daly	Cuba
Baila Esta Cumbia	Selena	United States, Mexico
Barlovento	Eduardo Serrano	Venezuela
Before the Next Teardrop Falls	Vivian Keith – Ben Peters	United States
Begin the Beguine	Cole Porter	United States
Bésame Mucho	Consuelo Velázquez	Mexico
Bilongo (La Negra Tomasa)	Guillermo Rodríguez Fiffe	Cuba
Blen Blen Blen	Chano Pozo	Cuba
Bonito y Sabroso	Beny Moré	Cuba
Borinquen	Pedro Flores	Puerto Rico
Brasil	Ary Barroso	Brazil
Bruca Manigua	Arsenio Rodríguez	Cuba
Burundanga	Oscar Muñoz Bouffartique	Cuba
Bururú Barará	Ignacio Piñeiro	Cuba
Cachita	Rafael Hernández – Bernardo Sancristobal	Puerto Rico
Camarón y Mamoncillo	Miguel Matamoros	Cuba
Camina Como Chencha la Gamba	Ñico Saquito (Benito Antonio Fernández Ortiz)	Cuba
Caminante del Mayab	Guty Cárdenas	Mexico
Caminemos	Heriberto Martins – Alfredo Gil	Mexico
Camino de Guanajuato	José Alfredo Jiménez	Mexico
Campanitas de Cristal	Rafael Hernández	Puerto Rico
Caña de Azúcar	Lorenzo Barcelata	Mexico
Cananea	Manuel S. Acuña	Mexico
Canción Mixteca	José López Alavés	Mexico
Candilejas (The Terry Theme)	Charlie Chaplin	United States
Cao Cao Maní Picao	José Carbó Menéndez	Cuba
Capullito de Alelí	Rafael Hernández	Puerto Rico
Caramelos (Caramelo a Kilo)	Roberto Puentes	Cuba
Carcelera	Felipe Rosario Goyco ("Don Felo")	Puerto Rico
Cartagenera	Vanella – Farías	Colombia
Cenizas	Wello Rivas	Mexico
Chacha Linda	Carlos y Pablo Martínez Gil	Mexico
Chango Ta Beni	Justi Barreto	Cuba
Cherry Pink and Apple Blossom White	Louis Guglielmi (Louiguy)	Spain/Italy
Cielito Lindo	Traditional	Mexico
Cómo Fue	Ernesto Duarte Brito	Cuba
Como México No Hay Dos	Pepe Guízar	Mexico
Compadre Pedro Juan	Luis Alberti	Dominican Republic
Con un Amor Se Borra Otro Amor	Arsenio Rodríguez	Cuba

Title	Composer	Country
Congoja	Rafael Hernández	Puerto Rico
Contigo Aprendí	Armando Manzanero	Mexico
Contigo en la Distancia	César Portillo de la Luz	Cuba
Contrabando y Traición	Angel González	Mexico
Convergencia	Bienvenido J. Gutiérrez – M. Guerra	Cuba
Corazón, Corazón	José Alfredo Jiménez	Mexico
Cu Cu Ru Cu Cu Paloma	Tomás Méndez	Mexico
Cuando el Destino	José Alfredo Jiménez	Mexico
Cuando Sale la Luna	José Alfredo Jiménez	Mexico
Cuando Salgo a Los Campos	D. R.	Mexico
Cuando Vuelva a Tu Lado[a]	María Grever	Mexico
Cuatro Caminos	José Alfredo Jiménez	Mexico
De Colores	Traditional	Mexico/United States
Delgadina	Traditional	Spain/Mexico
Demasiado Tarde	Roberto Cantoral	Mexico
Desvelo de Amor	Rafael Hernández	Puerto Rico
Dolor y Perdón	Beny Moré	Cuba
Dónde Estabas Tú?	Ernesto Duarte Brito	Cuba
Dos Arbolitos	Chucho Martínez Gil	Mexico
Dulce Habanera	Miguel Román – Rafael Ortiz	Cuba
Dundumbanza	Arsenio Rodríguez	Cuba
Échale Cinco al Piano	Felipe Valdés Leal	Mexico
Échame a Mi la Culpa	José Angel Espinoza "Ferrusquilla"	Mexico
El Abandonado	Traditional	Mexico
El Agua de Clavelito	Miguel Angel Pozo "Clavelito"	Cuba
El Andariego	Nicandro Castillo	Mexico
El Ausente (Ya Vine de Donde Andaba)	Traditional	Mexico
El Barzón	Miguel Muñiz	Mexico
El Bodeguero	Richard Egües	Cuba
El Bombón de Elena	Rafael Cepeda	Puerto Rico
El Brindis del Bohemio	Guillermo Aguirre y Fierro	Mexico
El Burrito de Belén (Mi Burrito Sabanero)	Hugo Blanco	Venezuela
El Caimán	Traditional	Colombia
El Cañaveral	Lorenzo Barcelata	Mexico
El Carretero	Traditional	Mexico
El Cascabel	Lorenzo Barcelata	Mexico
El Choclo	A. J. Villoldo	Argentina
El Cóndor Pasa	Daniel Alomía Robles	Peru
El Crucifijio de Piedra	Roberto Cantoral	Mexico
El Cumbanchero	Rafael Hernández – Bernardo Sancristobal	Puerto Rico
El Día Que Me Quieras	Alfredo Le Pera – Carlos Gardel	Argentina

Title	Composer	Country
El Eco y el Carretero	Pablito Márquez – Claudio Ferrer	Cuba, Puerto Rico
El Jamaiquino	El Niño Rivera	Cuba
El Jarabe Tapatío (Mexican Hat Dance)	Traditional	Mexico
El Jinete	José Alfredo Jiménez	Mexico
El Manisero (The Peanut Vendor)	Simons – Gilbert – Sunshine	Cuba, United States
El Moro de Cumpas	Leonardo Yañez Romo	Mexico
El Muerto Se Fue de Rumba	Rafael Blanco Suazo	Cuba
El Negrito del Batey	Medardo Guzmán	Dominican Republic
El Pájaro Carpintero	Di Lazzaro – Di Lazzaro – Brito	International
El Paralítico	Miguel Matamoros	Cuba
El Pata Rajada	Marcel Rey	Mexico
El Pavido Navido	G. Peña	Mexico
El Plebeyo	Felipe Pinglo Alva	Peru
El Preso No. 9	Roberto Cantoral – Antonio Cantoral	Mexico
El Que Siembra Su Maíz	Miguel Matamoros	Cuba
El Reloj	Roberto Cantoral	Mexico
El Rey	José Alfredo Jiménez	Mexico
El Rincón Caliente	Arsenio Rodríguez	Cuba
El Siquisirí	Traditional	Mexico
El Son de La Negra[b]	D. R.	Mexico
El Sube y Baja	Mario Montes	Mexico
El Túnel	Enrique Jorrín – Arturo Liendo	Cuba
El Último Adiós	Pedro Flores – Julio Venegas	Puerto Rico
El Zopilote Mojado	Miguel Macías Femat	Mexico
Elena la Cumbanchera	Gerardo Martínez	Cuba
Elige Tú Que Canto Yo	Joseito Fernández	Cuba
Ella	José Alfredo Jiménez	Mexico
Elube Changó	Alberto Rivera	Cuba
En la Cumbancha	Jorge Zamora	Cuba
En Mi Viejo San Juan	Noél Estrada	Puerto Rico
Entre Copa y Copa	Felipe Valdés Leal	Mexico
Escaleras de la Cárcel	Cuco Sánchez	Mexico
Escándalo	Chucho Navarro	Mexico
Escándalo	Rubén Fuentes	Mexico
Escarcha	Agustín Lara	Mexico
Esclavo y Amo	José Vaca Flores	Mexico
España Cañí	Pascual Marquina Narro	Spain
Espíritu Burlón	Miguel Jorrín	Cuba
Esta Noche Me Emborracho	Enrique Santos Discepolo	Argentina
Esta Tarde Vi Llover	Armando Manzanero	Mexico
Esta Tristeza Mía	Antonio Valdez Herrera	Mexico

Title	Composer	Country
Estrellita	Manuel M. Ponce	Mexico
Fallaste Corazón	Cuco Sánchez	Mexico
Falsa Moneda	Chucho Ramírez	Mexico
Falsaria	Carlos y Pablo Martínez Gil	Mexico
Farolito	Agustín Lara	Mexico
Flor	Guty Cárdenas	Mexico
Flor de Azalea	Z. Gómez Urquiza – Manuel Esperón González	Mexico
Francisco Guayabal	Pío Leiva	Cuba
Franqueza	Consuelo Velázquez	Mexico
Frenesí	Alberto Domínguez	Mexico
Fumando Espero	Juan Viladomat – Félix Garzó	Argentina
Gabino Barrera	Víctor Cordero	Mexico
Gavilán o Paloma	Rafael Pérez Botija	Spain
Gavilán Pollero	Ventura Romero Armendáriz	Mexico
Gema	Luis "Güicho" Cisneros Alvea	Mexico
Golondrina Viajera	Guty Cárdenas – Ricardo López Méndez	Mexico
Golondrinas Yucatecas	Ricardo Palmerín	Mexico
Gorrioncillo Pecho Amarillo	Tomás Méndez	Mexico
Granada	Agustín Lara	Mexico
Granito de Sal	C. Duarte Moreno – Pepe Domínguez	Mexico
Grítenme Piedras del Campo	Cuco Sánchez	Mexico
Guadalajara	Pepe Guízar	Mexico
Guajira	Armando Oréfiche	Cuba
Guajira Guantanamera	Joseito Fernández	Cuba
Guararé	Ricardo Fabrega	Cuba
Guitarras de Media Noche	José Alfredo Jiménez	Mexico
Hace un Año	Felipe Valdés Leal	Mexico
Hamaca	Luis Arcaráz	Mexico
Hipócrita	Carlos Crespo	Mexico
Historia de un Amor	Carlos Almarán	Panama
Humo en los Ojos	Agustín Lara	Mexico
Imposible	Agustín Lara	Mexico
Jacarandosa	Ñico Saquito (Benito Antonio Fernández Ortiz)	Cuba
Jamás Me Cansaré de Ti	Juan Gabriel	Mexico
Jesucita en Chihuahua	Traditional	Mexico
Juan Charrasqueado	Víctor Cordero	Mexico
Juancito Trucupey	Luis Kalaff	Dominican Republic
Juárez (No Debió de Morir)	Esteban Alfonso	Mexico
Julia	Francisco Moure Holguín	Julia
Júrame	María Grever	Mexico
La Adelita	Traditional	Mexico

Title	Composer	Country
La Bamba	Traditional	Mexico
La Banda del Caro Rojo	Paulino Vargas	Mexico
La Barca	Roberto Cantoral	Mexico
La Barca de Oro	Abundio Martínez	Mexico
La Bikina	Rubén Fuentes	Mexico
La Boa	José Carlos Reyes – Felix Reyna	Mexico, Cuba
La Boda de Luis Alonso	Gerónimo Giménez y Bellido	Spain
La Borinqueña	Felix Astol Artés	Spain, Puerto Rico
La Brisa y Yo	Ernesto Lecuona – Emilio de Torre	Cuba, Spain
La Cama de Piedra	Cuco Sánchez	Mexico
La Cama Vacía	Juan Manuel Pombo – Alberto Colantuoni	Argentina
La Canción del Molino Rojo	Auric – Engvick – De Llano	Mexico
La Chambelona	Felipe Neri Cabrera	Cuba
La Comparsa	Ernesto Lecuona	Cuba
La Copa Rota	Benito de Jesús Negrón	Puerto Rico
La Cucaracha	Traditional	Mexico
La Cumbancha	Agustín Lara	Mexico
La Cumbia del Sol	D. R.	Colombia
La Cumparsita	Gerardo Hernán Matos Rodríguez	Uruguay
La Diferencia	Juan Gabriel	Mexico
La Engañadora	Enrique Jorrín	Cuba
La Enorme Distancia	José Alfredo Jiménez	Mexico
La Feria de las Flores	Chucho Monge	Mexico
La Flor de la Canela	Chabuca Granda	Peru
La Gloria Eres Tú	José Antonio Méndez	Cuba
La Golondrina	Nicolás Juárez	Mexico
La Hiedra	Seracini – D'Acquisto – Molar	Italy
La Hija de Nadie	Romualdo García	Mexico
La Ley del Monte	José Angel Espinoza "Ferrusquilla"	Mexico
La Llorona	Traditional	Mexico
La Malagueña (Malagueña Salerosa)[b]	Elpidio Ramírez – Pedro Galindo	Mexico
La Mañanitas	Traditional	Mexico
La Media Vuelta	José Alfredo Jiménez	Mexico
La Mentira	Álvaro Carrillo	Mexico
La Mora	Eliseo Grenet	Cuba
La Mucura	Crescencio Salcedo	Colombia
La Muerte de un Gallero	Tomás Méndez	Mexico
La Nave de Olvido	Dino Ramos	Mexico
La Negra Noche	Emilio D. Uranga	Mexico
La Palma	Traditional	Mexico
La Paloma	Sebastián Yradier	Spain

Title	Composer	Country
La Pollera Colora	Wilson Choperana – Juan Madera	Colombia
La Que Se Fue	José Alfredo Jiménez	Mexico
La Ruñidera	Alejandro Rodríguez	Cuba
La Sitiera	Rafael López	Cuba
La Última Noche	Bobby Collazo	Cuba
La Virgen de la Macarena	B. Bautista Monterde – A. Ortiz Calero	Spain
La Zandunga	Traditional	Mexico
Lágrimas Negras	Miguel Matamoros	Cuba
Lamento Borincano	Rafael Hernández	Puerto Rico
Lamento Gitano	María Grever	Mexico
Lamento Jarocho	Agustín Lara	Mexico
Las Botas de Charro	José Alfredo Jiménez	Mexico
Las Isabeles	Luis Pérez Meza	Mexico
Las Llaves de Mi Alma	Vicente Fernandez	Mexico
Las Mañanitas	Traditional	Mexico
Las Posadas	Traditional	Mexico
Las Raspa	Traditional	Mexico
Las Rejas No Matan	Tomás Méndez	Mexico
Los Ejes de Mi Carreta	Atahualpa Yupanqui – Romildo Risso	Argentina
Lisboa Antigua	Portela – Galhardo – Do Vale	Portugal
Llego Borracho El Borracho	José Alfredo Jiménez	Mexico
Locas Por el Mambo	Beny Moré	Cuba
Los Laureles	Gilberto Parra	Mexico
Los Mandados	Jorge Lerma	Mexico
Los Tamalitos de Olga	José Fajardo	Cuba
Luna Arrabalera	Mario César Gomila – Carlos Marucci	Argentina
Luna Sobre el Jaragua	Luis Alberti	Dominican Republic
Malagueña	Ernesto Lecuona	Cuba
Mamá Yo Quiero (Mamãe Eu Quero)	Vicente Paiva – Jararaca	Brazil
Mambo del Ruletero	Dámaso Pérez Prado	Cuba
Mambo No. 5	Dámaso Pérez Prado	Cuba
María Bonita	Agustín Lara	Mexico
María Elena	Lorenzo Barcelata	Mexico
Mata Siguaraya	Lino Frías	Cuba
Matilde Lina	Leandro Díaz	Colombia
Me Caí de la Nube	Cornelio Reyna	Mexico
Me He de Comer Esa Tuna	Manuel Esperón González	Mexico
Me Lo Dijo Adela (Sweet and Gentle)	Otilio del Portal	Cuba
Me Voy Pal Pueblo	Mercedes Valdés	Cuba
Melao de Caña	Mercedes Pedroso	Cuba
Menéame la Cuna	Ñico Saquito (Benito Antonio Fernández Ortiz)	Cuba

Title	Composer	Country
Menudita	Ignacio Fernández Esperón "Tata Nacho"	Mexico
Mexicali Rose	Helen Stone – Jack B. Tenney	United States
México Lindo y Querido	Chucho Monge	Mexico
Mi Buenos Aires Querido	Alfredo Le Pera – Carlos Gardel	Argentina
Mi Cafetal	Crescencio Salcedo	Colombia
Mi Chorro de Voz	Salvador "Chava" Flores	Mexico
Mona Lisa^c	Jay Livingston – Ray Evans	United States, Mexico
Moneda Sin Valor	Néstor Pineda Maldonado	Mexico
Mujer	Agustín Lara	Mexico
Mulence	Arsenio Rodríguez	Cuba
Naufragio	Agustín Lara	Mexico
Nereidas	Amador Pérez Torres "Dimas"	Mexico
Ni en Defensa Propia	Ramón Ortega Contreras	Mexico
No Me Amenaces	José Alfredo Jiménez	Mexico
No Salgas, Niña, a la Calle	Carlos y Pablo Martínez Gil	Mexico
No Volveré	Manuel Esperón González – Ernesto E. Cortázar	Mexico
No, No y No	Osvaldo Farrés	Cuba
Noche Criolla	Agustín Lara	Mexico
Noche de Ronda	Agustín Lara	Mexico
Nosotros	Pedro Junco	Cuba
Nuestro Juramento	Benito de Jesus	Puerto Rico
Nunca	Guty Cárdenas	Mexico
Obsesión	Pedro Flores	Puerto Rico
Odiame	Rafael Otero	Peru
Ojos Tristes	Guty Cárdenas	Mexico
Pachito Eché	Alejandro Tobar	Colombia
Paloma Negra	Tomás Méndez	Mexico
Pelea de Gallos (La Feria de San Marcos)	Juan S. Garrido	Mexico
Pena Penita	Quintero, León y Quiroga	Spain
Perdón	Pedro Flores	Puerto Rico
Perdóname, Olvídalo	Juan Gabriel	Mexico
Peregrino de Amor	Guty Cárdenas	Mexico
Perfidia	Alberto Domínguez	Mexico
Piel Canela	Bobby Capó	Puerto Rico
Poquita Fe	Bobby Capó	Puerto Rico
Por Ti Aprendí a Querer	Lorenzo Barcelata	Mexico
Prisionero del Mar	Luis Arcaráz – Ernesto Cortázar	Mexico
Puño de Tierra	D. R.	Mexico
Qué Bonita es Mi Tierra	Rubén Fuentes	Mexico
Que Me Toquen las Golondrinas	Tomás Méndez	Mexico
Que Nadie Sepa Mi Sufrir	Angel Cabral – Enrique Dizeo	Argentina

Title	Composer	Country
Qué Te Ha Dado Esa Mujer?	Gilberto Parra	Mexico
Quiéreme Mucho	Gonzalo Roig – Agustín Rodríguez	Cuba
Quisiera	Guty Cárdenas	Mexico
Quizás, Quizás, Quizás	Osvaldo Farrés	Cuba
Ran-Kan-Kan	Tito Puente	Puerto Rico
Rayando el Sol	Manuel M. Ponce	Mexico
Rayito de Luna	Jesus "Chucho" Navarro	Mexico
Rayito de Sol (Por la Mañana)	Guty Cárdenas	Mexico
Recuerdo	Alberto M. Alvarado	Mexico
Recuerdos de Ypacaraí	Zulema de Mirkin – Demetrio Ortiz	Paraguay
Reina Rumba	Senén Suárez	Cuba
Renunclación	Antonio Valdez Herrera	Mexico
Rico Vacilón	Rosendo Ruiz Jr.	Cuba
Rival	Agustín Lara	Mexico
Rum and Coca Cola[b]	Lord Invader – Belasco – Amsterdam – Sullavan – Baron	Trinidad and Tobago, United States
Sabor a Mí	Álvaro Carrillo	Mexico
Salud, Dinero y Amor	Rodolfo Aníbal Sciammarella	Argentina
San Fernando	Lucho Bermúdez	Colombia
Santa	Agustín Lara	Mexico
Se Me Hizo Fácil	Agustín Lara	Mexico
Serenata Huasteca	José Alfredo Jiménez	Mexico
Serenata Sin Luna	José Alfredo Jiménez	Mexico
Si Me Comprendieras	José Antonio Méndez	Cuba
Si Nos Dejan	José Alfredo Jiménez	Mexico
Siboney	Ernesto Lecuona	Cuba
Siempre en Mi Mente	Juan Gabriel	Mexico
Sin Ti	Pepe Guízar	Mexico
Sin un Amor	Alfredo Gil – Jesús "Chucho" Navarro	Mexico
Solamente una Vez	Agustín Lara	Mexico
Sombras	Rafael Ramírez	Mexico
Son Tus Perjúmenes Mujer	Carlos Mejía Godoy	Nicaragua
South of the Border (Al Sur de la Frontera)	Kennedy – Carr – Valdés Leal	United States, Mexico
Suavecito	Ignacio Piñeiro	Cuba
Sun Sun Babae	Rogelio Martínez	Cuba
Talisman	Agustín Lara	Mexico
Tampico Hermoso	Alfredo M. Garza	Mexico
Tata Dios	Valeriano Trejo	Mexico
Tatalibaba	Florencio Santana	Cuba
Te Odio y Te Quiero	Enrique Alessio – Reinaldo Yiso	Argentina
Tequila	Chuck Rio (Daniel Flores)	United States
Tico Tico (Tico-Tico No Fubá)	Zequinha de Abreu	Brazil

Title	Composer	Country
Todos Vuelven	César Miró	Peru
Tragos Amargos	Ramón Ayala	Mexico, United States
Tres Lindas Cubanas	Antonio María Romeu	Cuba
Tú Me Acostumbraste	Frank Domínguez	Cuba
Tú Mi Delirio	César Portillo de la Luz	Cuba
Tu Recuerdo y Yo	José Alfredo Jiménez	Mexico
Tu Retirada	José Alfredo Jiménez	Mexico
Tú Sólo Tú	Felipe Valdés Leal	Mexico
Tu y Las Nubes	José Alfredo Jiménez	Mexico
Tumbando Caña	Blanco – Castro – Ramírez	Cuba
Un Mundo Raro	José Alfredo Jiménez	Mexico
Un Siglo de Ausencia	Alfredo Gil	Mexico
Un Viejo Amor	A. Esparza Oteo – A. Fernández Bustamante	Mexico
Una Copa Más	Chucho Navarro	Mexico
Una Pura y Dos Con Sal	Enrique Sánchez Alonzo	Mexico
Usted	Gabriel Ruíz – José Zorrilla	Mexico
Vaya con Dios	Russell – James – Pepper – Barrett	United States
Veinte Años	Felipe Valdés Leal	Mexico
Ven	Gonzalo Curiel	Mexico
Vendaval	Alexis Brau	Puerto Rico
Veracruz	Maria Teresa Lara	Mexico
Vereda Tropical	Gonzalo Curiel	Mexico
Viajera	Mario Molina Montes – Luis Arcaráz	Mexico
Vieja Luna	Orlando de la Rosa	Cuba
Viva Panamá!	Dagoberto "Yin" Carrizo	Panama
Volver Volver	Fernando Z. Maldonado	Mexico
Vuela Vuela Palomita	Lorenzo Barcelata	Mexico
Yambú	Machito – Ayala	Cuba
Yiri Yiri Bon	Silvestre Méndez	Cuba
Yo el Aventurero	Paco Michel	Mexico
Yo Soy Antillano	Claudia Ferrer	Puerto Rico
Yo Vendo Unos Ojos Negros	Donato Román	Chile
Zacatecas	Genaro Codina	Mexico

[a] Lyrics for the English version, "What a Difference a Day Makes," were written by Stanley Adams.
[c] For a discussion of disputes regarding the authorship of this song, consult the Wikipedia entry.
[b] The Spanish version of "Mona Lisa" is by P. Gamboa and Hermanos Reyes.

Sources

Books

Bronson, Fred. *The Billboard Book of Number 1 Hits*, 5th ed. New York: Billboard Books, 2003.

Laird, Ross. *Brunswick Records: A Discography of Recordings, 1916–1931*. Westport, CT: Greenwood Press, 2001.

Spottswood, Richard K. *Ethnic Music on Records*, vol. 4, *Spanish, Portuguese, Philippine, Basque*. Urbana: University of Illinois Press, 1990.

Websites

1	American Society of Composers, Authors and Publishers (ASCAP)	http://www.ascap.com/
2	BBC Radio 3	http://www.bbc.co.uk/
3	Biblioteca Luis Angel Arango (Colombia)	http://www.banrepcultural.org/blaa
4	Biblioteca Voces del Siglo XX (Venezuela)	http://www.fundacionjoseguillermocarrillo.org
5	Biografías de Puerto Rico	http://www.proyectosalonhogar.com/Biografias/
6	Broadcast Music, Inc. (BMI)	http://www.bmi.com/
7	Cancioneros	http://www.cancioneros.com/
8	Canciones del Ayer	http://www.cancionesdelayer.com/
9	Consejo Estatal para la Cultura y las Artes de Nayarit	http://www.cecan.gob.mx/
10	Cuba Encuentro	http://www.cubaencuentro.com/
11	Cuba Musical	http://cuba-musical.blogspot.com/
12	CUBARTE: El Portal de la Cultura Cubana	http://www.cubarte.cult.cu/
13	Danzonerox	http://www.wix.com/danzonerox/danzoteca3
14	Descarga	http://www.descarga.com/
15	.MUSIC (dotMusic)	http://music.us/
16	DurangoNet	http://www.durango.net.mx/
17	EcuRed: Enciclopedia Cubana	http://www.ecured.cu/
18	El Blog del Bolero	http://elblogdelbolero.wordpress.com/
19	El Cultural Electrónico (Madrid)	http://www.elcultural.es/
21	El Portal de Marieli	http://marielilasagabaster.net/
21	El Vallenato	http://www.elvallenato.com/
22	El Veraz (San Juan, Puerto Rico)	http://www.elveraz.com/
23	Emisora Cultural, Universidad de Antioquia, Colombia	http://emisora.udea.edu.co/
24	Folk Tango	http://www.folktan.com.ar/
25	Fundación Nacional para la Cultura Popular	http://www.prpop.org/
26	Guitarra Magazine	http://www.guitarramagazine.com/

27	Hispanópolis	http://hispanopolis.com/
28	Instituto de Cultura Puertorriqueña	http://www.icp.gobierno.pr/index.htm
29	La Biografía	http://www.labiografia.com/
30	La Guantanamera: Portal de La Cultura	http://www.gtmo.cult.cu/
31	Mi Cancionero	http://www.micancionero.com/index.jsp
32	Música de Chihuahua	http://musicadechihuahua.blogspot.com/
33	Musical AfroLatino	http://www.musicalafrolatino.com/
34	Pan American Symphony, Washington, DC	http://www.panamsymphony.org/
35	Pincelada Musical, Caracas, Venezuela	http://pinceladamusical.blogspot.com/
36	Prontuario de la Canción Mexicana	http://www.fomentar.com/Mexico/Cancionero/
37	Semanario Arquidiocesano de Guadalajara	http://www.semanario.com.mx/
38	Sociedad de Autores y Compositores Mexicanos (SACM)	http://www.sacm.org.mx/
39	Sociedad General de Autores y Editores (SGAE)	http://www.sgae.es/
40	Son Cubano	http://www.soncubano.com/
41	Soy Cubano	http://www.soycubano.com/
42	Toda Colombia	http://www.todacolombia.com/
43	Todo Tango	http://www.todotango.com/
44	Trovadores Yucatecos	http://www.trovadores-yucatecos.com/

In addition to the websites listed above, Wikipedia English (http://en.wikipedia.org/), Wikipedia Spanish (http://es.wikipedia.org/), and WorldCat (http://www.worldcat.org/) were also consulted.

Appendix B

Top Ten Songs

Of the thousands of titles in the Frontera Collection, these ten have the greatest number of releases. Five of these recordings are illustrated in figure 58.

Top Ten Songs

Rank	Title	No. of releases
1	Cielito Lindo	147
2	Gabino Barrera	98
3	Allá en el Rancho Grande	96
4	La Bamba	87
5	La Malagueña (Malagueña Salerosa)	64
6	Jarabe Tapatío / Mexican Hat Dance	58
7	Contrabando y Traición	58
8	La Cucaracha	57
9	El Rey	28
10	Noche de Ronda	24

Figure 58. The folkloric standard "Cielito Lindo" is the most recorded song in the Frontera Collection, with almost 150 renditions. This sample of five recordings, all 78s, illustrate the wide variety of artists who have interpreted the song in myriad styles, many with extended verses: Tito Guízar, with mariachi (Guadalajara 125), Narciso Martínez, in a huapango with accordion (Bluebird 3132), Los Rancheros, in a *canción huasteca* (Decca 10469), Guitarras Hawaianas, in a twangy instrumental (Okeh 16247) and tenor José Moriche, with semi-classical orchestra and castanets (Vocalion 8668). Photographs courtesy of the Arhoolie Foundation.

The Archivist's List: Seventy-eight Favorite 78s

List Compiled by Antonio Cuéllar

As the archivist in charge of digitizing the Frontera Collection, Antonio Cuéllar is the only person alive who has listened to all 32,000 sides of all 16,000 78s in the Frontera Collection, as well as countless 45s (fig. 59). Aside from diligence and patience, the Frontera archivist was required to have a good ear.

Cuéllar, who is Mexican American, grew up listening to traditional Mexican music because

Figure 59. Antonio Cuéllar, digital archivist for the Frontera Collection, in 2012. He is shown with the digital transfer equipment at the offices of the Arhoolie Foundation in El Cerrito, California. Photograph courtesy of Haley Ausserer.

his uncles had a mariachi band. He was much less familiar, however, with the regional border music at the heart of the Frontera Collection. And although he plays in a Bay Area punk band called La Plebe, he had never heard of the early rock recordings by a Texas native named Baldemar Huerta, known then as the Bebop Kid. Those tracks "had the essence of early rock, but in Spanish," Cuéllar noted, citing Huerta's cover version of Elvis Presley's "Don't Be Cruel," titled "No Seas Cruel," on the famed Falcon label, based in McAllen, Texas. "I had no idea they existed," said Cuéllar of those tracks by the artist who would go on to international fame singing in English as Freddy Fender.

Cuéllar was hired, said project manager Tom Diamant, "not for his knowledge of formal archiving, but for his knowledge of what musical instruments and the human voice should sound like when they are played back through a good pair of speakers." In the process, he has warmed to a whole new world of music on old 78 platters that are totally foreign to most in his generation. And he has emerged as an expert in the field.

Cuéllar writes, "I've heard so much great music in the past ten years, and I've thought about—and cried over—what is documented in these recordings. Being born in Mexico and growing up in the United States, I cannot ignore the history lesson that this music teaches. Much of what I know about my culture is due to this collection. The music has given me the tools to understand my place in history, and I've developed a greater appreciation of my heritage."

Here, then, are Cuéllar's picks from the tens of thousands of 78-rpm recordings he has listened to, one by one.

The Archivist's List: Seventy-eight Favorite 78s

Title	Artist	Label and no.	Comments
Antes y Después	Prieta Linda	Peerless 4786A	The singer complains about how things were great when the couple was dating, but now that they are married the relationship is filled with abuse. This plays into the machista attitude prevalent in Mexico.
Aventuras del West	Timoteo Cantú y Jesús Villa	Ideal 687-A	This song is about the riches to be made picking cotton in the US West. It offers advice to those who would go, warning of the discrimination they should expect. Cotton pickers should not say that they're Mexican, because the Germans there don't like Mexicans.
Capitán Charles Stevens, part 1	Lupe Martínez y Pedro Rocha	Vocalion 8280	I chose this track to highlight the influential dueto of Lupe Martínez and Pedro Rocha. This corrido is a tribute to Captain Charles Stevens, a Prohibition agent who was killed in the line of duty. It praises him for his valor and bravery.
Carga Blanca	Los Alegres de Terán	Falcon 1647	This corrido is about three men taking "white cargo," or cocaine, into the United States. They are betrayed and killed by the very people who paid them for the shipment in San Antonio. It is a classic tale of drugs and betrayal, themes that are ubiquitous in today's commercial regional music.
Cleto Rodriguez	Hermanitas Juanita y María	Globe 2003	Here Las Hermanas Mendoza are accompanied by Lydia Mendoza. This is a tribute to the heroics of Cleto Rodríguez, who went off to war to fight against the Japanese.
Contrabandistas Tequileros, part 1	Pedro Rocha y Lupe Martínez	Vocalion 8430	This corrido is about a tequila smuggler who is in jail awaiting his sentencing on March 17, 1930.
Contrabandistas Tequileros, part 2	Pedro Rocha y Lupe Martínez	Vocalion 8430-	In part 2, the smuggler is sentenced to time in the penitentiary for selling "tragos de tequila."
Corrido de Juan Reyna, part 1	Hermanos Bañuelos	Vocalion 8383	This corrido takes place on May 11, with no year given. Juan Reyna crashed into a police car and was brutally beaten by the cops before being taken to jail. Halfway through the corrido Juan Reyna is referred to as "El Mexicano," which implies that he is being abused because he is Mexican.
Corrido de Juan Reyna, part 2	Hermanos Bañuelos	Vocalion 8383-	The second part describes the trial of Juan Reyna. The Mexican community rallies behind him and collects money for his defense. Nonetheless, he is sentenced to one to ten years, just for defending his dignity.
Corrido de los Braceros	Los Braceros	Columbia 1290-C	This song tells about one aspect of the life of a bracero: the womanizing that goes on when men travel far away to work. While the men are enjoying the company of other women, their poor wives are at home, waiting for letters from their loved ones. Very interesting theme.
Corrido de Sidar, part 1	Salvador y Consuelo de Quirós	Columbia 3855-X	This is a tribute to an aviator named Pablo Sidar, who flew his plane to South America.

Title	Artist	Label and no.	Comments
Cuando Me Vine de Texas	Los Moreno	Cima 105-B	The singer tells of going to California to work in order to send money home to his girlfriend. The song uses caló slang and mentions large cities in California such as Hollywood, San Jose, and San Francisco.
Cuba y Puerto Rico	Sexteto Flores	Brunswick 41178	I chose this song to illustrate the fact that the collection also has Puerto Rican recordings. This is one of my favorites.
Delgadina	Cuarteto Carta Blanca	Okeh 16324	In this tragic song a father makes sexual advances to his daughter, Delgadina. She refuses, and the father punishes Delgadina by locking her up. She dies while in captivity.
El Chinito	El Cancionero Solitario	Bluebird B-3497-B	This is another example of the xenophobia that Mexicans and Mexican Americans often showed toward Asians. The lyrics would be very offensive by today's moral standards.
El Carnal	García y Cantú	Ideal 57	This sexual parody recounts the daily life of a gangster, pachuco, cholo, or equivalent for that time period. The themes and lyrics sound contemporary, evoking the tough, narco, gangster, or machista corridos of today. The use of "piruja" implies a prostitute or loose woman. This cut makes heavy use of caló.
El Chicano Valentón	Los Dos Manueles	Ideal 165	This was the first time the Ideal label used "Chicano" in a song title. Before the word took on a meaning of empowerment in the late 1960s, it was used as a derogatory term.
El Chinito	Quinteto Yucatán	Vocalion 8444	This song is about buying items from a Chinese vendor. It has passages that mimic or make fun of the Chinese language and Asian musical tones.
El Chino	Netty y Jesús Rodríguez	Vocalion 8917	This song parodies a conversation between a woman and a Chinese immigrant.
El Contrabando del Paso, part 1	Hermanos Bañuelos	Okeh 16354	My favorite version of this classic corrido.
El Corrido de Texas	S. Ramón y D. Ramírez	Columbia 3905-X	A very nice corrido played exclusively by strings. I like the rustic sound. The lyrics are a farewell from a man who will go to the US to pick cotton.
El Cuartelazo, part 1	Hermanos Chavarría	Columbia 4372-X	This corrido is about Madero's victory over Díaz and then his defeat and murder in 1913. Revolution corridos are very popular, and they provide nice details about events.
El Jornalero, part 1	Gaitán y Rodríguez	Vocalion 8482	In this corrido, set in the 1930s, the singers are returning to Mexico from San Antonio because people don't like Mexicans in Texas; they only like blacks and gringos. They say farewell to the city of San Antonio and to the women they loved.
El Jornalero, part 2	Gaitán y Rodríguez	Vocalion 8482	The singers praise the city of Nuevo León, Monterrey, where they will return. They praise and say farewell to all the woman they loved while they were in San Antonio.
El Lavaplatos, part 1	Hermanos Bañuelos	Vocalion 8349	This corrido is about a man who dreams of being a movie star and migrates to the US because of the revolution. He ends up meeting a friend in the US and begins to work in the fields. This corrido uses a lot of Caló.
El Lavaplatos, part 2	Hermanos Bañuelos	Vocalion 8349-	In the second part, the singer stops working in the fields because of the low wage and gets a job as a dishwasher. He returns to Mexico and abandons his dream of becoming a movie star. The complaints here are the same as in the modern-day "Lavaplatos."

Title	Artist	Label and no.	Comments
El Mojado	Timoteo Cantú y Jesús Maya	Ideal 259	"Mojado" (literally, wetback) is a derogatory word used to describe an undocumented person. The lyrics and the vocal style almost suggest that the singer is proud of this status as he boasts that he escaped deportation.
El Mojado, part 1	Gaytán, Cantú y Rodríguez	Vocalion 8516	This track depicts an immigrant, referred to as a "mojado" (wetback), being held by US immigration.
El Mojado, part 2	Gaytán, Cantú y Rodríguez	Vocalion 8516	The song goes on to critique the policies and practices of the US in relation to Mexican immigrants. It states that Chicanos are treated worse than African Americans and only courted when it is election time.
El Mosco Americano	Cancioneros Picarescos	Columbia 4371-X	This is a complaint about the American "mosquito," referring to tourists who go to Mexico. The song includes spoken dialog.
El Pastorcito	Los Alegres de Terán	Orfeo M-038	Very nice instrumental, dipping into a minor key. From the legendary Orfeo label.
El Reenganche, part 1	Luis Hernández y Leonardo Sifuentes	Victor 46615-A	This corrido recounts the journey and struggles of a Mexican immigrant—a track laborer—looking for work on the railroads. It mentions numerous cities in the United States.
El Reenganche, part 2	Luis Hernández y Leonardo Sifuentes	Victor 46615-B	Part 2.
El Tirili	Don Ramón Sr.	Master 2008	The song unapologetically talks about smoking marijuana and drinking. It praises the use of marijuana, making heavy use of caló slang. I like the humorous tone.
En las Islas Filipinas, part 1	Hermanos Ortiz	Martinez-Ortiz 602	This corrido is about the surprise attack on the United States by Japan on December 7, 1941, after which 200 artillery men from New Mexico were sent to the Philippines to fight the Japanese. The song praises the American flag as a symbol of freedom and liberty.
En las Islas Filipinas, part 2	Hermanos Ortiz	Martinez-Ortiz 602	Part 2.
El Registro	F. Montalvo y M. Rodríguez	Brunswick 41023-	This song is about the letter that was sent to men being drafted. The song describes them being taken to faraway lands to fight German troops. It also talks about arriving in France. The song laments everybody who was left behind at home, especially Mother.
General Emilio Zapata	Trío Luna	Columbia 2201-X	The song tells about General Zapata, who fought for the poor. He was valorous and well loved and respected by many. I like the delivery of Trío Luna.
Guerra . . . Guerra	Johnny Rodríguez	Decca 21067A	This is a call to prepare for war.
Guisa Gacha	Cuarteto Don Ramon, Sr.	Taxco 108	This is a different version than the one released on Discos Mexico BR-33-A. The tempo of this song is much faster and the lyrics are different, but the music is the same. This cut is heavy on caló.
La Crisis Actual, part 1	Los Cancioneros Alegres	Vocalion 8401	This corrido is about being deported back to Mexico after coming to the US illegally. It also tells of becoming a US citizen and getting better wages for being able to speak English.
La Crisis Actual, part 2	Los Cancioneros Alegres	Vocalion 8401-	The second part tells about the repatriation of the Mexican immigrant. First stop is jail for those who do not have passports, and then on to Mexico.
La Cucaracha	Flores y Montalvo	Bluebird B-2222-A	As in most other versions of this song, the main chorus and progression are the same. In this case the singers mention Pancho Villa going after Carranza and pulling him by his tail, which is unique to this recording.

Title	Artist	Label and no.	Comments
La Discriminación	Gaytán y Cantú	Ideal 305-A	This cut is about the discrimination that Latinos suffer in Texas and the apathetic stance taken by President Harry Truman.
La Guerra de Corea	Santiago Jiménez y Sus Valedores	Alamo 071A	This song is a farewell from an 18-year-old who had been drafted. He says that Tio Samuel (Uncle Sam) has called on him to fight in Korea. He bids farewell to his mother and his love.
La Inundación de California	Cancioneros Acosta	Columbia 4883-X	This corrido is about a flood that took place on March 13, 1928, in Southern California.
La Roña	Hermanos Areu	Brunswick 40560	The song parodies the way a Chinese man speaks.
La Televisión	Johnny López	Peerless 2543	This is a commentary about the arrival of television. The singer pleads for help in dressing nicely because you need more than just a good voice to appear on television.
La Tragedia del 29 de Agosto	Lalo Guerrero	Colonial 596	This corrido is about the Vietnam War protest that took place on August 29, 1970, in Los Angeles, during which the noted Mexican American journalist Ruben Salazar was killed by a sheriff's deputy.
Las Tres Elviras	El Ciego Melquiades	Bluebird B-3097-B	Very little is known about El Ciego Melquiades, but his violin playing is very honest and unpretentious. This is one of my favorite tracks.
Los Betabeleros	Conjunto Alamo	Alamo 074-B	A migrant laborer says farewell to his girlfriend, stating that he is going to strange and faraway lands for a season to pick beets with his parents.
Los Chinos	Gómez – Acosta	Columbia 2616-X	This anti-Chinese song demeans Mexican woman who date Chinese men. It's interesting to me, since one would think that the two ethnicities would come together and get along because they were both discriminated against. But that did not happen in this case.
Los Temblores en México, part 1	Hermanos Bolaños	Columbia 4441-X	Hawaiian-style guitar distinguishes this corrido that speaks of an earthquake that shakes, among other places, Oaxaca, and kills many people. I am unsure as to the year of the quake, though one can infer it to be an actual event, as many details are provided.
Los Temblores en México, part 2	Hermanos Bolaños	Columbia 4441-X	Part 2.
Los Tequileros	Timoteo Cantú y Jesús Maya	Ideal 253	This corrido talks about three men murdered at the Rio Grande as they were trying to cross over.
Luz Arcos, parts 1 and 2	Hermanos Chavarría	Columbia 4555-X	This corrido is about Luz Arcos, who shot and killed three men: Luciano, José, and Ildefonso Barrientes. Arcos was executed for these killings on November 7, 1930.
Luz Arcos, part 2	Hermanos Chavarría	Columbia 4555-X	Part 2.
Mal Hombre	Lydia Mendoza	Bluebird B-2200-A	This song was the one that catapulted Lydia Mendoza to stardom. It highlights her proficiency in playing her twelve-string guitar and her honest vocal stylings. The fact that it is sung from a woman's perspective is interesting because the majority of corridos take a male point of view, even if the singer is female.
Por Morfina y Cocaína, part 1	Manuel Valdez y Juan González	Bluebird B-2277-A	This corrido is about 26 convicts who are on their way to Leavenworth Prison to serve time. It names a few of the prisoners and describes their sadness and the family they are leaving behind.

Title	Artist	Label and no.	Comments
Por Morfina y Cocaína, part 2	Manuel Valdez y Juan González	Bluebird B-2277-B	Part 2.
Manuelita	Trío Huracán	Bluebird B-3157-B	This is a farewell from a soldier who is off to Germany.
Mateo Magdaleno	Los Madrugadores	Vocalion 8609	I have always had a fondness for music with a message. Here, the singer advises Mateo Magdaleno not to go into certain houses because they will give him "caldo" with foam, meaning beer. In essence, the advice is to stay away from bars and cantinas. The song uses caló.
El Zurco	Narciso Martínez	Bluebird B-3003-A	This is a very nice accordion instrumental with Narciso Martínez at his best. Narcisco was the grandfather of Tejano accordion, and this track is one of my favorites.
Los Mojados	Netty y Rodríguez	Bluebird B-2255-A	This is the first recording by Netty y Rodríguez for the Bluebird label. It is a spoken dialog between a man and his wife, who just got deported. The husband complains about the strictness of laws in the US, especially when it comes to beating one's wife. The song uses a lot of caló.
Por Culpa de una Trucha	Netty y Rodríguez	Bluebird B-2255-B	This is the B-side of the recording by Netty y Rodríguez on the Bluebird label. The spoken dialogue, using Caló, is between a comadre and a compadre. The comadre is sad because her husband is in jail and will get deported. She goes on to tell about the chain of events that led to his incarceration.
Nuevo Corrido de Pedro J. González	Los Montañeses del Alamo	Columbia 6629-X	This corrido is about the famed band leader of Los Madrugadores, who was incarcerated for seven years in San Quentin and released in 1940.
Pachuco Boogie	Orquesta Don Ramón	Discos Mexico BR338-B	This is a different label than San Antonio–based Discos México. Orquesta Don Ramón is Don Tosti's orchestra. Don Tosti was a band leader who spearheaded the Chicano pachuco movement in music. His songs had a certain realism to them that suggested pachucos sitting around and listening to his music. This song is heavy on caló.
Paricutín	Dueto Sánchez-Becerra	Peerless 1968	This corrido is about a volcano named Paricutín, which erupted on February 20, 1943. I chose it to highlight the theme of natural disasters in corridos.
Pin Pin	Conjunto Sonora Matancera	Latin American ERC-113-A	The song is a celebration of war victories, citing the fall of Berlin and Japan. War and victory became a common theme in the immigrant experience in the United States, as reflected in this song by La Sonora Matancera. It was most likely recorded in Cuba but was released on a Los Angeles-based label.
Qué Happy Estoy?	Monchito	Crown CR100B	This song expresses joy that there is no more war with Japan and the singer will soon be home.
The Mexican from New York	Netty y Jesús Rodríguez	Bluebird B-2344-B	In this spoken dialogue, a compadre is talking to a comadre about living in New York.
Un Chavo de la Paloma	Antonio Flores y Manuel Valdez	Bluebird B-3019-A	In this track, written in the caló pachuco style, a young man boasts about various criminal activities as well as his prowess with women.
Una Carta para Corea	Juanita y María Mendoza	Alamo 073-A	This is about a letter sent to the frontlines of Korea, where this woman's love was sent to fight. She pleads for his safe return. The song states that he left to fight for peace. Although soldiers' farewells and longing for their loved ones are a common theme in corridos, the Korean conflict is rarely mentioned, which makes this one interesting.

Title	Artist	Label and no.	Comments
Una Mañana de Enero, part 1	L. Barcelata y M. Apodaca	Vocalion 8930	This corrido is about a family that departs from the capital of Mexico for the United States. They left one morning in January, boarded a train, and made it to Nogales, Arizona. They had difficulty communicating there, since they could only answer "yes" to any question that was asked of them. They also had a difficult time finding someone who would take their money because all that was accepted was gold. From there they went to Tucson.
Una Mañana de Enero, part 2	L. Barcelata y M. Apodaca	Vocalion 8930	In part 2, the family still has trouble communicating. They missed their train because of broken luggage. For $30 they could get a ride in a car, but the man lost his wallet. The driver saw that they only had pesos and insulted them; the man slapped the driver and was thrown in jail.
Wine-O-Boogie	Don Ramón Sr.	Master 2008	A very good example of what a pachuco would be listening to. Instrumentally, this is influenced by Cab Calloway swing. The song is heavy on caló.
Ya Volvió Pedro J. González	Pedro J. González	Azteca 5101	This corrido is about the return of Pedro J. González, who was thrown in prison in 1933 after being framed for rape. It states that the justice system failed him and goes on to praise the Mexican community for their support, noting how friends and family visited and wrote. Pedro J. González was the leader of Los Madrugadores and had a Spanish-language radio show that was very popular.
Yo Soy el Bato	Lalo y Elena	Imperial 347-A	This is an interesting use of caló in a ranchera. It is rare for a ranchera to use so much slang in its lyrics. It shows a little of the influence that Mexican Americans had in making music.

Appendix D

Top Fifty Songwriters

For a collection specializing in Mexican and Mexican American border music, it is not surprising to find the field of top Frontera composers dominated by Mexican regional and Tex-Mex songwriters. In fact, seven of the top ten composers on this list from the Frontera catalog are key exponents of the norteño or conjunto genre, half of them based on the US side of the border, mostly in Texas.

For example, Francisco "Frank" Cantú and Juan Gaytán were prolific composers who were also popular performers in San Antonio, where they appeared as Gaytán y Cantú (no. 2) during the 1930s. José Morante (no. 3) was also a respected producer in San Antonio (fig. 60), home to many local labels that became a special target of collector Chris Strachwitz. At no. 22 is legendary accordion player Narciso Martínez, who helped develop the conjunto sound, a Texas trademark. And at no. 40 we find Lydia Mendoza, the Houston-born singer nicknamed the Lark of the Border (La Alondra de la Frontera). Mendoza, who is known much more for her vocals than for her songwriting, is most famous for her interpretation of a song with tango roots titled "Mal Hombre" (Bad Man). The Frontera Collection boasts twenty-four recordings that include the song, but only three give her songwriting credit, while most of the rest do not identify a composer.

Many of these artists and their works appear on those Texas labels that filled the void once major national record companies retreated from the local market during World War II. Rio Records, for example, was operated by businessman Hymie Wolf in the back room behind his record shop, which he had converted from a liquor store in downtown San Antonio. After Wolf's death, Strachwitz acquired all the Rio Records masters, which included works by beloved accordionist Fred Zimmerle (no. 44) of the Trío San Antonio, as well as early recordings by Tex-Mex conjunto star Tony de la Rosa (no. 20), who went on to gain fame as El Rey de las Polkas, the polka king of South Texas (fig. 61). Salomé Gutiérrez (no. 6) combined music and business as a popular singer-songwriter who also owned his own record label, D.L.B. Records, and retail outlet, Del Bravo Record Shop, in San Antonio.

Of course, the list also features stars of the norteño music field, Mexican cousins of their conjunto counterparts. Singer-songwriter Cornelio Reyna (no. 4) achieved international fame, along with Ramón Ayala, as the duo Los Relámpagos del Norte. One of the most acclaimed norteño acts of all time, the duo Los Alegres de Terán, ranks at no. 10, thanks to the songwriting success of Tomás Ortíz and Eugenio Abrego. California's Mexican

LOS CONQUISTADORES

Figure 60. José A. Morante (*center top*), prolific performer, composer, and producer, is shown here with his group, Los Conquistadores, in the 1950s. Morante served in the US Air Force during World War II and later ran his own record labels based in San Antonio. Though his records had limited distribution, his songs were so popular among his fellow artists on local Texas labels that he ranks third on the list of top songwriters in the Frontera Collection. Photograph courtesy of the Arhoolie Foundation.

American community is represented by prolific singer-songwriter Lalo Guerrero (no. 7), known as the father of Chicano music, whose song "Chucos Suaves" was featured in the smash Luis Valdéz play *Zoot Suit*.

But for all its concentration on border music, Frontera's list of top composers prominently features many artists from other areas and styles. Topping the list at no. 1, from Mexico City, is composer Víctor Cordero, who wrote songs used in over seventy motion pictures. His most famous corrido, "Juan Charrasqueado,"

was the basis of a 1948 movie of the same name directed by Ernesto Cortázar, a fellow Mexican songwriter who ranks at no. 14. The list also includes other internationally renowned Mexican artists, including famed ranchera songwriters Cuco Sánchez (no. 8) and Pepe Guízar (no. 24), as well as masters of the romantic bolero such as Gonzalo Curiel (no. 35) and Jesús "Chucho" Navarro (no. 38) of Trío Los Panchos, one of the most popular romantic trios of the 1940s and '50s. At no. 48 is singer-songwriter Guty Cárdenas, prime exponent of the lyrical song

Figure 61. Tony de la Rosa, known as the "Polka King of South Texas," was one of the most influential and innovative conjunto musicians of the post-World War II era. He appears on three lists from the Frontera Collection: top songwriters (appendix D), top performers (appendix E), and the top fifty favorite tunes selected by collector Chris Strachwitz (appendix G). Photograph courtesy of the Arhoolie Foundation.

style from southern Mexico known as "canción yucateca," which is accompanied by lilting guitars and influenced by the romantic, gently rhythmic music of the Caribbean.

Three artists from the Caribbean made it to the top twenty: prolific Puerto Rican composers Rafael Hernández (no. 12) and Pedro Flores (no. 16), along with Cuba's mambo king Pérez Prado (no. 19). The list also includes blind Cuban bandleader Arsenio Rodríguez (no. 43), considered the godfather of salsa; semi-classical Cuban composer Ernesto Lecuona (no. 46), who penned the enduring pop tunes "La Malagueña" and "Siboney"; and another Puerto Rican, Bobby Capó (no. 34), author of the Latin American standard "Piel Canela."

All in all, this list of the top fifty composers is a well-rounded, international representation of some of the best and most successful Latin music songwriters of the twentieth century.

The list was compiled by using the browsing function of the UCLA Frontera database to identify the artists with the greatest number of songs next to their names and eliminating artists with less than thirty listings. These names were then cross-checked in the Arhoolie Encyclopedia, the most complete archive of the Strachwitz collection. In most cases, that secondary search added many more credits to each songwriter, since the Arhoolie Encyclopedia contains many more entries than the one still being assembled from it by the UCLA Digital Library.

To some small degree, undeserved credits may have boosted a songwriter's ranking on the list, as is the case with Lydia Mendoza's "Mal Hombre," as noted above. However, such songwriting discrepancies do not substantially affect most of the top-ranking writers, whose works for the most part are well known and properly documented.

Top Fifty Songwriters

Rank	Songwriter	No. of recordings
1	Víctor Cordero	458
2	Francisco Cantú and Juan Gaytán (Gaytán y Cantú)	455
3	José A. Morante	281
4	Cornelio Reyna	252
5	José Alfredo Jiménez	245
6	Salomé Gutiérrez	241
7	Lalo Guerrero	221
8	Cuco Sánchez	210
9	Rubén Fuentes	205
10	Tomás Ortíz and Eugenio Abrego (Los Alegres de Terán)	205
11	José L. Moreno	183
12	Rafael Hernández	157
13	Jesús Ramos	144
14	Ernesto Cortázar	135
15	Daniel Garzés	121
16	Pedro Flores	115
17	Chencho Cárdenas	110
18	Pedro Ayala	105
19	Dámaso Pérez Prado	103
20	Tony de la Rosa	99
21	Manuel S. Acuña	93
22	Narciso Martínez	92
23	Alfonso Esparza Oteo	89
24	Pepe Guízar	82
25	Gabriel Ruíz	82
26	Gilberto Parra	80
27	Lalo González "El Piporro"	78
28	Miguel Salas	78
29	Felipe Bermejo	76
30	Lorenzo Barcelata	73
31	Fernando Z. Maldonado	70
32	Rubén Méndez	66
33	Arturo Mosqueda	65
34	Bobby Capó	64
35	Gonzalo Curiel	64
36	Leopoldo González	64
37	José Guadalupe Prado	59
38	Jesús "Chucho" Navarro	58

Rank	Songwriter	No. of recordings
39	Pedro Galindo	57
40	Lydia Mendoza	57
41	María Grever	54
42	Agapito Zúñiga	53
43	Arsenio Rodríguez	53
44	Fred Zimmerle	50
45	Daniel Santos	46
46	Ernesto Lecuona	45
47	Ignacio Fernández Esperón "Tata Nacho"	44
48	Guty Cárdenas	43
49	Juan S. Garrido	43
50	Luis Pérez Meza	40

Appendix E

Top Fifty Performers

Like the list of top songwriters list, this list of top per¬formers represents the artists with the greatest number of recordings held in the Frontera Collection. Compared to the songwriters, this group of fifty performing artists is much more homogenous in musical style. Indeed, forty-five of the fifty performers on the list are of Mexican origin, in keeping with the archive's focus as a collection of Mexican and Mexican American music. In this regard, the list of top performers, more than any of the other lists, most faithfully reflects the collector's intentions. Chris Strachwitz was most interested in border music, and this is the type of recording he set out to acquire. It's no surprise, then, that these performers account for twenty of the songs picked by Strachwitz for his personal list of fifty favorites from the collection (see appendix G). Strachwitz picked three songs by Los Alegres de Terán, the norteño music superstars who top this list of performers, with 811 separate recordings.

Texas-born singer Lydia Mendoza, another Strachwitz favorite, comes in at no. 2, with 679 songs. She is followed at no. 3 by Lalo Guerrero, the Tucson-born and LA-based singer-songwriter who is considered the father of Chicano music and who also appears on the composer list. Mendoza and Guerrero are among the twenty recording artists in the top fifty who

lived and worked on the US side of the border, primarily in Texas. Others include Flaco Jiménez (no. 17), the internationally renowned accordion player from San Antonio, as well as his father, the legendary Santiago Jiménez Sr. (no. 25). Also on the list are Tony de la Rosa (no. 8), the polka king of South Texas; Narciso Martínez (no. 9), the father of conjunto music; and two Tex-Mex superstars, Little Joe (no. 35) and Freddy Fender (no. 41) (fig. 62).

The late Cornelio Reyna, a prime exponent of the norteño genre, is the only artist who appears twice on the list, once as a solo artist at no. 31 and again as part of the influential norteño duo Los Relámpagos del Norte, which also included accordion player Ramón Ayala. If all the records on which Reyna performed were combined, the total number would make him no. 9 on the list.

Also notable is the number of Mexican duets on this list, representing a format popular during the first half of the twentieth century. At no. 5, Las Hermanas Padilla lead this group of eleven, which includes Strachwitz favorites Los Alegres de Terán (no. 1) and Los Donneños (no. 13).

Although not a specific target of the collection, superstar singers from Mexico's golden era of mariachi music are well represented here, with Pedro Infante (no. 11), Miguel Aceves

LITTLE JOE AND THE LATINAIRES RECORDING ARTISTS FOR **EL ZARAPE RECORDS**

Figure 62. A new generation of Texas artists emerged in the 1960s and '70s, coinciding with the cultural and political awakening known as the Chicano Movement. They sang in English and Spanish, played electric guitars, and created a fusion style known as Tejano, or Tex-Mex. They are represented among the top performers in the Frontera Collection by singer Freddy Fender (no. 41) and bandleader Little Joe (no. 35). Fender, born Baldemar Huerta, had national hits with "Before the Next Teardrop Falls" and "Wasted Days and Wasted Nights." Little Joe, born José María de León Hernández, went on to win four Grammy Awards with his band, La Familia, most recently in 2010. Little Joe is shown here, holding his guitar, with his brother Johnny in the early 1960s, when he led Little Joe and the Latinaires. Photographs courtesy of the Arhoolie Foundation.

Mejía (no. 15), Pedro Vargas (no. 24), Lola Beltrán (no. 33), José Alfredo Jiménez (no. 42), and Cuco Sánchez (no. 46). The latter two also appear prominently on the composer list. Another act that enjoyed huge popularity in Mexico during the 1940s and '50s is Trío Los Panchos (no. 12), the only act representing the many romantic guitar trios that appear in the collection in lesser numbers. The romantic bolero, one of the biggest genres in the collection, is represented by two of its most renowned interpreters, female vocalists Chelo Silva (no. 6) and Eva Garza (no. 32).

The first of the five non-Mexican artists on the list does not appear until halfway down.

The Castilians (no. 26) was a Latin pop orchestra based in New York that was famous for schmaltzy versions of Valentino tangos. The other four non-Mexican performers are all respected singers and bandleaders from the Caribbean, including Puerto Rican stars Daniel Santos (no. 39) and Bobby Capó (no. 40), the latter also a well-known songwriter. Rounding out the list are two bandleaders heavily identified with the mambo craze, Cuban pianist Pérez Prado (no. 43) and Puerto Rican *timbalero* Tito Puente (no. 50). Puente recorded many 78-rpm records before going on to a long career as a salsa and Latin jazz superstar until his death at the end of the century.

This list was compiled with the same procedure used to assemble the composer list. Artists were first selected from song counts provided in the UCLA Frontera database, and their names were then run through the Arhoolie Encyclopedia using the "artist" search function. The results were filtered to eliminate LPs, CDs, and cassettes to avoid inflating the rank of some artists, since the encyclopedia database counts each track of an LP as a separate entry. Thus, only 78s and 45s were counted to create this list, representing the only two formats in the UCLA database as of this date. Duplicates were eliminated from the results to determine a final rank.

Some performers from the 1920s and '30s, such as singer Pilar Arcos (no. 22), ranked relatively high on the list despite having only 78-rpm recordings in the collection. Other more contemporary artists, such as Little Joe, are ranked exclusively on the basis of their 45-rpm recordings, since they are too young to have recorded in the older format. Due to their career longevity, the top-ranked Alegres de Terán have many recordings released in both formats.

Top Fifty Performers

Rank	Artist	No. of recordings
1	Los Alegres de Terán	811
2	Lydia Mendoza	679
3	Lalo Guerrero	463
4	Beto Villa	421
5	Las Hermanas Padilla	420
6	Chelo Silva	364
7	Dueto Azteca	349
8	Tony de la Rosa	349
9	Narciso Martínez	313
10	Carmen y Laura	303
11	Pedro Infante	302
12	Trío Los Panchos	298
13	Los Donneños	286
14	Conjunto Bernal	273
15	Miguel Aceves Mejía	269
16	Hermanos Banda	260
17	Flaco Jiménez	252
18	Valerio Longoria	248
19	Luis Pérez Meza	232
20	Gaytán y Cantú	215
21	Los Montañeses del Alamo	211

Rank	Artist	No. of recordings
22	Pilar Arcos	206
23	Dueto Estrella	205
24	Pedro Vargas	203
25	Santiago Jiménez Sr.	196
26	The Castilians	195
27	Rubén Vela	192
28	Agapito Zúñiga	191
29	Dueto Río Bravo	189
30	Los Relámpagos del Norte	184
31	Cornelio Reyna	153
32	Eva Garza	151
33	Lola Beltrán	146
34	Las Jilguerillas	145
35	Little Joe	144
36	Los Mañaneros de Nuevo León	142
37	Juan Montoya	138
38	Fernando Rosas	137
39	Daniel Santos	137
40	Bobby Capó	135
41	Freddy Fender	133
42	José Alfredo Jiménez	133
43	Pérez Prado	133
44	Hermanos Maya	128
45	Marcelo y Aurelia	126
46	Cuco Sánchez	125
47	Pedro Yerena	124
48	Rubén Reyes	120
49	Trío San Antonio	117
50	Tito Puente	116

Top Twenty Genres

Like the lists of top songwriters and performers, this list of top musical genres represents a wide array of styles from many countries and regions. Again, as expected, Mexican styles dominate, accounting for more than half the total number of songs on the list. Rancheras, the top-ranking genre, include many songs that people recognize as mariachi music, but the style may also be performed by guitar duets, trios, accordion conjuntos, and Tex-Mex orchestras.

There is ample cross-pollination between genres, as the list of subgenres suggests. The no. 2 category, bolero, includes seventy-two separate subgenres, such as bolero ranchero and bolero mambo. This resulted in an occasionally capricious allocation of songs that could belong to either of two categories. For example, "Corazón de Mi Vida," by the norteño duet El Palomo y El Gorrión, is counted in the database, and thus on this list, as a bolero ranchero within the bolero genre. But a song in similar style, "Por Favor" by Rafael Cantú, is listed as a ranchero bolero and thus counted here within the ranchera genre. Such inconsistencies in the archive are under review, but they don't materially alter the result of the overall count, since only a limited number of subgenres directly overlap and the total number of songs in these cases is relatively small.

The tabulation for this table was based entirely on the UCLA Frontera searchable archive, which lists all genres and subgenres alphabetically. However, the database counts only those tracks where a genre was identified directly on the label, a task that was occasionally subject to the whims, and guesswork, of record companies. Still, based on listening to thousands of tracks, the categorization seems to be generally accurate. A record tagged as a bolero, in other words, tends to actually be a bolero. The practice of specifying genres directly on record labels was much more consistent in the old days, largely disappearing in the US market after 45s were introduced. This count, therefore, is weighted toward the older records on which genres were specified (fig. 63).

Since the archive counts subgenres separately, they were manually grouped under the larger main headings. Duplicate subgenres, such as mambo-instrumental and instrumental mambo, were then aggregated for the final count. Fine distinctions among subgenres were allowed to stand alone, such as "instrumental mambo bop," a category that includes only one title, "Whatever It Means" by Miguelito Valdés.

One final note: The no. 7 genre, the son, encompasses such a broad category of music that it merits a separate breakdown. A son can take many forms, with many sounding very distinct from the others. Perhaps the most commonly known is the Cuban son, a precursor of salsa that was popularized in the United States recently by the Buena Vista Social Club. Equally popular, though completely different in style, are the son varieties from Mexico, such as the son jarocho from the southern state of Veracruz, typified by "La Bamba," and the mariachi-style son from the western state of Jalisco, represented by another emblematic dance number, "El Son de la Negra." Clearly, even the Mexican sones feature a variety of sounds and styles. In recognition of these distinctions, sones are ranked in two broad subcategories by region: son caribeño and son mexicano.

Figure 63. Although not the focus of the Frontera Collection, the mambo and other non-Mexican genres form a significant part of the archive. On this tune, "El Mambo en Broadway," pianist Alfredito Valdés is accompanied by Los Diablos del Mambo (The Mambo Devils), under the direction of a young Tito Puente in one of his earliest recordings. The label SMC (Spanish Music Center), founded by New York music store owner Gabriel Oller, recorded the top names in Afro-Cuban music of the mambo era, the late 1940s and 1950s. Photograph courtesy of the Arhoolie Foundation.

Top Twenty Genres

Rank	Genre	No. of songs	No. of subgenres
1	Ranchera	15,572	44
2	Bolero	8,685	72
3	Corrido	4,019	34
4	Canción	3,578	0
5	Polka	3,424	33
6	Vals	1,847	45
7	Son	901	73
	Son caribeño	555	44
	Son mexicano	346	29
8	Guaracha	866	30
9	Cumbia	836	13
10	Tango	777	25
11	Mambo	676	47
12	Huapango	560	19
13	Balada	480	16
14	Paso doble	395	21
15	Rumba	374	37
16	Schottis	300	6
17	Danzón	297	11
18	Blues	228	15
19	Cha cha chá	227	17
20	Norteña	219	3

My Fifty Favorite Mexican and Latin Recordings

by Chris Strachwitz

This list contains recordings that are remarkable for their performance quality. I've included a range of genres and styles. You'll find many classics and several recordings that are sure to be a surprise. These are my favorites, but they are presented in no particular order (fig. 64)!

Figure 64. Los Alegres de Terán, Tomás Ortíz (*left*) and Eugenio Abrego (*right*), joined producer Chris Strachwitz on the occasion of the premier of the documentary *Chulas Fronteras* in 1976. Los Alegres appear in the film, which debuted at Pacific Film Archives Theatre in Berkeley. Photograph courtesy of the Arhoolie Foundation.

My Fifty Favorite Mexican and Latin Recordings

Title	Artist (label and no.)	Comment
Canción Mixteca	Los Donneños (Oro 233, Arhoolie CD 7001)	The most emotional and gutsy rendition of this classic Mexican song by one of the best norteño conjuntos. A real classic!
Yo Me Enamoré	Fred Zimmerle and Steve Jaramillo (Perla 1001)	To my ears, an incredibly emotional rendition of this song, with just two guitars and of course the two voices in the old rural crying style.
El Troquero	Regionales de Texas (Conde 1924; original Del Valle 959)	An all-time classic norteño song. Del Valle had the original recording and it was a huge hit. On a tour of California, Los Regionales recorded the song again for this tiny California label, but with the full rhythm section. I like both recordings!
Tu Conciencia	Dueto Río Bravo con Los Alegres de Terán (Columbia 9086)	The emotions are obvious in the gorgeous voices which deliver this great song—and with superb backing by Los Alegres de Terán. I have loved this record for forty years.
Viva Seguín	Santiago Jiménez (Imperial 232, Arhoolie CD 7023)	The first recording by the composer of this delightful and widely popular classic polka.
Corre, Corre, Camioncito	Las Norteñitas (Falcon 1193)	One of my favorite female duets, but not all their recordings are as good as this one. These strong singers are backed here by the Prado brothers with their typical driving Monterrey sound at its zenith. The accordion blends perfectly with an alto sax, backed by a good bajo sexto and string bass—a heavenly sound!
Cuando Cae la Tarde	Santiago Jiménez (Globe 2012, Arhoolie CD 7023)	Santiago at first only recorded accordion instrumentals, but in the early 1950s he suddenly introduced his voice in traditional duet style and made a classic version of this wonderful ranchera.
Canción Mexicana	Lucha Reyes (Victor 70-7099 and RCA Victor 23-6398)	The first ranchera queen is in top form here, giving it all she's got on this wonderful Lalo Guerrero composition, with great backing by the mariachis.
Mariquita	Mariachi Coculense Rodríguez (Victor 46375, Arhoolie CD 7011)	Dr. Rodríguez was only the patron of this mariachi by Cirilo Marmolejo (the guitarrón player). He brought these mariachis from Cocula to Mexico City, where they were the first mariachi to make electrical recordings. This wonderful son in the pre-trumpet mariachi tradition is a pure delight!
Mañana en Adelante	Mariachi Tapatío (Victor 75238, Arhoolie CD 7012)	Led by José Marmolejo, a nephew of Cirilo, this is probably the first mariachi to record with a trumpet player (in the mid-1930s), Jesús Salazar. I love the way he plays this ranchera with the same sadness but also joy that I hear in the sound of the vocal duet.
La Primavera	Mariachi Tapatío (Victor 75727, Arhoolie CD 7012)	Another ranchera by this wonderful mariachi, where the trumpet blends perfectly with the violins and does not yet go out on its own virtuoso trip. Such drive and gusto—love it!
La Pena Mía	Lola Beltrán (Peerless 3656)	Lola Beltrán followed the great Lucha Reyes into the world of ranchera divas. The recording strikes me as remarkable—her young and strong yet controlled voice sings music that is pure and wide open. If only the mariachis had been a bit more simpatico.
Rinches de Texas	Dueto Reynosa (Oro 230)	A superb corrido composed by the label's owner, Willie Lopez, about a melon strike viciously broken up by the hated "rinches," or Texas Rangers. The singers and the conjunto on this performance really dig in behind this true story to create a classic.

Title	Artist (label and no.)	Comment
Camioncito Pasajero	Conjunto Tamaulipas (RyN 176; alternate version on Arhoolie CD 425)	I love this regional ranchera composed by Leonardo Salazar. It is performed with such feeling by this conjunto, both on the 45 and in their performance on the sound track to our film, *Del Mero Corazón*.
Zenaida	Los Madrugadores (Vocalion 8596, parts 1 and 2, Arhoolie CD 7020; or an alternate, Hermanas Mendoza, RCA 23-5543)	I can't get this wonderful melody out of my head—I try to sing or hum it constantly. Los Madrugadores (los hermanos Sánchez y Linares) were the first to record this story about Zenaida, and they did it in two parts. Great singers, they were very popular in the mid-1930s, and the song soon gained widespread popularity as well. A shorter but still good version is by Las Hermanas Mendoza (Juanita and María Mendoza, with Lydia playing her twelve-string), whose voices I also adore.
Al Pie de la Tumba	Los Alegres de Terán (Falcon 2003, or Conjunto Tamaulipas, Arhoolie CD 425)	I love the sound of these two men, the fathers of norteño music: Eugenio Abrego and Tomás Ortíz. I enjoy almost any song they sing, but this one, rather sad and almost morbid, somehow has stuck with me. During the filming of *Del Mero Corazón*, I requested the song by the Conjunto Tamaulipas, and their version, as you can hear and see in the film, is almost equally appealing.
Prenda del Alma	Los Alegres de Terán (Falcon 1479; alternate version recorded live for our film *Chulas Fronteras*, Arhoolie CD 425)	A lovely song I just can't get out of my head. They also sang it for our film *Chulas Fronteras* in their superb style. Also check out the earlier version by the great activist, organizer, composer, and radio personality from the 1930s, Pedro J. González, on Azteca 5102.
Pancho Villa	Hermanos Chavarría con Trío San Antonio (Falcon A323)	The Chavarría brothers were probably the fiercest singers ever to record. They started recording in the late 1920s and continued into the 1930s, but then fell out of style. Traditionalist Fred Zimmerle befriended them in San Antonio in the late 1940s and got them to record for the last time with his conjunto, backing them to create this masterpiece.
Marihuana Boogie	Lalo Guerrero (Imperial 535)	I love this classic pachuco song from the father of Chicano music, here accompanied by a jazzy quintet. Lalo covered every aspect of Mexican American music—a true giant who performed and composed for over six decades.
Chicano Boogie	Cuarteto Don Ramón Martínez (actually Don Tosti's Quartet) (Taxco 117, Master 2007, Arhoolie CD 7040)	This pachuco boogie brings together all the elements: boogie, be-bop, slang, Chicano swing, caló. It's all there in this delightful recording!
Mi Único Camino	Conjunto Bernal (Ideal 1637, Arhoolie CD 9060)	The classic version of this wonderful, powerful song performed by Paulino Bernal and his conjunto.
Luzita (mazurka)	Narciso Martínez (Bluebird 2920, Arhoolie CD 7016; or Ideal 135)	This lovely old-time mazurka is played on the accordion by the father of the norteño accordion style. It starts in a minor key but then modulates to major and back again, which is how many older dance tunes were played until the 1950s, when that tradition was no longer in demand. Another classic!
Atotonilco	Tony de la Rosa (Ideal 1570, Arhoolie CD 362)	A fantastic old polka brought up to date in the 1950s by the polka king of South Texas, Tony de la Rosa. I love it!
There's No Tortillas	Lalo Guerrero (Ambiente 33 100)	I had to list at least one more by the incredible Lalo Guerrero. He composed and recorded so many different types of songs, from corridos to this funny parody.
Ándale, Vamos Platicando	Medina River Boys (Bluebird 3041, Arhoolie CD 7018)	This rare mix of gringo country and Mexican singing is a jewel. I love the steel guitar and the fine singing on this San Antonio recording from the 1930s. I wish they had made more records!

Title	Artist (label and no.)	Comment
La India Bonita	Banda Típica de Mazatlán (Columbia 2548-C, Arhoolie CD 7048)	I love this charming old waltz, especially as performed by this banda. It is one of the first recordings of banda sinaloense, a regional music that was not recorded until the early 1950s.
Mexicano Hasta las Cachas	Banda El Recodo de Cruz Lizarraga (RCA Camden 33-289, Arhoolie CD 7048)	This killer version of an older song is brought up to date in the 1950s. It is sung with corazón and gusto by Las Hermanas Sarabia in front of this most famous of all bandas sinaloenses.
Me Voy a Baracoa	Sexteto Machin (Brunswick 41118, Arhoolie CD 7003)	This is a gorgeous 1929 recording of a son cubano by one of the best Cuban sextets, with a perfect balance between percussions, strings, and voices. Pure joy to listen to!
Quiéreme, Camagueyana!	Sexteto Bolona (Brunswick 40158, Arhoolie CD 7006)	I had to name one more of these delightful Cuban sones. This one is by the Sexteto Bolona, with their crying voices and superb rhythms.
El Gato Negro	El Ciego Melquiades (Bluebird 3188, Arhoolie CD 7045)	The last of a vanishing breed, this blind fiddler, Melquiades Rodríguez, played at house parties and restaurants in San Antonio, Texas. He recorded this superb polka in the mid-1930s with guitar and violoncello—what pure old-time joy!
Carga Blanca	Los Cuatesones (Manuel C. Valdez and André Álvarez) (Corona 2032, Arhoolie CD 7053)	I love the tune of this still enormously popular corrido about smuggling heroin and especially this version by the composer. Whenever I request this seminal song, a part of the roots of the narcocorrido, the conjuntos still all know it! Los Alegres de Terán also do a fine rendition.
Josefina, Josefina	Los Reyes de la Plena (Brunswick 40752, Arhoolie CD 7037)	From Puerto Rico came much fine regional music, and this one is one of my favorites, with an accordion, a trumpet, strings, and percussion—and that funky rural-sounding lead singer.
Los Canedistas	Orquesta de Guadalupe Acosta (Okeh 16783, Arhoolie CD 7017)	A great polka composed of many parts and performed by this lovely old world–sounding salon orchestra. Recorded in San Antonio in 1930, this track takes you back to a gentler era. Acosta was a well-known musician, music shop proprietor, and record scout.
Sobre las Olas (Over the Waves)	Banda Mochis de Porfirio Amarillas (Columbia 4020, Arhoolie CD 7048)	This waltz by Mexican composer Juventino Rosas became famous all over the world. Here in the US, it was especially popular among country musicians and among jazz musicians who were first exposed to it by the huge Mexican brass band that played at the cotton festival in New Orleans toward the end of the nineteenth century. I love this version by a typical banda sinaloense, this one obviously from Los Mochis.
Lupita	Mariachi Coculense de Cirilo Marmolejo (Victor 75517, Arhoolie CD 7011)	This track is by the first electrically recorded mariachi. By this time the Victor engineer in Mexico City had become really good at recording the guitarrón up front with plenty of volume, and in those days the guitarrón player had to really pluck that thing like a string bass!
Elena	Las Hermanas Degollado (Brunswick 108, Arhoolie CD 486)	I am a sucker for female duets, and here is another of my favorites: Adele and Panchita Degollado backed by the powerhouse Monterrey conjunto of Los Hermanos Prado, with that gorgeous blending of alto sax and the accordion. Nobody can create this sound today.
A Puñaladas	Hermanos Prado (Del Valle 339, Arhoolie CD 7001)	This is one of my favorites by the Prado brothers: Guadalupe Prado, accordion; Anselmo Prado, first voice and guitar; and Homero Prado, second voice and bajo sexto. Rudolfo Hernández plays alto sax plus string bass. What a gem!
Sin Tu Cariño	Valerio Longoria y su Conjunto (Corona 2238, Arhoolie CD 7001)	This is a lovely bolero by the man who introduced this more genteel musical genre into the Tejano conjunto repertoire. But Valerio was also a master of cumbias, rancheras, corridos, etc.

Title	Artist (label and no.)	Comment
Gregorio Cortez	Los Hermanos Banda (Del Valle 347, Arhoolie CD 7001)	This important border ballad is well documented. You can listen to the first recording of it by Pedro Rocha and Lupe Martínez (billed as Trovadores Regionales), but that version is in two parts (Vocalion 8351, AR CD 7019). For a shorter version you can't beat this superb rendition by the Banda brothers, Rodolfo and Armado. The song is still popular all along the Río Bravo!
El Sube y Baja	Los Donneños (Falcon 294, Arhoolie CD 9057)	I wanted a superb polka by this conjunto. This one features the accordionist Mario Montes, supported by his excellent bajo sexto player, Ramiro Cavazos, who still plays and operates RyN Records in McAllen, Texas. Another all-time classic!
La Guacamaya	Conjunto Alma Jarocha (Arhoolie CD 354)	The son jarocho is still very popular in the Veracruz area, and this recording, which I made in Boca Del Río, just south of Veracruz, is one of my favorites. It features strong harp players, which I miss in most of the contemporary groups.
La Bamba	Andrés Huesca (Victor 70-7538)	Andrés Huesca was the superb singer and harp player who put Jarocho music on the map by making many bestselling commercial recordings. If you have to hear "La Bamba," then I love this early version from the voice of the master.
Indita Mía	Freddy Fender (Ideal 2222, Arhoolie CD 366)	One of my most favorite old songs is "Indita Mía," and although there are many fine versions, I always liked Freddy Fender's. His pure, beautiful voice eventually made him famous.
La Chileca	Conjunto Alma de Apatzingán de Juan Pérez Morfín (Alborada Cass. 31, Arhoolie CD 426)	Probably the best conjunto michoacano (or conjunto arpa grande) ever recorded. This is my favorite from the fine album recorded by Alborada Records, an Apatzingán, Michoacán firm that produced and preserved great local music. The engineer also knew how to bring out the driving power of the harp.
El Gustito	Los Caporales de Panuco (Arhoolie CD 431)	A typical Huastecan trio with violin, huapangera, and jarana, and of course falsetto singing—one of the many strong regional traditions still flourishing in Mexico. This is my favorite son from their album, which I recorded in a hotel room in Tampico, Tamaulipas, in 1978.
Mexico-Americano	Rumel Fuentes accompanied by Los Pingüinos del Norte (Arhoolie CD 507)	A wonderful song about pride. Recently popularized by Los Lobos and Los Cenzontles, it is sung here by the composer. It was recorded outdoors during my filming of the documentary *Chulas Fronteras*.
The Free Mexican Airforce	Peter Rowan and Flaco Jiménez (Arhoolie CD 3027)	I'm addicted to this silly, crazy, but very catchy song by Peter Rowan. I recorded this version in San Antonio. Although it is perhaps not fully representative of Flaco's music, he nevertheless gets in fine licks and a long solo toward the end.
Comprende Cariño	Isidro (El Indio) López (Ideal 2496, Arhoolie CD 9042)	My favorite Tejano orquesta singer and alto saxophonist, with a fine vals ranchera. I love the way his trumpeter plays behind Isidro's vocals.
El Cheque en Blanco	Chelo Silva with Flaco Jiménez (Arhoolie CD 423)	The queen of Tejano bolero, but also hugely popular all over Mexico, Chelo Silva was an emotional singer with a haunting, husky voice who sang almost exclusively boleros. I was fortunate enough to capture Chelo, during what was probably her last public appearance, on my car radio as I approached an outdoor park in San Antonio where KCOR was broadcasting live. A very emotion- charged performance with wonderful accordion backing from Flaco Jiménez.
El Canoero	Valerio Longoria (Arhoolie CD 336)	This great musician from San Antonio learned this fine cumbia by listening to shortwave radio from Colombia. He included it when I recorded him in 1989, and I have always loved his rendition of this catchy tune.

Appendix H

What Is a Corrido?
Thematic Representation and Narrative Discourse

by Guillermo E. Hernández

Introduction: Antecedents in the Study of the Genre

Corridos have been sung for almost two hundred years, yet the genre has tended to remain distant or misunderstood to outsiders of this important ballad tradition of Mexico and the United States. One reason for this situation has been the apparent obscurity of the texts, which are difficult to interpret due to their local references and conventions. As a result, corridos have flourished in relative isolation, preserving the views of marginal communities; that is, corridos convey unofficial versions of history. Indeed, composed, transmitted, and consumed by rural and urban working classes—people distant from circles of power and prestige—the genre expresses viewpoints that often contradict or stand in direct opposition to dominant perspectives.

This article originally appeared in Studies in *Latin American Popular Culture* 18 (1999): 69–92. Copyright 1999 by University of Texas Press. All rights reserved.

An important factor in the evolution of the corrido has been its shift from oral transmission to commercial consumption via broadsides and recordings.[1] Despite this substantial transformation from folklore to popular culture, corridos have maintained a number of important characteristics. As in the past, texts seem obscure to outsiders, events are narrated within a historical or realistic dimension, and emphasis is given to stories of tragic or dramatic quality.[2] The genre also continues to be fundamentally a poetic medium of expression that combines metrics, rhythm, and melody to convey issues of significant importance to the audience.[3]

Corridos have evolved into brief narratives that seem to lack critical information about the events described.[4] As before, contemporary authors and audiences share a significant basis of knowledge and opinion to warrant utmost textual brevity. This shared information, however, is no longer immediate, as it was when the genre was transmitted orally and local community issues provided the basic subject matter that inspired corrido composers. Yet, even today, a competent listener must possess basic cultural information to decode the meaning of the narrative. A second important aspect that comes to the aid of all corrido audiences is familiarity with the conventions of the genre. Since experienced audiences have listened to a considerable number of corridos, a few musical beats and several allusive words may suffice to distinguish originality and value in a corrido. Naturally, corrido audiences are aesthetically predisposed to enjoy the genre, have personal repertoires of favorites, and are sensitive to the cultural nuances in the compositions they hear.

The bibliography and discography available for the study of the corrido have emerged in three overlapping phases. A first or initial phase began in the first half of the twentieth century, when oral and literary texts were published in broadsides, in songbooks, cited within other texts, or recorded. Sound recordings, of course, maintain a fuller dimension of the actual performance, since the textual transcriptions rarely included musical illustrations.[5] A second or pioneering phase began in the middle 1930s with the publication of collections and analyses of the corrido corpus. During this period researchers established the basis for the study of the corrido as a serious and significant area of intellectual concern.[6] A third or contemporary phase has emerged in the last twenty-five years when, continuing previous efforts, a larger and representative corrido corpus became available and the study of the genre was revitalized.[7]

During the second phase, the term "corrido" was formally defined. An early and influential notion that helped establish the parameters of the genre was the literary definition of the corrido advanced by Armando Duvalier (1937): an "epic-lyric poem, ranging between twenty and thirty octosyllabic quatrains and subject to six basic primary formulas" (16). In addition, Duvalier suggested eight secondary formulas that may occasionally appear in corridos.[8] According to Duvalier, the primary formulas that shape the overall narrative structure of the poem are

(1) Singer's initial address to the audience
(2) Place, time, and name of the main character
(3) Antecedents to the arguments of the main character
(4) Message
(5) Main character's farewell
(6) Composer's farewell

These primary formulas need not all appear in a particular corrido, although all samples of the genre must include at least three: (2) place and name of the main character, (4) message, and (5 or 6) the farewell. They must also maintain an arrangement of four or six lines per stanza.

Another important and influential contribution to the definition of the genre appeared in Vicente T. Mendoza's monumental *El romance español y el corrido mexicano* (1939). Mendoza's work provided a foundation for study of the corrido. In his *Lírica narrativa de México: El corrido* (1964), he defined the corrido as

> an epic-lyric-narrative genre—with quatrains with variable rhyme, either assonant or consonant on even lines—a literary form based on a musical phrase of four members, describing events that cause a deep impact on the masses. (9)

A most significant stage in the study of the genre came from the United States. In his monograph on the ballad of Gregorio Cortez, *"With His Pistol in His Hand": A Border Ballad and Its Hero* (1958), Américo Paredes focused on the complex interrelationship between the history, the legend, and the corrido variants dedicated to this heroic figure. A most valuable aspect of Paredes's study was his insistence on the relation between the corrido of Cortez and the rich cultural tradition of balladry that existed along the US-Mexico border during the second half of the nineteenth century. Paredes's approach represents a model of research demonstrating the interdisciplinary requirements involved in the analysis of a genre as multifarious as the corrido.

In contrast with Américo Paredes, whose emphasis was on American folklore, Merle E. Simmons applied methods from literary criticism to suggest a continental diffusion of the Spanish romance that resulted in the eventual creation of the Mexican corrido. In "The Ancestry of Mexico's Corridos" (1963), Simmons provided evidence of how a slow gestation took place from the colonial period to the present. His thesis provoked an immediate rebuttal from Américo Paredes. In "The Ancestry of Mexico's Corridos: A Matter of Definitions" (1963), Paredes reaffirmed his position on the border as a geographic and cultural origin of the corrido. Paredes also challenged Vicente T. Mendoza's earlier argument for the Mexican state of Michoacán as a probable site for such an origin. This debatable issue was further magnified by Celedonio Serrano Martínez, who, in his monograph *El corrido no deriva del romance español* (1973), proposed an indigenous or prehispanic corrido origin, although he provided no documentary evidence to back up his claim. These discussions on the genealogy of the corrido, although important, tended to eschew earlier questions regarding the definition of the genre and the contours of its corpus. Indeed, efforts to define the corrido are necessary to advance our understanding of the formal characteristics and the parameters of the corpus, circumscribing factors that will prove fundamental in any eventual elucidation of the creation and diffusion of the genre.

John Holmes McDowell undertook the task of reformulating basic questions on the distinguishing features of the corrido corpus. His work can be said to represent the beginning of the third, contemporary phase in the study of the corrido. In "The Mexican *Corrido*: Formula and Theme in a Ballad Tradition" (1972), McDowell successfully applied Parry and Lord's influential oral-formulaic theory to the corrido tradition, finding that the "the world-view of the corrido makes available to the corridista a set of themes, legends, and personages." Furthermore, the formula in the corrido represents "a means of including the peripheral themes and developing the central theme, all within the metric and rhyme stipulations of the genre" (220).

In "The Corrido of Greater Mexico as Discourse, Music, and Event" (1981), McDowell reveals a complex set of conditions evident in the corrido. Regarding discourse, he considers that "the corrido is narrative, reflexive, and propositional in semantic intent and poetic in technique." Musically, he observes, "two autonomous systems, the poetic and the musical, are brought into parity through minor adjustments of the verse line to the musical phrase." Finally, he finds the corrido to be "a performance event which calls into play a wide range of communicative resources belonging to the native expressive ecology, articulating them by means of an impressive inventory of esthetic, social, economic, and political variables" (40, 70, 73).

Another major contribution to the study of the corrido corpus was the publication of Cuauhtémoc Esparza Sánchez's *El corrido zacatecano* (1976). This collection provides a detailed documentation of the longest living Mexican corrido tradition available. Esparza Sánchez includes as his earliest example a corrido narrative, with music, whose heroic protagonist is the leader of the Mexican independence, Miguel Hidalgo y Costilla, describing his entrance and imprisonment in Guadalupe, Zacatecas, during 1811. Other examples are included that help to identify a vital regional tradition in existence throughout the nineteenth century. Such a discovery represents a major contribution to the study of the corrido, its corpus, and the evolution and characteristics of the genre.

Our current knowledge of the corrido has been greatly enhanced by these efforts to revise the genre's definition and characteristics as well as its origins and evolution. In addition, the numerous corrido collections that have been compiled during the last fifty years demand a reexamination of the genre's nature and contours.[9] It is a task that, undoubtedly, will continue to demand the attention of students of this important ballad tradition. With these considerations in mind, I propose to discuss, on the basis of thematic representation and narrative discourse, the formal characteristics as well as the basis for composition and dissemination that act as a complex interplay of factors binding a corrido tradition.

Thematic Representation

Thematic representation in the corrido indicates a composer's treatment of the tale's subject matter. Four areas or modes of thematic representation are evident in a traditional corrido text: (1) character, (2) values and qualities, (3) time and setting, and (4) language. These modes, naturally, do not occur in isolation, but rather appear simultaneously, sustaining and intensifying each other's significance. The cultural importance of these modes cannot be underestimated: each reflects the worldview of corrido communities and, in turn, produces a substantial impact on the beliefs and practices

of corrido audiences. Each of these modes has distinct components.

The first mode, character, includes protagonists, allies, enemies, witnesses, or community members, audiences, and narrators (composers, performers). The second mode, value, can be broken down into positive values and qualities, on the one hand, and negative values and qualities, on the other. Positive values include good, truth, courage, virtue, love, loyalty, strength, charisma, kindness, generosity, pride, humility, gratefulness, righteousness, care, and competency. Negative values encompass evil, deception, cowardice, corruption, hate, treachery, weakness, awkwardness, cruelty, selfishness, shame, arrogance, ungratefulness, wrongfulness, mistreatment, and unfitness. The third mode, time and setting (of the narration or the performance), comprises spaces or times that may be public, private, official, ordinary, geographic, historic, or imagined. The fourth mode concerns language, which may be poetic, formal, informal (colloquial, dialectal), concise, or direct, and articulated as monologue or dialogue.

Character

The corrido possesses a number of characteristics that serve to identify the genre and aid in its interpretation. Foremost among these characteristics is the portrayal of human beings whose acts conform to the experiences and expectations of corrido listeners. That is, the characters depicted are people whose behavior is credible in daily life but who have participated in actions that have had a deep impact on local communities. This is particularly true in the case of the protagonist, who generally serves as a model of conduct under extraordinary circumstances. Francisco I. Madero, the leader of the Mexican Revolution, is thus portrayed in a popular corrido from the period:

> Ah qué Madero tan hombre,
> le conozco sus acciones:
> derecho se fue a la cárcel
> a echar fuera las prisiones.
> ¡Virgen Santa de Guadalupe
> lo llene de bendiciones!
> ("Nuevo Corrido de Madero," in Hernández
> 1985, 39–41)

Madero is a man who is known ("le conozco"), courageous ("tan hombre"), just, and resolute in liberating oppressed prisoners ("derecho se fue a la cárcel / a echar fuera las prisiones"), and who deserves the blessing of the most popular Mexican religious figure ("¡Virgen Santa de Guadalupe / lo llene de bendiciones!")

Characters within a corrido are represented comparatively. That is, their actions and attitudes within the narrative are interdependent and help define their respective roles as allies, enemies, witnesses, community members, or narrators. For example, in the introductory stanza to the corrido about the Mexican-Texan hero Gregorio Cortez, a number of characters are identifiable:

> En el condado del Carmen
> miren lo que ha sucedido:
> murió el Sheriffe Mayor,
> quedando Román herido.
> ("Gregorio Cortez," in Strachwitz 1994, 25–33)

Here, the narrators (composer and performers) address an audience within and without the narrative, composed of allies, witnesses, and community members ("miren"). Then, the sole mention of the "Sheriffe Mayor" suffices to identify his figure as an enemy, given his affiliation with the oppressive Texas Rangers, and his death signals the gravity of the situation. Finally, the narrator alludes to the protagonist's brother Román, whose wound intensifies the Gregorio's predicament, as an ally.

The protagonist's defeat is generally a tragic, although heroic, event. Like other corrido figures, Cortez demonstrates moral authority despite his vulnerable situation. Alluding to the distress suffered by his loved ones magnifies the human dimension of his plight.

> Cuando llegan los sheriffes
> Gregorio se presentó:
> —Por la buena si me llevan
> porque de otro modo, no.—
>
> Ya agarraron a Cortez,
> ya terminó la cuestión,
> la pobre de su familia
> la lleva en el corazón.
> ("Gregorio Cortez," in Strachwitz 1994, 25–33)

The qualities ascribed to protagonists may also include humor. Often the negative qualities demonstrated by the enemy merit irony and sarcasm from the narrator. Running in the middle of battle is a mark of cowardice:

> Los de Yurécuaro andaban,
> al golpetear la carrera,
> que parecían golondrinos
> por entre la zacatera.
>
> Los de Yurécuaro andaban
> que no hallaban ni qué hacer,
> llorando como chiquitos
> cuando ya querían correr.
> ("Corrido de Yurécuaro y Tanhuato," in
> Hernández 1985, 25–28)

The representation of characters includes narrators, who may be either composers or performers. This is evident in "Jesús Leal," a corrido dedicated to a hero from the state of Michoacán who was apprehended and executed in 1873:

> Adiós Jesusito Leal,
> yo me despido de ti,
> estos versos te compuso
> una joven de Tepic.
> ("Jesús Leal," in Hernández 1985, 28–32)

Here the composer-narrator bids farewell ("yo me despido de ti") and addresses the protagonist Leal ("de ti"). It is noticeable that, after she indentifies herself ("una joven de Tepic"), her words will be repeated by all succeeding performer-narrators singing the corrido, although untrue in their cases. This shift in narrative voice, from composer to performer, may modify a narrative. In "Jesús Leal" this shift accentuates the narrator's awareness of the act of creation ("estos versos te compuso / una joven"), demonstrating, as McDowell has noted, the genre's capacity for reflexivity.

Variations in narrative voice are common in the corrido. For example, in "Kiansis," the performer-narrator informs the listening audience ("La mujer de Alberto Flores"), then re-creates a dialogue—within the narrative—between a cowboy's mother (¿Qué razón me da de mi hijo?") and her son's boss (*caporal*) ("Señora, yo le diría, / pero se pone a llorar"). In the last stanza there is a return to the narrative voice of the performer, first addressing the audience ("Ya no tengo que cantarles"), and then continuing the narrative ("aquí termina"):

> La mujer de Alberto Flores
> le pregunta al caporal:
> —Déme razón de mi hijo
> que no lo he visto llegar?—
>
> —Señora, yo le diría,
> pero se pone a llorar:
> lo mató un toro frontino
> en las trancas de un corral.—
>
> Ya con ésta me despido
> por el amor de mi querida,
> ya les canté a mis amigos
> los versos de la corrida.
> ("Kiansis," in Paredes 1976, 54)

Although corrido protagonists are predominantly male figures with characteristics denoting local Mexican culture, the genre easily admits other identities that conform to these norms. Such flexibility explains the enormous success, in the 1970s, of "Contrabando y

traición," a corrido portraying a woman who conducts herself as a model protagonist:

> Sonaron siete balazos,
> Camelia a Emilio mataba;
> la policía sólo halló
> una pistola tirada,
> del dinero y de Camelia
> nunca mas se supo nada.
> ("Contrabando y Traición," in Vélez 1982, 68)

Indeed, Camelia is able to escape punishment for her execution of Emilio and keep the money; she is never seen again. Previous heroines of corridos were, frequently, negative models who were censured for violating codes of behavior. A new day for the role of gender in the corrido is also marked by a narrative voice that blames Emilio for his fate and does not condemn Camelia:

> Una hembra, si quiere a un hombre
> por él puede dar la vida,
> pero hay que tener cuidado
> si esa hembra se siente herida;
> la traición y el contrabando
> son cosas incompartidas.
> ("Contrabando y Traición," in Vélez 1982, 68)

Such adaptability helps explain why the genre throughout its history has shown the capacity to portray protagonists with such a wide variety of occupations, regional characteristics, political affiliations, and social identities. Indeed, this versatility enables corridos to deploy even nonhuman protagonists, such as horses, as long as their treatment conforms to its heroic canons. In the corrido "El potro lobo gateado," for example, the role of the horse is equal to the role played by the cowboy.[10]

> Montó el charro en su caballo:
> —Esa carrera les gano.
> Mi caballo es muy violento:
> se va venir como rayo,
> le va ganar a la yegua.
> ¡Prepárenle otro caballo!

A las primeras pasturas
el caballo no se vía,
se cubrió de polvadera.
¡Qué caballo tan violento!
Nomás alas le faltaban
para volar por el viento.
("El Potro Lobo Gateado," in Hernández 1985,
    26–27)

Values and Qualities

The representation of corrido characters adheres to a traditional code of ethics according to which the actions of individuals are judged either in positive or in negative terms. That is, as McDowell (1981) points out, the corrido is propositional. It is a genre of exemplary narratives where conflictive situations find a resolution in the defeat or victory of an opponent. Although characters may represent a single value or quality, their portrayal generally includes a variety or a combination of characteristics. Nevertheless, given the heroic nature of the tradition, courage is one of the qualities commonly attributed to protagonists. For example, in the corrido "Arnulfo," the two protagonists are described as charismatic ("qué bonitos son los hombres"), and righteous ("defendiendo su derecho"), but it is their courage ("que se matan pecho a pecho") that provides them with a larger-than-life dimension.

¡Qué bonitos son los hombres
que se matan pecho a pecho,
cada uno con su pistola,
defendiendo su derecho!
("Arnulfo," in Ortiz Guerrero 1992, 28–29)

Enemy characters are often denigrated, and the negative representation of their values and qualities stands in contrast to the virtues of heroic opponents. Such is the treatment accorded Victoriano Huerta, responsible for the coup d'état against the revered revolutionary president Francisco I. Madero. In "The Battle

of Zacatecas," Huerta is portrayed as corrupt ("borracho"), awkward ("patas chuecas"), and weak in battle (Zacatecas) after suffering a stunning defeat at the hands of his adversary, Pancho Villa.

Ahora sí, borracho Huerta,
harás las patas más chuecas
al saber que Pancho Villa
ha tomado Zacatecas.
("La Toma de Zacatecas," in Hernández 1985,
    68–69)

Satirical intent underlies General Inez Chávez García's treatment of an aspiring follower:

Decía Rafael Espinoza:
—Señor, lo acompañaré.
Y don Inez le decía:
—¿Para qué lo quiero a usté?
("Corrido de Inez Chávez García," in Hernández
    1985, 112–15)

The audience will certainly notice the ridiculous treatment (foolishness) of Rafael Espinoza (an enemy) after Chávez García (protagonist) rejects his request to join Chávez's forces. Local contemporaries—who knew Rafael Espinoza and the reasons for such disdain—must have appreciated the scene and fully comprehended its significance.[11] Narrators frequently include such revealing textual and contextual details that describe the roles and reputations of the characters represented.

The corrido may be employed in favor of any partisan cause or figure. While admiring composers created a cycle of corridos representing Francisco Villa as a heroic protagonist, his opponents painted him with the ridiculousness associated with enemies. Thus, in the stanzas below Villa is portrayed as an arrogant ("No te las eches") and inept soldier, reminding him of his defeat at Celaya ("las más hechas se van") and of his civilian name (Arango). Villa's followers were represented as ineffectual soldiers who recognize their sorrowful conditions ("Ya no semos tan temidos"). In their weakness ("pobrecita gente"), they are prone to have false beliefs ("se les afiguraba") and confuse military prowess with corruption ("que tomaban a Celaya / como tomar aguardiente").

No te las eches Arango
ni te las vayas a echar,
ni las cuentes tan seguras
que las más hechas se van.

Decían los pobres villistas:
—Ya no semos tan temidos,
por dondequiera rodamos,
parecemos armadillos.

Ya se les afiguraba
a esa pobrecita gente
que tomaban a Celaya
como tomar aguardiente.
("Derrota de Villa en Celaya," in Hernández 1985, 79–82)

Time and Setting

Time and setting refer to the chronology and geography of events in corrido narratives. The backgrounds mentioned tend to reflect the time and place that are customary in daily life: "En la ciudad de Linares / serían más o menos / cinco de la tarde ("Subteniente de Linares," in Ortiz Guerrero 1992, 71–72). Quite often a scene only provides a point of reference: "Kilómetro once sesenta, / carretera nacional ("Arturo Garza Treviño," in Ortiz Guerrero 1992, 68–69). To experienced corrido listeners such outlines are sufficient, since previous knowledge and imagination help re-create the suggested scene. For example, in the corrido "San Pedro de los Ruedas," the yearly festivities are minimally listed ("juego de pelota . . . peleas de gallos") while the gathering of a large number of people is barely mentioned ("La gente llegó en camiones / otros a pie y a caballo"). The only time alluded to is the annual event ("cada año").

Había juego de pelota,
también peleas de gallos;
la gente llegó en camiones
otros a pie y a caballo
pa' celebrar una fiesta
que se festeja cada año.
("San Pedro de los Ruedas," in Ortiz Guerrero 1992, 91)

Commonly mentioned corrido settings include the plaza, street, dance hall, bar, or battlefield. Natural settings are frequent: a road, a sierra or a hill, a mine, or an agricultural field. Although less usual, the portrayal of an official setting also occurs, such as a church, a military installation, or an office. Although scenes in corridos often display public settings where the narrated events occur, sometimes the settings are private, as in the home or in a dialogue. Chronological references are common. Generally, any mention of time is limited either to the hour, the day, or the year when an event takes place. As with other modes, corridos are flexible in adopting a variety of settings, yet maintain adherence to times and locations that are traditionally employed. Indeed, time and setting are important elements of representation in the corrido, since geography and chronology imprint a sense of realism that provides historical credibility and relevance to the actions of the characters:

En mil novecientos quince,
Jueves Santo en la mañana,
salió Villa de Torreón
a combatir a Celaya.
("La Toma de Celaya," in Hernández 1985, 69–70

Language

An important linguistic aspect of corridos is their observance of dialectal patterns and adherence to traditional speech. Their vocabulary is often distinctively regional and follows

Mexican Spanish rural traditions. In their usage speakers employ words such as "vía" for "veía," "ora" for "ahora," "suidad" for "ciudad," "usté" for "usted," and "ahi" and "haiga" for "haya." The pronunciation and inflection of performers will parallel local dialectal tonalities serving as a marker to corrido audiences that the message conveys their social and cultural assumptions. The narrative, however, may also contain significant linguistic and cultural information. For example, in the corrido of "Manuel Lozada," listeners are aware of speech usage in a trilingual community of northern Mexico (Huichol, Cora, and Spanish), in addition to local conventions such as playing the tambora:

> Llegaron a los portales
> gritando en huichol y cora:
> que les dieran aguardiente y
> tocaran la tambora.
> ("Corrido de Manuel Lozada," in Esparza
>   Sánchez 1976, 25–28)

The listener, therefore, is expected to possess knowledge of local linguistic customs in order to appreciate nuances in a narrative. "Filadelfo Robles," a corrido from the "Costa Chica," an Afro-Mestizo region in the Mexican state of Guerrero, uses African ancestral conventions ("sombra pesada") and local vocabulary ("broza").[12]

> Ese Filadelfo Robles
> tenía la sombra pesada.
> Él andando con su broza
> ni los perros le ladraban.
> ("Filadelfo Robles," in Aguirre Beltrán 1985,
>   176)

Similarly, the influence of English language among Spanish speakers is present among the US-Mexico border populations. In "El Contrabando del Paso," an office, a location, and a vehicle are mentioned as a result of linguistic borrowings: "corte" from "court," "dipo" from "depot," and "coche" from "coach."

> Nos sacaron de la corte
> a las ocho de la noche,
> nos llevaron para el dipo,
> nos montaron en un coche.
> ("El Contrabando del Paso," in Strachwitz 1994,
>   100–104)

Although the corrido must convey an everyday, factual perception of the world, its language is constructed on the basis of poetic rhythms. The poetic form is customarily based on variable octosyllabic quatrains with a rhyme scheme that coincides in the even lines, as is customary in the copla:

A-ño-de-mil-no-ve-cien-tos	A 8
muy-pre-sen-te-ten-go-yo,	B 8
que en-un-ba-rrio-de-Sal-ti-llo,	C 8
Ro-si-ta-Al-ví-rez-mu-río.	B 8

("Rosita Alvirez," in Ortiz Guerrero 1992, 29–30)

Some corridos, however, have six or seven syllables; less frequently, others may be found with eleven and more syllables per line.[13]

A-gus-tín-ba-ja-ba,	A 6
ba-ja-ba y-su-bí-a,	B 6
él-per-dío-la-vi-da	C 6
por-Ma-rí-a-Gar-cí-a.	B 6

("Agustín Jaime," in Ortiz Guerrero 1992, 31)

Los-sol-da-dos-que-vi-nie-ron-des-de-Te-xas,	A 12
a-Pan-cho-Vi-lla-no-po-dían-en-con-trar, (11+1)	B 12
ya-fas-ti-dia-dos-de o-cho ho-ras-de-ca-mi-no,	C 12
los-po-bre-ci-tos-se-que-rían-re-gre-sar. (11+1)	B 12

("La Expedición Punitiva," in Hernández 1985, 69–70)

Rhyme schemes may show a degree of variation from the traditional patterns. Some composers utilize rhymes that coincide in both the odd and the even lines, but even these deviations tend to maintain a basic dependence on the norm. In "Pistoleros Famosos," two lines are added to the quatrain, but although the first

(A) and the third (A) lines rhyme, only the sixth (B) line maintains the traditional rhyming scheme with the second (B) and the fourth (B) lines:

Por-las-már-ge-nes-del-Rí-o,	A 8
De-Rey-no-sa has-ta-La-re-do,	B 8
se a-ca-ba-ron-los-ban-di-dos,	A 8
se a-ca-ron-los-pa-ter-os;	B 8
y-ya-se es-tán-a-ca-ban-do	C 8
a-to-dos-los-pis-to-le-ros.	B 8

("Pistoleros Famosos," in Ortiz Guerrero 1992, 120)

While the above examples maintain a strict metrical and rhyming regularity, it is frequent to find deviations from these norms. Irregularities are more common among older corridos whose oral diffusion increases the possibility for the creation of variants. In contrast, contemporaneous corridos are generally transmitted through electronic means of production and communication and, therefore, tend to maintain a single narrative textual version and regular metrics. This poetic tendency in modern corridos also influences their linguistic conventions: they are products of popular culture rather than oral tradition.

Narrative Discourse

Narrative discourse in the corrido tradition can be divided into seven sections: (1) fate, (2) pursuit, (3) challenge, (4) confrontation, (5) defeat, (6) judgment, and (7) farewell. Since these sections of narrative discourse are thoroughly familiar to knowledgeable corrido listeners, alluding to or mentioning one or more of them will suffice in a narrative. That is, a process of reconstruction takes place in the mind of an experienced listener whereby the scene in a corrido is automatically placed within the familiar context of narrative discourse. This relation between a section and the entire narrative discourse corresponds to the literary reliance of a text on a master or meta-narrative.

Each of the discursive sections may include different elements. Fate encompasses anticipation, omen, and chance. Pursuit may involve plans, coercion, chase, and escape. Challenge may take the form of ridicule, offense, defiance, provocation, aggression. The confrontation may be a duel, a battle, an attack, or a skirmish. Defeat may comprise capture, imprisonment, sentence, execution, and death. The judgment involves thought, reflection, deduction, advice, experience, and lamentation. The farewell encompasses remembrance, memory, nostalgia, and reputation.

All corridos display several narrative sections, although it is rare to find one that includes all. Since the existence of the genre is directly proportional to the presence of these narrative sections, their absence may exclude a song from the corrido corpus. Indeed, without their presence—especially the sections of challenge, confrontation, and defeat—corridos lack the emotional power characteristic of the genre and may be excluded from its corpus.

Fate

All references to the misfortune that eventually befalls a character are included under the narrative section "fate." The identification of a vice will be an indication that tragedy is awaiting a culprit; usually recklessness or breaking the norms of good conduct causes the unfortunate end. Such is the example of Reyes Ruiz, a protagonist who disregards his mother's advice to abstain from attending the celebration of Mexican Independence Day on the 16th of September. In spite of a parental prohibition ("a ese dieciséis no vas") and his peers' warning ("lo mejor será no ir"), Reyes's violation of the omen ("no sabes tu porvenir") leads him to his death.

> Su mamá le respondió:
> Hijo de mi corazón,
> a ese dieciséis no vas,
> ahí irás en otra ocasión.
>
> Sus amigos le decían:
> Lo mejor será no ir,
> si tu madre te lo evita,
> no sabes tu porvenir.
> ("De Reyes Ruiz," in Mendoza 1964, 262–63)

Ill fortune may also occur to an arrogant character who mistreats those who are economically, politically, or socially weak. Reckless disdain in "Asesino a sueldo" leads the hired murderer to declare his intentions, suffering fatal consequences for this mistake:

> —Vengo a matar a tu padre.
> Así dijo el gatillero;
> el niño no era cobarde
> y lo sorprendió primero:
> lo fusiló con un mauser
> y cinco balas de acero.
> ("Asesino a Sueldo," in Ortiz Guerrero 1992, 114–115)

Pursuit

A common scene in corridos portrays a heroic protagonist who is chased by a group of enemies under overwhelming and unjust conditions. In the corrido "Gregorio Cortez," for example, the large number of lawmen pursuing Cortez through the state of Texas highlights his solitary figure attempting to escape the injustice awaiting him. The inhumanity of his pursuers leads them to employ bloodhounds to hunt him down. The picture of a humble and vulnerable man who successfully evades his ferocious pursuers provides Cortez with a larger-than-life stature:

> Soltaron los perros jaunes
> pa' que siguieran la huella,

> pero seguir a Cortez
> era seguir una estrella.
> ("Gregorio Cortez," in Strachwitz 1994, 25–33)

The pursuit of a character includes numerous narrative aspects involving pursuers and the pursued: plans for capture and escape, mental and physical activities, peculiarities of the pursuit, and description of the escape and attendant conditions. The unequal conditions of this situation coincide with the role of the corrido as a medium of expression to convey local community history:

> Agarró los diez mil pesos,
> los amarró en su mascada,
> y le dijo al comandante:
> —Prevéngase su Acordada.
>
> —Prevéngase su Acordada
> y escuadrón militar,
> y vámonos a Durango
> a traer a Heraclio Bernal.
> ("Heraclio Bernal," in Hernández 1985, 32–35)

Often this persecution takes a symbolic form that involves the coercion or intimidation of the protagonist by someone who has a higher position of authority or social and political prominence. The coercion demonstrated toward the main character also produces a double response on the part of the listener: sympathy toward the misfortunes of the protagonist and a deep sense of antagonism for the injustices perpetrated by the oppressors. In "Belén Galindo," for example, the narrative voice reconstructs the malicious words of the evil mother-in-law as she transmits the immoral proposition of a possible suitor:

> Llega la suegra y le dice:
> Belén, te vengo a avisar,
> don Marcos te quiere mucho,
> te da plata pa' gastar.
> ("Mañanas de Belén Galindo," in Esparza Sánchez 1976, 37–38)

Challenge

The values advocated by the corrido favor exemplary behavior supporting community norms. The pride and courage of heroic protagonists justify their open defiance of their enemies. Such boldness, however, must not be interpreted as arrogance or vanity, flaws of character usually ascribed to enemies. That is, the challenge serves to mark offended righteousness, highlighting the vices of opponents and asserting the positive values guiding the actions of favored characters. The audience appreciates the scorn launched against a powerful enemy (Porfirio Díaz) who has inept soldiers ("que les mande otros mejores") fighting an invincible and defying protagonist (Ignacio Parra):

> Les gritaba Ignacio Parra:
> —Lástima de tiradores,
> díganle a Porfirio Díaz
> que les mande otros mejores.
> ("Ignacio Parra," in Hernández 1985, 21–22)

An offended hero is often entirely justified in expressing rage at the dishonorable actions of an enemy:

> González bajó el cabresto
> y se lo llevó un amigo.
> Roberto de su caballo
> le gritaba, enfurecido:
> —Yo creí que tú eras hombre,
> no pensé que eras vendido.
> ("La Chiva Colgada," in Ortiz Guerrero 1992, 66–67)

This scene describes the act of seizing a goat that hangs from a moving rope by a rider on a horse running at full gallop. It represents a public performance of a feat requiring great skill. Martínez is the man in charge of manipulating the rope, and Roberto's failure and his accusation of fraud are both serious affronts in the eyes of the community.

Confrontation

The confrontation constitutes a narrative element that is central to the corrido. Whether described or alluded to, the clash of two incompatible opponents who resolve a fundamental disagreement helps define the critical issues on which the entire composition rests. The genre can be considered as epic-tragic because it poses a denouement that cannot admit of a happy resolution for both adversaries. Given the respect expected toward elders, the indignant rejection ("váyase de aquí") on the part of Belén Galindo toward her immoral mother-in-law, demonstrating her innocence ("yo no soy de esas"), justifies the following showdown:

> Váyase de aquí, señora,
> no me venga a molestar.
> Mire que yo no soy de ésas,
> no me doy ese lugar.
> ("Mañanas de Belén Galindo," in Esparza Sánchez, 37)

In "Valente Quintero" the conflict is resolved in a duel where Valente Quintero and Martín Elenes kill each other.

> Se tomaron de la mano,
> se apartaron de la bola,
> y a los poquitos momentos:
> seis disparos de pistola.
> ("De Valente Quintero," in Mendoza 1964, 197–98)

The confrontation may involve nonhuman opponents, such as the two horses vying for first place in "El Moro de Cumpas." Although the horserace involves two owners (Rafael Romero and Pedro "Piter"), and two riders (Trini Ramírez and Chendo Valenzuela), engaged in their respective contests, the two horses (Relámpago and Moro) are the real challengers:

> Por fin dieron el "Santiago,"
> el Moro salió adelante
> con la intención de ganar:
> Ramírez le tupió al zaino

y arriba de medio taste
dejaba al Moro para atrás.
("El Moro de Cumpas," in Serna Maytorena
1988, 38–39)

The clash may also occur between forces of nature and humans, as is commonly portrayed in corridos based on disasters. For example, in the corrido regarding the broken dam at Santa Clarita, California, in 1928, the flood is described as a formidable enemy on a path that crushes human life. Here the lament for the helpless human victims of the catastrophe overwhelms the audience of the corrido:

El torrente caminaba
destrozando las regiones,
y dejando tras su paso
muchos tristes corazones.
("Inundación de California," in Hernández
1978, 25–28)

Defeat

The defeat of one of the opponents is an important turning point in corrido narratives. The success of a protagonist and the downfall of the enemy define the nature of the conflict, the values at stake, and the respective personalities of the contenders. As mentioned before, because corridos generally depict the misfortune of principal characters, the genre has acquired predominant tragic qualities. These courageous but fatal conditions often provide corrido protagonists with an aura of martyrdom. Thus, a national figure of the stature of Francisco I. Madero, murdered for political reasons, is portrayed as a victim of heartless enemies:

Señores, les contaré
lo que en México pasó:
que una bola de asesinos
a Madero asesinó.
("El Cuartelazo," in Hernández 1985, 42–46)

Corridos may also convey the sorrow suffered in the community when local figures perish in a confrontation. Such protagonists are treated as heroic victims of painful and useless sacrifices:

—Hijo de mi corazón,—
decía su padre llorando,
—has muerto como los hombres,
en tu caballo peleando.
("Alejos Sierra," in Paredes 1976, 79–80)

Judgment

The subject matter of the narrative is often judged within the corrido tale itself. This is usually a commentary on the actions described, a reflection on the personalities of the characters involved, or a thought on a particular human problem. The word thus expressed may include the identity of the narrator ("se apellida Salazar"), demonstrating poetic humility for his composition ("El que compuso estos versos / No tuvo conocimiento"), addressing the listening audience directly:

El que compuso estos versos
no tuvo conocimiento;
los compuso un subteniente
del segundo regimiento.

Si quieren saber su nombre
lo voy a decir ahorita
se apellida Salazar,
fue constitucionalista.
("La Toma de Matamoros," in Hernández 1985,
100–102)

Such commentaries, expressed by the performer within the text of the corrido, may also highlight the exemplary nature of the events narrated and the role of corridos in prescribing community behavior. In "Carga Blanca," for example, one of the first corridos to include the topic of drugs, the narrative voice advises against drug trafficking, warning of the negative consequences awaiting the transgressors:

Despedida se las diera
pero ya se me perdió,
dejen los negocios chuecos:

ya ven lo que sucedió.
("Carga Blanca," in Ortiz Guerrero 1992,
182–83)

Farewell

The narrative voice often mentions the significance of the name, qualities, or actions of the protagonist. The enumeration of a character's attributes has the purpose of reminding the audience of the extraordinary life and death of the characters praised in the narrative. The tragic end met by many of the corrido protagonists is usually formulated as an earthly farewell, often with religious allusions, for a voyage to an eternal world.

Ya se acabó Benjamín,
ya no lo oyirán mentar.
Ya está juzgado de Dios,
ya so alma fue a descansar.
("Benjamín Argumedo," in Hernández 1985,
47–53)

Conclusions

Throughout a history that is now almost two hundred years old, the corrido has had two major processes of transmission: at first it was communicated through an oral network until it was recorded commercially and became a product of popular culture. Throughout this time the corrido has tended to portray heroic actions emphasizing the tragic qualities of life. The history of the study of the genre, however, began in the early twentieth century, and it has continued to the present throughout three periods or overlapping phases: an early phase of publication of texts, a second or pioneer phase of analysis, and a third or contemporary phase when an international group of scholars and aficionados has revitalized the study of the genre.

The large corrido corpus gathered in the last fifty years merits revision of some of its basic features. The present study suggests the identification of corridos and the contours of the corpus according to two aspects: thematic representation and narrative discourse. Thematic representation in the corrido indicates the treatment given by a composer to the subject matter in the tale. Four areas or modes of thematic representation are evident in a traditional corrido text: (1) character, (2) value, (3) time and setting, and (4) language. These modes, naturally, do not occur in isolation, or in any particular order, often appearing partially or simultaneously, sustaining and intensifying each other's significance. Narrative discourse in the corrido tradition refers to the logical arrangement of events. This arrangement can be divided into seven sections: (1) fate, (2) pursuit, (3) challenge, (4) confrontation, (5) defeat, (6) judgment, and (7) farewell. Since these sections of narrative discourse are thoroughly familiar to knowledgeable corrido listeners, they may appear in any order and they need not be fully developed to be understood by an experienced corrido audience.

Corridos recount stories of heroic and often tragic figures who left us their example as they confronted difficult situations in their communities. Many of the names of narrators and characters as well as their trials and tribulations remain only in that collective and unofficial history that is the corrido tradition.

Lo sacaron a la orilla
por ver si sabía jugar,
le dieron tres puñaladas
al pie de un verde rosal.
("De Lucio Pérez," in Mendoza 1964, 260–62)

Ese año de ochenta y seis,
presente lo tengo yo:
que murió Lino Rodarte,
el gobierno lo mató.
("Corrido de Lino Rodarte," in Esparza
Sánchez 1976, 30–32)

Notes

1. Nicolopulos (1997) discusses various views of the epic corrido, its "second orality" as well as its survival in our own days. Limón (1992) discusses the survival of the corrido of "Greater Mexico" in "residual" form.

2. A distinction must be made between corridos that are indeed based on strict historical fact and others that are predominantly fictional. The latter are often the creation of professional, urban composers who emulate, with various degrees of success, the realistic tradition of corridos based on historical fact.

3. There is an erroneous though, unfortunately, widespread conception that corridos serve a role in oral communication similar to the function played by newspapers in literate societies. As John McDowell has appropriately stated: "The purpose of the corrido is not, as some scholars have supposed, to convey news. News travels readily enough through less formal channels such as gossip, anecdote, etc. Generally speaking, the corrido depends on a prior transmission of news; its purpose is to interpret, celebrate, and ultimately dignify events already thoroughly familiar to the corrido audience" (1981, 47).

4. The advent of the commercially recorded corrido was especially significant in the development of brief corridos. The recordings in 78-rpm discs originally employed both sides for a single corrido. Later, record labels reduced the length of the composition and recorded two per side. This practice was guided exclusively by business: a disc including two corrido titles could attract a larger number of buyers. Since that period, corridos have a tendency toward briefness—six to nine stanzas—in comparison with older samples that often exceeded fifteen stanzas. In the introduction to his recorded collection, Strachwitz (1994) discusses "The Golden Age of the Recorded Corrido." Spottswood (1990) has gathered a monumental discography of the recordings made in the United States.

5. Important collections from this early period include, among others, those by Higinio Vázquez Santa Ana (Guanajuato), Vicente T. Mendoza (Mexico), Américo Paredes (Texas), Gonzalo Aguirre Beltrán (Guerrero), Celedonio Serrano Martínez (Guerrero), Mario Colín (Estado de México), Armando de María y Campos and Celestino Herrera Frimont (Mexican Revolution), Eduardo Guerrero and Vanegas Arroyo (Broadsides), and Vicente Acosta (Arizona).

6. Notable pioneers during the second phase were Armando Duvalier, Vicente T. Mendoza, Américo Paredes, Merle E. Simmons, Cuauhtémoc Esparza Sánchez, Celedonio Serrano Martínez, John Donald Robb, Daniel Castañeda, and Héctor Pérez Martínez.

7. This phase is distinguished by the establishment of a relatively large international network of corrido scholars and aficionados engaged in teaching and lecturing as well as the publication of articles and books on the genre based on archival and field research.

8. Duvalier's secondary formulas are (1) insistence on remembering a particular event, (2) outcry or reflection on an event narrated, (3) biographical discussion of the character described, (4) summary of the events narrated, (5) appeal for the purchase of the corrido, (6) corridista announces end of first part and next part or sequel, 7) name of composer, and 8) beginning of the second part or any other corrido that follows.

9. In addition to the collection from Zacatecas, other important regional collections have been available in the last quarter of the twentieth century. Among others that should be mentioned is the Arhoolie collection of commercial recordings dating from the 1920s to the present. Numerous corrido anthologies and recordings are now available from the states of Durango, Guanajuato, Guerrero, Michoacán, Morelos, Nuevo León, New Mexico, Sonora, Tamaulipas, Tehuantepec (Istmo), Texas, and Veracruz, as well as general collections in Mexico and in the United States.

10. Most corridos depicting horse races portray the horse as protagonist and its owner as a secondary character. Dual protagonists, such as in the corrido of "El potro lobo gateado," are rare. Their existence may be explained as a story-within-the-story: a cowboy defies a rich hacienda owner and the horse race is a subaltern narrative which could also stand on its own.

11. Guadalupe García Torres (1997) discusses the historical context for the cycle of corridos dedicated to this revolutionary.

12. Filadelfo's "heavy shadow" indicates his status as an extraordinary individual. Aguirre Beltrán (1985) discusses this concept as a surviving African spiritual belief. "Broza" is a gang or group of followers.

13. There is a type of composition, identified as a corrido, found primarily in the Mexican state of Morelos, with long lines of fourteen and more syllables. Although identified as corridos, this branch of musical compositions must first be studied comparatively in order to assess its degree of similarity and difference with the tragic corrido found in other parts of Mexico and the United States. A similar study should be conducted with the valona. Razo Oliva (1987) discusses the possibility of a link between corrido and valona.

Works Cited

Acosta, Vicente S. 1951. "Some Surviving Elements of Spanish Folklore in Arizona." Thesis, University of Arizona.

Aguirre Beltrán, Gonzalo. 1985. *Cuijla: Esbozo etnográfico de un pueblo negro.*

Lecturas Mexicanas 90. Mexico City: Secretaria de Educación Pública y Fondo de Cultura Económica.

Castañeda, Daniel. 1943. *El corrido mexicano: Su técnica literaria y musical.* Mexico City: Editorial Surco.

Colín, Mario. 1972. *El corrido popular en el Estado de México.* Toluca, Mexico: Biblioteca Enciclopédica del Estado de México.

De María y Campos, Armando. 1962. *La revolución mexicana a través de sus corridos populares.* 2 vols. Mexico City: Instituto Nacional de Estudios Históricos de la Revolución Mexicana.

Duvalier, Armando. 1937. "Romance y corrido." *Crisol: Revista de Crítica* 3543: 8–16, 35–41.

Esparza Sánchez, Cuauhtémoc. 1976. *El corrido zacatecano.* Mexico City: Instituto Nacional de Antropología e Historia.

García Torres, Guadalupe. 1997. "Los corridos de Inés Chávez García: Lírica de una leyenda moderna." *Aztlán: A Journal of Chicano Studies* 22, no. 49: 49–71.

Guerrero, José E. 1924. *Canciones y corridos populares.* 2 vols. Mexico: Author's private printing.

———. 1931. *Corridos históricos de la Revolución Mexicana desde 1910 a 1930 y otros notables de varias épocas.* Mexico City: Eduardo Guerrero Collection at the Biblioteca Nacional de México.

Hernández, Guillermo E. 1978. *Canciones de la Raza: Songs of the Chicano Experience.* Berkeley, CA: Fuego de Aztlán.

———, ed. 1985. *The Mexican Revolution, The Heroes and Events, 1910–1920 and Beyond: A Collection of Corridos from Early Historic Recordings.* Booklet accompanying Folklyric Records 7041–7044. Cerrito, CA: Arhoolie.

———. 1986. "La punitiva: El corrido norteño y la tradición oral, impresa y fonográfica."

Heterofonía (Conservatorio Nacional de Música) 29: 46–64.

Herrera Frimont, Celestino. 1934. *Los corridos de la Revolución.* Pachuca, Mexico: Ediciones del Instituto Científico y Literario.

Hubbel, Linda J. 1968. "Historicity Study of Mexican Corridos about Zapata." *Kroeber Anthropological Society Papers* 38: 68–81.

Limón, José E. 1992. *Mexican Ballads, Chicano Poems: History and Influence in Mexican-American Social Poetry.* Berkeley: University of California Press.

McDowell, John Holmes. 1972. "The Mexican *Corrido*: Formula and Theme in a Ballad Tradition." *Journal of American Folklore* 85, no. 337: 205–20.

———. 1981. "The Corrido of Greater Mexico as Discourse, Music, and Event." In *'And Other Neighborly Names': Social Process and Cultural Image in Texas Folklore,* edited by Richard D. Bauman and Roger D. Abrahams, 44–75. Austin: University of Texas Press.

Mendoza, Vicente T. 1939. *El romance español y el corrido mexicano.* Mexico City: Universidad Nacional Autónoma de México, Instituto de Investigaciones Estéticas.

———. 1964. *Lírica narrativa de México: El corrido.* Mexico City: Universidad Nacional Autónoma de México, Instituto de Investigaciones Estéticas.

Nicolopulos, James. 1997. "The Heroic Corrido: A Premature Obituary?" *Aztlán: A Journal of Chicano Studies* 22, no. 1: 115–38.

Ortiz Guerrero, Armando Hugo. 1992. *Vida y muerte en la frontera: Cancionero del corrido norestense.* Monterrey, Mexico: Hensa Editores.

Paredes, Américo. 1963. "The Ancestry of Mexico's Corridos: A Matter of Definitions." *Journal of American Folklore* 76, no. 301: 231–35.

———. 1976. *A Texas-Mexican Cancionero: Folksongs of the Lower Border*. Urbana: University of Illinois Press.

———. 1990. *"With His Pistol in His Hand": A Border Ballad and Its Hero*. Austin: University of Texas Press. First published 1958.

———. 1993. "The Mexican Corrido: Its Rise and Fall." In *Folklore and Culture on the Texas-Mexican Border*, edited by Richard Bauman, 129–41. Austin: University of Texas, Center for Mexican American Studies.

Razo Oliva, Juan Diego. 1987. *Testimonios del viento: Cancionero folklórico salmantino*. Tlahuapan, Puebla, Mexico: Dirección General de Culturas Populares, Secretaria de Educación Pública/Premiá Editora de Libros.

Serna Maytorena, Manuel A. 1988. *"En Sonora así se cuenta . . .": El corrido en Sonora y Sonora en el corrido*. Hermosillo, Mexico: Gobierno del Estado de Sonora.

Serrano Martínez, Celedonio. 1973. *El corrido mexicano no deriva del romance español*. Mexico: Centro Cultural Guerrerense.

Simmons, Merle E. 1963. "The Ancestry of Mexico's Corridos." *Journal of American Folklore* 76, no. 299: 1–15.

Spottswood, Richard K. 1990. *Ethnic Music in Records: A Discography of Ethnic Recordings Produced in the United States, 1893 to 1942*. Foreword by James H. Billington. 7 vols. Urbana: University of Illinois Press.

Strachwitz, Chris. 1994. *Corridos y tragedias de la frontera: First Recordings of Historic Mexican-American Ballads (1928–37)*. Folk-lyric Records 7019–7020. Cerrito, CA: Arhoolie.

Vázquez Santa Ana, Higinio. 1925. *Canciones, cantares y corridos mexicanos*. 2 vols. Mexico: Imprenta León Sánchez.

Vélez, Gilberto. 1982. *Corridos mexicanos*. Mexico: Editores Mexicanos Unidos.

Two-Part Corridos in the Frontera Collection

Before LPs were introduced in the 1950s, performers often could not fit an entire corrido on one side of a 78-rpm disc, such as the one shown in figure 65. Recording corridos in two parts became a common practice. The Frontera Collection contains perhaps the most extensive collection of these rare discs, listed here alphabetically by title.

Figure 65. "El Lavaplatos" (The Dish Washer) is a famous two-part corrido about a Mexican immigrant who seeks success in Hollywood but finds only menial labor and dashed dreams. This version was recorded by Los Hermanos Bañuelos on Vocalion. The Frontera Collection contains other two-part versions of this Depression-era song, including the 78-rpm release on Victor by its composer, Jesús Camacho Osorio, in a duet with Manuel "El Perro" Camacho. Photograph courtesy of the Arhoolie Foundation.

Two-Part Corridos in the Frontera Collection

Title	Label and no.	Artist
Alejos Sierra	Ideal 93	Gaytán y Cantú
Alejos Sierra	Vocalion 8475	Pedro Rocha y Lupe Martínez
Almazán	Columbia 4609-X	Hermanos Chavarría
Aquí Hemos Venido Porque Hemos Llegado	Victor 81647-A	Luis Hernández – Leonardo Sifuentes
Asalto del Banco de Ciudad Juárez	Aguila 5011-A	Dueto Lunas – Salas
Asesinato del General Sandino	Decca 10096A	Montalbo y Berlanga
Aurelio Pompa	Columbia 2097-X	Trío Luna
Aviador Carranza	Columbia 3223-X	Cancioneros de Sonora
Ay! Qué Muchachas	Vocalion 8724	Hernández y Sifuentes
Baldo Prieto	Victor 30496-A	Justo Mireles y Juan Gaitán
Benito Canales	Bluebird B-2502-A	Desiderio García y Santos Guerrero
Benjamín Argumedo	Decca 10041A	Morales y Romero
Benjamín Argumedo	Universal 4050-A	Dueto Hureta-González
Benjamín Argumedo	Vocalion 8241	González y Hernández
Capitán Charles Stevens	Vocalion 8280	Lupe Martínez y Pedro Rocha
Chavela	Victor 46582-A	Silvano Ramos y Daniel Ramírez
Chávez y Ofilio Herrera	Bluebird B-2215-A	Tamez y Martínez
Chocala, Fierros	Vocalion 8358	Ramón Jazo y Silvano Ramos
Consejo al Maje	Vocalion 8582-A	Ezequiel Nevárez y José Elicciri
Consejos al Maje	Okeh 16826	Los Madrugadores
Contestación a "Zenaida"	Vocalion 8875	Gaytán y Cantú
Contrabandistas Tequileros	Vocalion 8430	Pedro Rocha y Lupe Martínez
Convictos de Colorado	Vocalion 8615	Hernández y Sifuentes
Corrido a Senador Chávez	Coast 1	Tito Guízar
Corrido de Bonifacio Torres	Vocalion 8369	Hermanos Bañuelos
Corrido de Guty Cárdenas	R.M.M. L-0156	Nacho y Chicharo
Corrido de Inés Chávez García	Vocalion 8312	Hermanos Bañuelos
Corrido de Jesús Cadena	Coast 7041	Martín y Malena
Corrido de Joaquín Murrieta	Decca 10036A	Hnos. Sánchez y Linares
Corrido de Joaquín Murrieta	Columbia 1811-C	Los Madrugadores
Corrido de Juan Reyna	Columbia 4339-X	Roca y Amador
Corrido de Juan Reyna	Vocalion 8383	Hermanos Bañuelos
Corrido de la Huichapa y Baltares	Columbia 4035-X	Hermanos Bañuelos
Corrido de la Muerte del Aviador Sidar	Brunswick 41026	Hermanos Bañuelos
Corrido de Lola Huichapa y Armando Baltares	Vocalion 8318	Catalina Laform y Luis Vizcarra
Corrido de los Bootleggers	Bluebird B-2381-A	Francisco Montalvo y Andrés Berlanga
Corrido de Los Hermanos Hernández	Decca 10018A	Hnos. Sánchez y Linares
Corrido de Pancho Tirado	Peerless 1732	Dueto Sánchez-Becerra

Title	Label and no.	Artist
Corrido de Raúl Galván	Vocalion 8715	Del Valle y Rivas
Corrido de Sidar	Columbia 3855-X	Salvador y Consuelo de Quirós
Corrido de Toral	Vocalion 8220	Trovadores Tapatíos
Corrido de Yurécuaro y Tanhuato	Brunswick 41192	Hermanos Bañuelos
Corrido del Coronel Fierro	Columbia 4251-X	Hermanos Bañuelos
Corrido del General Cárdenas	Vocalion 8722	Del Valle y Rivas
Corrido del General Fierro	Victor 30534-A	Guzmán y Hernández
Corrido del Gral. Gorostieta	Vocalion 8237	Trío Mayo
Corrido del Hampa	Vocalion 8833	Flores y Durán
Corrido del Petrolero	Vocalion 8451	Pedro Rocha y Lupe Martínez
Corrido del Tri Army	Bluebird B-3105-A	Santos Guerrero y Antonio Hernández
Corrido Historia y Muerte del General Francisco Villa	Brunswick 40045-A	Moré – Rubi – Vivo
Derrota de Villa en Celaya	Decca 10141A	Pedro Rocha y José Angel Colunga
El "Bootlegger"	Columbia 4336-X	Roca y Amador
El Arreglo Religioso	Columbia 3650-X	Cancioneros de Sonora
El Barco Ligero	Vocalion 8897	Los Madrugadores
El Brindis del Bohemio	Victor 30411-A	Manuel C. Bernal
El Caballo Canciller	Vocalion 8327	Ramon Jazo
El Contrabandista	Vocalion 8585-A	Gaytán y Cantú
El Contrabando de El Paso	Victor 80755-A	Luis Hernández – Leonardo Sifuentes
El Contrabando de El Paso	Universal 4041-A	Dueto Hureta-González
El Contrabando de San Antonio	Okeh 16728	Justo Mireles y Juan Gaitán
El Contrabando del Paso	Brunswick 40467	Hermanos Bañuelos
El Corrido de Escobar	Victor 46408-A	Genaro Rodríguez y Ezequiel Mandujano
El Corrido del Agrarista	Columbia 3689-X	Trovadores Tamaulipecos
El Cruzado en Palestina	Decca 10001A	Gonzales y Rosales
El Cuartelazo	Columbia 4372-X	Hermanos Chavarría
El Deportado	Columbia 4041-X	Luna y Gallegos
El Deportado	Vocalion 8287	Hermanos Bañuelos
El Deportado	Victor 46719-A	Grupo Azteca
El Descarrilamiento	Columbia C-4051	Trío Nava
El Desdichado	Vocalion 8824	Del Valle y Rivas
El Dorado de Villa	Vocalion 8977	Gaytán y Cantú
El Hijo Desobediente	Decca 10086A	Montalbo y Berlanga
El Huérfano	Okeh ONY 16382	Trío Matamoros
El Huérfano	Victor 81240-A	Luis Hernández – Leonardo Sifuentes
El Jornalero	Vocalion 8482	Gaitán y Rodríguez
El Lava Platos	Okeh 16716	Gómez y Romano
El Lavaplatos	Victor 46944-A	Osorio y Camacho

Title	Label and no.	Artist
El Lavaplatos	Columbia 4218-X	Chaves y Lugo
El Lavaplatos	Brunswick 41063	Cancioneros del Repertorio
El Maldito Permanente	Vocalion 8880	Santos Guerrero y Antonio Hernández
El Mojado	Vocalion 8516	Gaytán, Cantú y Rodríguez
El Obrero	A. Martin & Co. RR 1437	Emilia Navarrete
El Pablote	Vocalion 8450	Norverto González y José Rosales
El Petrolero	Columbia 4395-X	Hermanos San Miguel
El Radiograma	Brunswick 41398	G. Guzmán y J. Rosales
El Reenganche	Victor 46615-A	Luis Hernández y Leonardo Sifuentes
El Soltero Empedernido	Decca 10140A	Trío Melodías Mexicanas
El Vuelo de Carranza	Vocalion 8173	Ramos Trío
El Vuelo de Sidar	Victor 46772-A	Grupo Azteca
Emilio Carranza	Vocalion 8150	Cuadro México
En el Rancho de Lucero	Vocalion 8431	Salas y Herrera
En las Islas Filipinas	Martinez-Ortiz 602	Hermanos Ortiz
Esos Enamorados	Decca 10101A	Hermanos Chavarría
Felipe Ángeles	Decca 10042A	Morales y Romero
Felipe Ángeles	Brunswick 40895	Guerra y Guerra
Fidel Espinoza	Decca 10122A	Hermanos Chavarría
Francisco Sarabia	Decca 10443A	Chucho y Marín
Fusilamiento de Felipe Ángeles	Vocalion 8679	Bernardo San Román y Luis Vera
Fusilamiento de Toral	Vocalion 8211	Dúo Mexicano
Inez Chávez García	Universal 4103-A	Trío Iglesias – Calvo – Silva
Inundación de Tampico	Brunswick 41588	Fierra y Gómez
Irapuato	Bluebird B-2239-A	Hermanos Pizano
Juan Reyna	Okeh 16759	González y Hernández
Julia del Real	Columbia 4565-X	Ramón Jazo
La Adelaida	Decca 10281A	Adelita y Chicho
La Carolina	Vocalion 9070	Chicho y Margarita
La Carretera	Vocalion 8405	Salas y Herrera
La Condenada	Victor 46760-A	Cancioneros Acosta
La Crisis Actual	Vocalion 8401	Los Cancioneros Alegres
La Expedición Punitiva	Brunswick 40826	F. Montalvo y M. Rodríguez
La Historia de Pancho Villa	Victor 46650-A	Hermanos Atilano
La Inundación de León	Columbia C-4075	Trío Nava
La Inundación de Nogales	Victor 30381-A	Sifuentes y Guzmán
La Inundación de Piedras Negras	Vocalion 8481	Luna y Delgado
La Modesta	Vocalion 8390	Pedro Rocha y Lupe Martínez
La Modesta	Decca 10404A	Los Madrugadores

Title	Label and no.	Artist
La Muerte de Juan Reyna	Columbia 4526-X	Cancioneros de Chihuahua
La Muerte de Obregón	Vocalion 8151	Cuadro México
La Muerte de Pancho Villa	Victor 77438-A	Alcides Briceño y Jorge Añez
La Piedrera	Victor 46392-A	Luis Hernández y Leonardo Sifuentes
La Punitiva	Victor 46437-A	Luis Hernández y Leonardo Sifuentes
La República en España	Columbia 4504-X	Guty y Añez
La Senaida	Decca 10071A	Montalbo y Berlanga
La Toma de Celaya	Columbia 3463-X	Hermanos Bañuelos
La Toma de Celaya	Brunswick 41169	Hermanos Bañuelos
La Toma de Jiménez	Victor 46391-A	Luis Hernández y Leonardo Sifuentes
La Toma de Jiménez	Universal 4106-A	Dúo Plá-Ruiz
La Toma de Matamoros	Brunswick 41281	Lara y Novelo
La Tragedia de Guty Cárdenas	Brunswick 41441	Dueto Ruffino
La Tragedia de Oklahoma	Columbia 4584-X	Ramos y Ortega
Las Casadas	Brunswick 41261	Guzmán y Hernández
Las Cuarenta Cartas	Victor 46994-A	Posada y Pérez
Las Huelguistas	Bluebird B-2451-A	Cuco Luevano y Luis Vera
Las Pajamas	Bluebird B-2251-A	Flores y San Román
Las Pizcas de Algodón	Vocalion 8438	Salas y Herrera
Las Posadas	Columbia 3690-X	Trovadores Tamaulipecos
Las Quejas de Zenaida	Decca 10191A	Flores y Valdez
Los Convictos de las Cruces	Vocalion 8445	Norverto González y José Rosales
Los Tacinques Vacilando	Brunswick 41319	Hernández y Flores
Los Temblores de Oaxaca	Victor 30317-A	Sifuentes y Guzmán
Los Temblores de Oaxaca	Brunswick 41287	Hermanos Bañuelos
Los Temblores en México	Columbia 4441-X	Hermanos Bañuelos
Máquina 501	Victor 30502-A	Sifuentes y Guzmán
Margarito El Tigre de Santiago	Brunswick 41260	González y San Miguel
Marijuana La Soldadera	Brunswick 40955	Hermanos Bañuelos
Memorias de Pancho Villa	Victor 30937-A	Estudiantina Mexicana
Mexicanos Que Van Para el Norte	Vocalion 8624	Hernández y Sifuentes
Monterrey	Vocalion 8409	Pedro Rocha y Lupe Martínez
Monterrey, Sultana del Norte	Okeh 16816	Cuarteto Monterrey
Muerte de Sidar	Columbia 4142-X	Hermanos Bañuelos
Muerte del Aviador Carranza	Victor 81485-A	Contreras y Carrillo
Nuevo Contrabando de San Antonio	Vocalion 8388	Salas y Herrera
Nuevo Corrido de Laredo	Melotone MS16084	Salas y Mendoza
Obregón	Columbia 3224-X	Cancioneros de Sonora
Ortiz Rubio	Vocalion 8325	La Bella Netty y Jesús Rodríguez

Title	Label and no.	Artist
Pablo Sidar	Columbia 3915-X	Cancioneros de Sonora
Pájaro Prisionero	Vocalion 8745	Hernández y Sifuentes
Pancho Villa y Carranza	Okeh 16646	Genaro Rodríguez y Juan Chávez
Poemas de Mi Patria	Vocalion 8740	Los Madrugadores
Poemas de Mi Patria	Columbia 4177-X	Hermanos San Miguel
Por Morfina y Cocaína	Bluebird B-2277-A	Manuel Valdez y Juan González
Radios y Chicanos	Columbia 4335-X	Roca y Amador
Rendición de Pancho Villa	Vocalion 8246	Lupe Martínez y Pedro Rocha
Rendición de Pancho Villa	Universal 4058-A	Dueto Chihuahuense
Severo Cruz	Vocalion 8625	Hernández y Sifuentes
Suicidio de Juan Reyna	Vocalion 8425	Nacho y Justino
Tampico Hermoso	Bluebird B-2438-A	Paz Flores y Bernardo San Román
Tragedia de Amado Garza	Decca 10195A	Hermanos Chavarría
Tragedia de Los Estudiantes	Victor 30493-A	T. Guizar y S. Espinal
Tragedia de Los Hermanos Carrillo Puerto	Victor 77788-A	Alcides Briceño y Jorge Añez
Tragedia de Miguel e Ignacia Ozada	Vocalion 8402	Pedro Rocha y Lupe Martínez
Tragedia de Nicaragua	Columbia 4503-X	Guty y Añez
Tragedia de Polanco	Bluebird B-3225-A	Asunción Romero y Manuel González
Tragedia del General Obregón	Victor 81486-A	Contreras y Carrillo
Un 16 de Septiembre	Vocalion 8251	José H. Bernal
Una Mala Mujer	Brunswick 41419	G. Guzmán y J. Rosales
Una Mañana de Enero	Vocalion 8930	L. Barcelata y M. Apodaca
Unión de Nueceros	Vocalion 8700	Leopoldo Cruz y Valentín Gutiérrez
Vera Cruz	Columbia 4621-X	Hermanos Chavarría
Viernes Santo	Decca 10287A	Los Madrugadores
Zenaida	Vocalion 8596	Los Madrugadores

Appendix J

Thirty Corridos that Define the Genre

These corridos were selected by Guillermo Hernández to illustrate particular attributes of the corrido genre (see appendix H). Most of the songs cited in his essay are included in the Frontera Collection, many in different versions, including the one shown in figure 66.

Figure 66. This recording of "Agustín Jaime," a well-known corrido, is by Ortíz y Maldonado with Dueto Abrego, a precursor to the famed duet Los Alegres de Terán of Eugenio Abrego and Tomás Ortíz. Early pre-Alegres material was released on the hard-to-find Orfeo label, which features an Orpheus figure and the English slogan "As Sonorous as His Lyre." The genre of this tune is listed on the label as "tragedia," a term often substituted for "corrido." Photograph courtesy of the Arhoolie Foundation.

Thirty Corridos that Define the Genre

Title	Quality or attribute
Agustín Jaime	Poetic structure
Arnulfo González	Courage as key quality
Arturo Garza Treviño	Local setting
Asesino a Sueldo	Arrogance as fatal flaw
Belén Galindo	Persecution by person in authority
Benjamín Argumedo	Farewell
Carga Blanca	Judgment against drug trafficking
Contrabando y Traición	Women as protagonists
El Contrabando de El Paso	Linguistic borrowings
El Cuartelazo	Martyrdom in defeat
El Moro de Cumpas	Competition
El Potro Lobo Gateado	Heroic horses
El Subteniente de Linares	Time and place
Gregorio Cortez	Moral authority
Heraclio Bernal	Evading pursuit by superior forces
Ignacio Parra	Challenge and defiance
Inez Chávez García	Satirizing the enemy
Jesús Leal	Female narrator
La Chiva Colgada	Expressing outrage
La Expedición Punitiva	Rhyme scheme and variations
La Inundación de California	The force of Mother Nature
La Toma de Matamoros	Commentary by composer
La Toma de Zacatecas	Virtue and villains
Lino Rodarte	Oral history
Reyes Ruiz	Fate
Rosita Alvírez	Poetic rhythm
Valente Quintero	Confrontation
Yurécuaro y Tanhuato	Humor and sarcasm
El Nuevo Corrido de Madero	The heroic protagonist
La Derrota de Villa en Celaya	Taking sides in a conflict

Appendix K

Forty Notable Mariachi Recordings

List Compiled by Jonathan Clark

The Frontera Collection tracks the development of the mariachi genre from the earliest days of studio recording through the 1950s. It is one of most important archives of recorded mariachi music in the world, making a large repository of early mariachi recordings accessible to the public. Jonathan Clark, a mariachi scholar and musician, picks his forty favorite mariachi tunes from the Frontera Collection (fig. 67).

Figure 67. Mariachi musician Juan Marmolejo in Mexico City during the early 1980s, celebrating the release of two LPs featuring the mariachi of his father, Cirilo Marmolejo. Juan is flanked here by author Jonathan Clark (*left*) and producer Chris Strachwitz, who compiled the albums from 78-rpm records now in the Frontera Collection. The younger Marmolejo appears as a boy, holding a vihuela, in the cover photo of the album held by Clark. Photograph courtesy of the Arhoolie Foundation

Forty Notable Mariachi Recordings

	Artist	Title	Label and no.	Comment
1	Cuarteto Coculense	La Malagueña	Columbia C-270	A highly unusual son, and one of the few recordings by this prototype mariachi where vestiges of the guitarrón can actually be heard.
2	Mariachi Coculense de Cirilo Marmolejo	El Camino Real	Victor 79413-B	The earliest recording of "Camino Real de Colima." The highly percussive vihuela strum resembles not only that of the huapango, but popular South American strum patterns as well.
3	Mariachi Tapatío de José Marmolejo	La Tierra del Mariachi	Victor 75795-A	Theme song from the 1938 film of the same name that features Mariachi Tapatío and Lucha Reyes.
4	Mariachi Tapatío de José Marmolejo	Jarabe Ranchero	ASP 101-B	A folkloric dance medley of great musical interest.
5	Mariachi Vargas de Tecalitlán	Mavi	Anfión 20-036-B	A rare recording of an older waltz seldom performed today. Recorded in Los Angeles by Mariachi Vargas in the mid-1940s.
6	Mariachi Vargas de Tecalitlán	La Pelusa	Victor 70-7759-A	Miguel Martínez's earliest recorded trumpet showpiece. This polka of German origin appears in Jorge Negrete's 1942 film *El Peñón de Las Ánimas*.
7	Mariachi Pulido	La Trompeta del Diablo	Peerless 4065	Dating from 1952, one of the earliest trumpet duet recordings by this group. It features trumpeters Miguel Martínez and Jesús Córdoba.
8	Mariachi Pulido	La Texanita	Peerless 3969	One of best-known compositions of Bonifacio Collazo, architect of the Mariachi México sound.
9	Mariachi México [de Pepe Villa]	Las Alteñitas	Musart M1154	One of Mariachi México's very first polka hits.
10	Mariachi México [de Pepe Villa]	Rosas de Mayo	Victor 23-6211	Miguel Martínez composed this popular instrumental at the end of his one-year tenure with Mariachi México, in late 1953.
11	Mariachi Perla de Occidente	Camino al Baño	Columbia 3042-C	Although this polka remains popular in certain regions, few recordings of it exist. This highly unusual recording features a trombone, in homage to group founder Marcelino Ortega Sr.
12	Mariachi [de] Miguel Díaz	Diez de Mayo	Peerless 3866	Among the earliest mariachi recordings to feature a trumpet duet, predating Mariachi Pulido's first two-trumpet recordings. Trumpeters are Miguel Martínez and Arcadio Elías.
13	Los Dos Palomos con el Mariachi Chapala	Los Guayabos	Azteca 5256	The duet of Ricardo González (high voice) and Heriberto Molina (low voice) in a canción ranchera full of double entendres.
14	Mariachi Los Abajeños	El Zopilote Mojado	Peerless 1927	One of the oldest and most traditional of the Mexican paso dobles.
15	Pepe Gutiérrez y sus Charros de Atotonilco	Los Arrierros	Victor 76526-B	Unusual lyrics, and a more complete version of this son than Mariachi Vargas ever recorded. Somewhat similar to the Mariachi México version of the same piece.
16	Hermanos Quintero con los Charros de Atotonilco	La Madrugada	Columbia 6179-X	The Quintero brothers were early members of Mariachi Vargas; they left to form Los Charros de Atotonilco. Rafael Quintero (high voice) and Jerónimo Quintero (low voice).
17	Mariachi Coculense "El Costeño"	Tierra Mía	Vocalion 9193	The corrido-like lyrics of this son chronicle the adventures of a mariachi from Jalisco in Los Angeles.
18	Mariachi Los Coyotes	El Mocho Lencho	Peerless 4039	This spirited recording of a traditional march popular in Jalisco features both a trumpet and a clarinet.

	Artist	Title	Label and no.	Comment
19	Mariachi Guadalajara [Los Angeles, CA]	Pueblo de Ameca	Master Music 313-A	While this remains a popular regional son, recordings of it are difficult to find.
20	Mariachi Guadalajara [Fresno, CA]	Carmen	Mexicanos 009	A classic waltz dating from the time of the Mexican Revolution.
21	Diego Villanueva and his Guadalajara Charros	Los Javalines	Trilón 157-B	A classic son also known as "El Jabalí."
22	Mariachi de Juan Güitrón	El Tesmo	Peerless 4508-B	A fine rendition of this seldom-heard son.
23	Mariachi de Mendoza	La Mujer de Chuchu	General 5005-A	An unusual early mariachi recording of a huapango.
24	Mariachi Reyes de Chapala	Arriba Jalisco	Tri-Color 584-B	This boisterous, irreverent medley by Pepe Guízar gives every member of the mariachi an opportunity to declaim a poetic verse.
25	Mariachi Reyes de Chapala	El Son de la Negra	Águila 5010-A	A version of this classic mariachi anthem that is quite distinct from what we are accustomed to hearing today. Similar to José Marmolejo's recording of this son.
26	Los Jumileros de Rafúl	Camioncito Flecha Roja	Bluebird B-3265-A	Original hit recording of this hit song, featuring an unusual regional variant of mariachi instrumentation.
27	Los Trovadores Tapatíos	El Petate	Victor 75194-B	Two important figures in mariachi music, Lucha Reyes and Pepe Gutiérrez, accompanied by the magnificent guitar of Antonio Bribiesca.
28	Ray y Laurita con los Charros de Ameca	Pajarillo	Bluebird 3521-A	The duet of Ray Pérez y Soto and Laurita Rivas sing on what was trumpeter Miguel Martínez's first recording session.
29	Pepe y Juanita con los Charros de Atotonilco	La Mula	Bluebird B-3365-B	Pepe Gutiérrez in duet with singing partner Juanita Escoto.
30	Martín y Malena con el Mariachi Vargas	Alma Llanera	Imperial 148-A	One of the earliest recordings of a Venezuelan joropo by a mariachi. Erroneously listed on the label as a corrido.
31	Hermanas Padilla con el Mariachi "Los Costeños"	El Bato Gacho	Columbia 1312-C	A aggressive, man-bashing ranchera atypical of lyrics of that period. This song was later made famous by Las Jilguerillas.
32	Hermanas Padilla con el Mariachi México de Pepe Villa	El Quelite	Columbia 3960	Note how the energetic two-trumpet sound of Mariachi México contrasts with that of previous recordings by the Padilla sisters.
33	Dueto Azteca con el Mariachi Chapala	Cantinas y Mujeres	Columbia 2857-C	Memo Quintero of Mariachi Vargas and María Padilla of Hermanas Padilla, in their famous vocal duet.
34	Jorge Negrete con el Mariachi Vargas de Tecalitlán	Amanecer Ranchero	Victor 70-7682-B	A lesser-known early hybrid arrangement by Manuel Esperón that anticipated later musical trends.
35	Pedro Infante con el Mariachi Tapatío Marmolejo	El Durazno	Peerless 2000	A classic ranchera from Pedro Infante's very first recording session for Peerless, in October 1943.
36	Miguel Aceves Mejía [con el Mariachi Vargas de Tecalitlán]	Oyes, Lupita	Victor 23-5141-B	This Silvestre Vargas composition is one of Aceves Mejía's earliest ranchera recordings.
37	Miguel Aceves Mejía con el Mariachi Vargas de Tecalitlán	A Buscar la Muerte	Victor 23-5531	A rare recording by Aceves Mejía of an obscure José Alfredo Jiménez composition.
38	José Alfredo Jiménez	Cuatro Primaveras	Columbia 3566-C	One of José Alfredo Jiménez's lesser-known treasures.
39	José Alfredo Jiménez	El Derrotado	Columbia 2273-C	An obscure ranchera recently revived by Vicente Fernández.
40	Lola Beltrán [con el Mariachi Vargas de Tecalitlán]	Tú Ya No Me Quieres	Peerless 5110	Lola and Mariachi Vargas in top form, with a brilliant trumpet performance by Miguel Martínez.

Notes

A Cultural Treasure

1. The terms *Mexican*, *Mexican American*, and *Latino* are used throughout the text in ways consistent with the context. In general, *Latina/o* is used sparingly as an umbrella term to describe anybody or anything from Latin America. More specific terms such as *Mexican*, *Peruvian*, *Cuban*, and so on, are used whenever the specific nationality or ethnic origin is known. The term *Mexican American* is used for people of Mexican descent living in the Unites States, as well as for their music and culture. However, given the constant interchange of people and ideas across the border, the distinction between *Mexican* and *Mexican American* can be fluid and blurred. Generally, *Mexican American* implies a certain degree of assimilation within US culture and society. For an in-depth discussion of the complexity of ethnic nomenclature, see Suzanne Oboler, *Ethnic Labels, Latino Lives: Identity and the Politics of (Re)Presentation in the United States* (Minneapolis: University of Minnesota Press, 1997).

2. The Frontera Collection can be accessed at http://frontera.library.ucla.edu/index.html. Because of copyright restrictions, recordings are fully accessible only from computers on the UCLA campus. Users that are off campus have access to metadata, images, and the first fifty seconds of the recording.

3. Tom Diamant, "Archiving the Arhoolie Foundation's Strachwitz Frontera Collection of Mexican and Mexican American Recordings" (paper presented at conference on "Sound Savings: Preserving Audio Collections," Harry Ransom Humanities Center, University of Texas, Austin, July 24–26, 2003), available on Association of Research Libraries website, http://www.arl.org/preserv/sound_savings_proceedings/Arhoolie-2.shtml.

About the Frontera Collection

1. Diamant, "Archiving the Arhoolie Foundation's Strachwitz Frontera Collection."

2. Ibid. Nowhere is this cross-cultural and cross-border interplay more apparent than in the genre of the narrative corrido, discussed at length in a later chapter. Indeed, the eminent border scholar Américo Paredes posits the concept of Greater Mexico, a social and cultural state that exists on both sides of the border, nourished by the interaction of ideas and by movement of people in both directions. For a comprehensive exposition of the concept, see Américo Paredes, *Folklore and Culture on the Texas-Mexican Border* (Austin: Center for Mexican American Studies, University of Texas, 1993). And for an analysis of how transborder culture is manifested in other fields, including literature, film, and even comedy, see David R. Maciel and María Herrera-Sobek, eds., *Culture across Borders: Mexican Immigration and Popular Culture* (Tucson: University of Arizona Press, 1998).

3. "The Collection," Strachwitz Frontera Collection of Mexican and Mexican American Recordings, UCLA Library, Digital Collections, http://frontera.library.ucla.edu/collection.html.

4. The Frontera Collection contains an extensive sample of banda music, in the broadest sense of the term. It includes an early 1950s 78-rpm version of "El Sinaloense," written by Severiano Briseño and performed in classical banda fashion by the Banda Sinaloense de Mazatlán (Peerless 4510B) and by Los Guamuchileños de Culiacan (Columbia 3030-C). Today the song is considered a classic of the genre, with seven versions in the archives so far, some transposed to mariachi accompaniment. Contemporary banda music is generally associated with the popular style of brass and percussion groups from the state of Sinaloa. But the genre is not limited to that western state, or even to northern Mexico, for that matter. The related style known as "tamborazo" is associated with the north-central state of Zacatecas and is represented in the Frontera Collection by Genaro Codina's "La Marcha de Zacatecas," a quintessential example of the genre. Among the versions of the rousing march is one by the Banda Especial de la Guarnición de México, typical of the military and police brass bands that were quite popular in the nineteenth and twentieth centuries. These military bands, of which the collection has many fine examples, are considered precursors to the civilian musical groups that came to be known as banda.

5. Diamant, "Archiving the Arhoolie Foundation's Strachwitz Frontera Collection."

Chris Strachwitz

1. Chris Strachwitz, telephone interview by Agustin Gurza for the *Los Angeles Times*, January 2005. For the article based on the interview, see Agustin Gurza, "In a Mexico Groove: Arhoolie Records' Owner Will Share His Vast Collection via a UCLA Project," *Los Angeles Times*, February 5, 2005, Calendar sec.

2. Chris Strachwitz, liner notes to *Arhoolie Records 40th Anniversary Collection: The Journey of Chris*

Strachwitz, 1960–2000 (El Cerrito, CA: Arhoolie, 2000), CD box set.

3. Senator Newlands, whose Reno mansion is now a National Historic Landmark, married Clara Adelaide Sharon, the daughter of another Nevada politician and Wild West pioneer named Senator William Sharon. Strachwitz's great-great-grandfather was a banker, stock speculator, and alleged scoundrel whose exploits in silver mining are documented in the biography *The Infamous King of the Comstock: William Sharon and the Gilded Age in the West*, by Michael J. Makley (Reno: University of Nevada Press, 2006).

4. Elijah Wald, liner notes to *Arhoolie Records 40th Anniversary Collection: The Journey of Chris Strachwitz, 1960–2000* (El Cerrito, CA: Arhoolie, 2000), CD box set.

5. Chris Strachwitz, telephone interview by Agustin Gurza for the *Los Angeles Times*, January 2005.

6. Ibid.

7. Wald, liner notes to *Arhoolie Records 40th Anniversary Collection.*

8. Chris Strachwitz, telephone interview by Agustin Gurza for the *Los Angeles Times*, January 2005.

9. Ibid.

10. Wald, liner notes to *Arhoolie Records 40th Anniversary Collection.*

11. Ibid.

12. Chris Strachwitz, telephone interview by Agustin Gurza for the *Los Angeles Times*, January 2005.

13. Ibid.

14. Larry Benicewicz, "Chris Strachwitz and the Arhoolie Story," *BluesART Journal*, BluesArtStudio, November 29, 2010, http://www.bluesart.at/NeueSeiten/pageA54.html.

15. Ibid.

16. "Q&A with Chris Strachwitz," GlobalVillageIdiot (UK, site discontinued).

17. Al Reiss, "Contagious Enthusiasm: Talking with Arhoolie Records' Chris Strachwitz," *Dirty Linen*, August/September 1996.

18. Chris Strachwitz, telephone interview by Agustin Gurza for the *Los Angeles Times*, January 2005.

19. Michael Fox, "Simon and Gosling Play Strachwitz's Tunes," Sf360.org, San Francisco Film Society, September 23, 2009, http://www.sf360.org/Articles/In-Production/?pageid=12458.

20. Larry Rohter, "Still the Address of Down-Home Sounds," *New York Times*, November 24, 2010.

21. Chris Strachwitz, interview by Agustin Gurza, El Cerrito, CA, January 14, 2009.

Story of the Frontera Collection

1. *El Mundo del Corrido de Guillermo Hernández*, ed. Maureen Gosling (Arhoolie Foundation, 2008), DVD.

2. Ibid.

3. Ibid.

4. Chris Strachwitz, interview by Agustin Gurza, January 14, 2009.

5. Ibid.

6. Joel Selvin, "Music Man," *San Francisco Chronicle*, January 13, 2008.

7. Chris Strachwitz, interview by Agustin Gurza, January 14, 2009.

8. Chris Strachwitz, telephone interview by Agustin Gurza for the *Los Angeles Times*, January 2005.

9. Chris Strachwitz, interview by Agustin Gurza, January 14, 2009.

10. Wald, liner notes to *Arhoolie Records 40th Anniversary Collection.*

11. Chris Strachwitz, telephone interview by Agustin Gurza for the *Los Angeles Times*, January 2005.

12. Ibid.

13. "The History of Arhoolie Records by founder and president, Chris Strachwitz," in "About Us" on the Arhoolie Records website, http://www.arhoolie.com/about-us.html?sl=EN.

14. *The Jaxyson Records Story*, CD produced, compiled and annotated by Opal Louis Nations (PID, 2008).

15. Strachwitz, liner notes to *Arhoolie Records 40th Anniversary Collection.*

16. "Q&A with Chris Strachwitz," GlobalVillageIdiot (UK, site discontinued).

17. Barbara Schultz, "Arhoolie Records' Chris Strachwitz," *Mix Magazine*, August 1, 2002, http://mixonline.com/recording/interviews/audio_arhoolie_records_chris/.

18. Selvin, "Music Man."

A Century of Corridos

1. Guillermo E. Hernández, "What Is a Corrido? Thematic Representation and Narrative Discourse," *Studies in Latin American Popular Culture* 18 (1999). Reprinted in this volume as appendix H.

2. Generally, record labels used their own criteria to identify songs they considered to be corridos. Those criteria did not always match the definition used by scholars and other experts to decide what constitutes a true corrido. Thus, as Strachwitz notes, sometimes songs are identified on the record labels as corridos when they are actually just standard love songs. In many postwar cases a corrido is simply identified as a "ranchera," as with "Los Rinches de Texas" on ORO Records. Also, labels sometimes used alternative terms to identify corridos, such as "tragedias." Finally, the record companies did not always include a genre description on every label; this is especially true on more recent discs. If a label has no

identified genre, that category is left blank in the song's metadata file within the Frontera online archive.

3. The UCLA database identifies a genre or style for a musical piece only when one is specifically printed on the record label itself, yielding a vast variety of distinct genres and subgenres. In some cases a simple descriptive term on a label, such as "comedic dialog," is listed as a separate genre. For further discussion of the process of categorizing the archive, see appendix F.

4. James Nicolopulos, "Reversing Polarities: Corridos, Fronteras, Technology, and Counterdiscourses," in *Reflexiones 1998: New Directions in Mexican American Studies*, ed. Yolanda C. Padilla (Austin: Center for Mexican American Studies, University of Texas, 1999), 23. Nicolopulos died in 2010.

5. The *Corridos sin Fronteras* website is at http://www.corridos.org/.

6. Guillermo E. Hernández, "Discovering the Tradition of Corridos—as Far Back as the 17th Century" (presentation at seminar on "The Latinization of Art & Culture in America: Understanding Its Impact and Why It Matters," Western Knight Center for Specialized Journalism, Los Angeles, October 19, 2005), http://www.wkconline.org/index.php/seminars/speakerpage/?sid=1584&seminarid=94.

7. Vicente T. Mendoza, *El romance español y el corrido mexicano* (Mexico City: Universidad Nacional Autónoma de México, 1939); *El corrido mexicano* (Mexico City: Fondo de Cultura Económica, 1954); *Lírica narrativa de México: El corrido* (Mexico City: Universidad Nacional Autónoma de México, Instituto de Investigaciones Estéticas, 1964).

8. Nicolopulos, "Reversing Polarities," 23.

9. Hernández, "Discovering the Tradition of the Corridos."

10. Américo Paredes, "The Ancestry of Mexico's Corridos: A Matter of Definitions," *Journal of American Folklore* 76, no. 301: 231–35.

11. Richard Bauman, introduction to *Folklore and Culture on the Texas-Mexican Border*, by Américo Paredes (Austin: Center for Mexican American Studies, University of Texas, 1995), xvii.

12. Américo Paredes, "The Mexican *Corrido*: Its Rise and Fall," chap. 6 in *Folklore and Culture on the Texas-Mexican Border*, 140.

13. "Cortina, Juan Nepomuceno," in *Handbook of Texas Online*, Texas State Historical Association, http://www.tshaonline.org/handbook/online/articles/CC/fco73.html.

14. Paredes, *Folklore and Culture on the Texas-Mexican Border*, 140.

15. Manuel Peña, foreword to *A Texas-Mexican Cancionero: Folksongs of the Lower Border*, by Américo Paredes (Austin: University of Texas Press, 1995), xxix.

16. Manuel Peña, "Música fronteriza/Border Music," *Aztlán: A Journal of Chicano Studies* 21, nos. 1–2 (1992–96): 191–225.

17. Shelley Streeby, *American Sensations: Class, Empire, and the Production of Popular Culture* (Berkeley: University of California Press, 2002), 282.

18. Ibid., 279.

19. Peña, "Música fronteriza / Border Music."

20. Américo Paredes, *"With His Pistol in His Hand": A Border Ballad and Its Hero* (Austin: University of Texas Press, 1958).

21. Chris Strachwitz, interview by Agustin Gurza, January 14, 2009.

22. Nicolopulos, "Reversing Polarities," 30–32.

23. Ibid., 35.

24. Chris Strachwitz, interview by Agustin Gurza, January 14, 2009.

25. Edward Larocque Tinker, *Corridos & Calaveras* (Austin: University of Texas Press, 1961), 7.

26. José Eduardo Limón, *Mexican Ballads, Chicano Poems: History and Influence in Mexican-American Social Poetry* (Berkeley: University of California Press, 1992), 16.

27. Chris Strachwitz, telephone interview by Agustin Gurza for the *Los Angeles Times*, January 2005.

28. For a comprehensive, firsthand account of the contemporary narcocorrido and its composers and interpreters, see Elijah Wald, *Narcocorrido: A Journey into the Music of Drugs, Guns, and Guerrillas* (New York: Harper Collins, 2001).

29. James Nicolopulos, liner notes to *The Roots of the Narcocorrido*, Arhoolie CD 7053 (El Cerrito, CA: Arhoolie, 2004).

30. Guillermo E. Hernández, "En busca del autor de 'El contrabando de El Paso," *Aztlán: A Journal of Chicano Studies* 30, no. 2 (2005): 139–56.

31. Chris Strachwitz, telephone interview by Agustin Gurza for the *Los Angeles Times*, January 2005.

32. Nicolopulos, "Reversing Polarities," 37.

33. Edward J. Escobar, *Race, Police, and the Making of a Political Identity: Mexican Americans and the Los Angeles Police Department, 1900–1945* (Berkeley: University of California Press, 1999), 140–41.

34. Luis Miguel Gómez Garrido, "Una versión del romance de Delgadina tradicional en la Vega de Santa María (Ávila)," *Culturas Populares: Revista Electrónica* 4 (January–June 2007), http://www.culturaspopulares.org/textos4/articulos/gomezgarrido.htm.

35. Emma Pérez, *The Decolonial Imaginary: Writing Chicanas into History* (Bloomington: Indiana University Press, 1999), 102.

36. Ibid., 115.

37. Hernández, "En busca del autor de 'El contrabando de El Paso,'" 153. Translation mine.

38. All quotations from Hernández in this section of the chapter are from "What Is a Corrido?," which is reprinted in this volume as appendix H.

39. Trovadores Regionales was the name used by Pedro Rocha and Lupe Martínez, a popular duo from San Antonio who were *corridistas*, or interpreters of corridos. The Strachwitz Frontera Collection has since acquired a copy of this record in better playing condition, but that version has not yet been added to the UCLA database.

40. Chris Strachwitz, notes on the manuscript of this book, November 6, 2011.

41. As of this writing, the Tigres versions had not been uploaded to the UCLA Frontera Collection database.

42. Nicolopulos, "Reversing Polarities," 33.

43. Strachwitz, notes on the manuscript of this book, November 6, 2011.

44. In addition to the Trío Nava recording on the UCLA website, the complete Frontera archive maintained by the Arhoolie Foundation shows a total of eleven releases of this corrido by six different artists: Los Alegres de Terán, Los Broncos de Reynosa, Chalino Sanchez, Pedro de Lara, Los Rieleros del Norte, and Beto Quintanilla. They include two on 45s, four on LPs, three on cassettes, and one on an Arhoolie compilation CD, *The Mexican Revolution*, compiled and annotated by Guillermo Hernández in 1996.

45. Chris Strachwitz, notes on the manuscript of this book, November 6, 2011.

Transcending Machismo

1. See "Entrevista Inédita con Carlos Monsiváis," by Alfonso Quiñones, DiarioLibre.com, June 22, 2010, http://aquinones.diariolibre.com/?p=155.

2. Vicente T. Mendoza, "El machismo en México al través de las canciones, corridos y cantares," *Cuadernos del Instituto Nacional de Antropología* (Buenos Aires) 3 (1962): 75.

3. Américo Paredes, "The United States, Mexico, and *Machismo*," in *Perspectives on Las Américas: A Reader in Culture, History, and Representation*, ed. Matthew C. Gutmann, Félix V. Matos Rodríguez, Lynn Stephen, and Patricia Zavella (Malden, MA: Blackwell, 2003), 329–41.

4. Ibid., 332.

5. Ibid., 333.

6. Felipe Montemayor, "Postemio Antropológico," in *Picardía Mexicana*, ed. A. Jiménez (Mexico City: Libro Mex, 1960), 229–30. Translated and quoted in Paredes, "The United States, Mexico, and *Machismo*," 329.

7. Carolina Acosta-Alzuru, "Telenovelas, Boleros, Tangos and Rancheras," *Telenovelas* (blog), August 24, 2008, http://telenovelas-carolina.blogspot.com/2008/08/telnovelas-boleros-tangos-and-rancheras.html.

8. Consuelo "Chelo" Silva (1922–88) was one of the few Mexican American artists from the border region to achieve international success on a par with such Mexican superstars as Javier Solís and Lola Beltrán. The Brownsville, Texas, native got her first break in show business in 1939 when she was invited to sing on a hometown radio program hosted by Américo Paredes, the author, poet, and composer who would become her husband. (The couple later divorced.) In 1952, at age thirty, Silva made her first recording for Discos Falcon of McAllen, Texas, marking the start of a prolific studio career that also included a successful stint with Columbia Records. The singer, known as La Reina del Bolero, is featured on 360 titles in the Frontera Collection, ranking no. 6 on the list of artists with the most recordings in the archive (see appendix E). See also Juan Carlos Rodríguez, "Silva, Consuelo [Chelo]," *Handbook of Texas Online*, Texas State Historical Association, http://www.tshaonline.org/handbook/online/articles/fsind.

9. There are four other versions of this song in the collection, all on 78-rpm discs. But this is the only version with these unusual lyrics. The other four have the same melody and the same opening line, but they continue with standard or even clichéd romantic lyrics about love and women.

Gringos, Chinos, and Pochos

1. For a comprehensive analysis of racial attitudes toward blacks in Latin America and the impact of the growing presence of Afro-Latinos in the United States, see Anani Dzidzienyo and Suzanne Oboler, eds., *Neither Enemies nor Friends: Latinos, Blacks, Afro-Latinos* (New York: Palgrave Macmillan, 2005).

2. The roots of war and ethnic conflict between the two nations can be traced to the 1835 Texas War of Independence against Mexico, led by Anglo immigrants who had been allowed to settle there and later revolted. See David Montejano, *Anglos and Mexicans in the Making of Texas, 1836–1986* (Austin: University of Texas Press, 2006).

3. Thomas R. Hietala, *Manifest Design: American Exceptionalism and Empire* (Ithaca, NY: Cornell University Press, 2003), 156.

4. Guillermo E. Hernández, "Las características cómicas del pocho y del pachuco: Sus antecedentes literarios y populares," article presented under the auspices of the Faculty Senate Research Committee, University of California, Los Angeles, http://www.chicano.ucla.edu/center/events/caracter.html. It is based on an earlier, shorter version delivered to the "Simposio sobre literatura mesoamericana y chicana en honor al Dr. Luis Leal," Monterrey, Nuevo León, Mexico, November 6–9, 1985.

5. For an in-depth historical study of the multiple manifestations of La Malinche as represented in texts since the colonial period, see Sandra Messinger Cypess, *La Malinche in Mexican Literature: From History to Myth* (Austin: University of Texas Press, 1991).

6. Peña, "Música Fronteriza / Border Music."

7. Américo Paredes, "The Anglo-American in Mexican Folklore," in *New Voices in American Studies*, ed. Ray Browne (Lafayette, IN: Purdue University Press, 1966), 115.

8. Chris Strachwitz, telephone interview by Agustin Gurza, November 2008.

9. Gustavo Arellano, "¡Ask a Mexican!" *OC Weekly* (Orange County, CA), March 24, 2005, http://www.ocweekly.com/2005-03-24/columns/ask-a-mexican/.

10. For a historical look at the mass migration of Chinese to Mexico in the decades following passage in the United States of the Chinese Exclusion Act of 1882, see Robert Chao Romero, *The Chinese in Mexico, 1882–1940* (Tucson: University of Arizona Press, 2010).

11. Hernández, "Las características cómicas del pocho y del pachuco."

12. Peter Clair Haney, "Carpa y Teatro, Sol y Sombra: Show Business and Public Culture in San Antonio's Mexican Colony, 1900–1940" (PhD diss., University of Texas, Austin, 2004).

13. Hernández, "Las características cómicas del pocho y del pachuco."

El Mariachi

1. See Jesús Jáuregui, *El mariachi: Símbolo musical de México* (Mexico City: Santillana Ediciones, 2007), 104; Jonathan Clark, "Mariachi Tapatío de José Marmolejo, el Auténtico," liner notes to *Mexico's Pioneer Mariachis, Vol. 2: Mariachi Tapatío de José Marmolejo*, Arhoolie/Folklyric CD 7012 (El Cerrito, CA: Arhoolie, 1994).

2. See Hermes Rafael, *Origen e historia del mariachi* (Mexico City: Editorial Katún, 1982), 123; Jonathan Clark, "Mariachi Vargas de Tecalitlán," liner notes to *Mexico's Pioneer Mariachis, Vol. 3: Mariachi Vargas de Tecalitlán*, Arhoolie/Folklyric CD 7015 (El Cerrito, CA: Arhoolie, 1992).

3. Rafael Méndez Moreno, *Apuntes sobre el pasado de mi tierra* (Mexico City: Costa Ámic, 1961), 130–33.

4. Arhoolie CD 7036 includes almost all the sones recorded by Cuarteto Coculense.

5. Miguel Martínez plays on most of the Peerless recordings by Trío Guayacán. He is also featured on certain songs with Hermanos Martínez Gil, Gregorio Sierra, Los Panchos, and others.

6. Emilio García Riera, *Breve historia del cine mexicano* (Mexico City: Instituto Mexicano de Cinematografía, 1988), 210.

7. For further reading, see Daniel Sheehy, *Mariachi Music in America: Experiencing Music, Expressing Culture* (New York: Oxford University Press, 2006).

Los Tigres del Norte

1. All quotes attributed to Jorge Hernández in this chapter come from an unpublished interview conducted by Agustin Gurza at the offices of Los Tigres del Norte, San Jose, CA, August 19, 2009.

2. Chuy Varela, "Hear Los Tigres Roar," *San Francisco Chronicle*, November 5, 2006, PK-20.

3. Chris Strachwitz, interview by Agustin Gurza, El Cerrito, CA, July 2009.

Guide to the Strachwitz Frontera Collection of Mexican and Mexican American Recordings

Lizette Guerra

Archive:	UCLA Chicano Studies Research Center Library
Collection Number:	128
Inclusive Dates:	Approximately 1905–1999
Extent:	Approximately 63,212 sound recordings
Creator:	Chris Strachwitz
Provenance:	The Arhoolie Foundation
Physical Location of Sound Recordings:	Arhoolie Records, El Cerrito, California
Location of Digitized Files:	UCLA Digital Library
	http://frontera.library.ucla.edu/index.html
Restrictions on Use and Reproduction:	Copyright has not been assigned to the UCLA Chicano Studies Research Center nor the UCLA Library. Some of the digitized printed ephemera and many, if not all, of the websites in the collection and elements incorporated into the websites are protected by the U.S. Copyright Law (Title 17, U.S.C.). The materials may also be subject to publicity rights, privacy rights, or other legal interests. Transmission or reproduction of materials protected by copyright beyond that allowed by fair use requires the written permission of the copyright owners.
Access:	Due to copyright restrictions the digital collection is only fully accessible from computers on the UCLA campus. Users that are off campus have full access to the metadata, the images of the labels, and a fifty-second sample from the beginning of each recording.
Related Materials:	Arhoolie Foundation Projects:
	The Arhoolie Encyclopedia
	Frontera Collection Image Archive
	Documenting and Cataloging the Mexican Peerless Label
	http://www.arhoolie.org/

Anthony Beltramo Collection of Cancioneros
UCLA Chicano Studies Research Center Library and Archive
Mexican Sheet Music Collection, 1920–1936
University of New Mexico Center for Southwest Research
Encyclopedic Discography of Victor Recordings
University of California, Santa Barbara Libraries
http://victor.library.ucsb.edu
Border Cultures: Conjunto Music
The University of Texas at Austin
http://www.lib.utexas.edu/benson/border/index.html

Contact: Lizette Guerra or Michael Stone
UCLA Chicano Studies Research Center
193 Haines Hall
Box 951544
Los Angeles, CA 90095-1544
www.chicano.ucla.edu
(310) 206-6052 /
(310) 825-0648
lguerra@chicano.ucla.edu
mstoneic@ucla.edu

Scope and Content

The Arhoolie Foundation's Strachwitz Frontera Collection of commercially produced Mexican and Mexican American sound recordings is the largest repository of Mexican and Mexican American vernacular sound recordings in existence. Although Mexican and Mexican American music comprises the majority of the Frontera Collection, it also includes many notable samples of other popular Latin music styles from several countries throughout the Spanish American world. Despite the global origins of the music, most of the recordings in the Frontera Collection were made in the United States on domestic record labels, large and small. The collection can be divided into three distinct eras in Mexican and Mexican American recording history. The first era represents the first half of the twentieth century and is comprised of 33,472 individual performances on 78-rpm discs, including the first corridos ever recorded. The second is comprised of 25,090 45-rpm records representing some 50,000 performances from the mid-1950s to the 1990s. Many of the 45s were produced by small regional record labels serving the burgeoning immigrant community along the border. The last section contains approximately 4,000 albums (33⅓-rpm long-play recordings) and 650 cassette tapes from around 1955 to 1990. Because of the depth and breadth of these three sections, the Strachwitz Frontera Collection is unique and irreplaceable.

Navigating the Collection on the UCLA Digital Library

Browse Function

Researchers are able to browse the collection by:

Title
Label
Genre
Subject
Name
Performer
Composer

Each list is organized alphabetically.

Advance Search Function

Researchers are able to search the collection by using any or all of the following search functions:

Keyword
Composer
Performer
Title
Subject
Label
Genre
Format

Subject and keywords searches may be done in either English or Spanish.

Alphabetical lists are available for each of the above categories within the browse function. These lists will help researchers narrow their search.

Selected Bibliography

Benicewicz, Larry. "Chris Strachwitz and the Arhoolie Story." *BluesART Journal*, BluesArtStudio, November 29, 2010. http://www.bluesart.at/NeueSeiten/pageA54.html.

Benson Latin American Collection, University of Texas at Austin. "Border Cultures: *Conjunto* Music." http://www.lib.utexas.edu/benson/border/index.html.

Clark, Jonathan. "Mariachi Tapatío de José Marmolejo, el Auténtico." Liner notes to *Mexico's Pioneer Mariachis, Vol. 2: Mariachi Tapatío de José Marmolejo.* Arhoolie/Folklyric CD 7012. El Cerrito, CA: Arhoolie, 1994.

———. "Mariachi Vargas de Tecalitlán." Liner notes to *Mexico's Pioneer Mariachis, Vol. 3: Mariachi Vargas de Tecalitlán.* Arhoolie/Folklyric CD 7015. El Cerrito, CA: Arhoolie, 1992.

Corridos Sin Fronteras: A New World Ballad Tradition. Smithsonian Institution Traveling Exhibition Service and Smithsonian Center for Latino Initiatives. http://www.corridos.org/.

Cypess, Sandra Messinger. *La Malinche in Mexican Literature: From History to Myth.* Austin: University of Texas Press, 1991.

Dzidzienyo, Anani, and Suzanne Oboler, eds. *Neither Enemies nor Friends: Latinos, Blacks, Afro Latinos.* New York: Palgrave Macmillan, 2005.

Escobar, Edward J. *Race, Police, and the Making of a Political Identity: Mexican Americans and the Los Angeles Police Department, 1900–1945.* Berkeley: University of California Press, 1999.

Fox, Michael. "Simon and Gosling Play Strachwitz's Tunes." SF360. org, San Francisco Film Society, September 23, 2009. http://www.sf360.org/Articles/In-Production/?pageid=12458.

Gómez Garrido, Luis Miguel. "Una versión del romance de Delgadina tradicional en la Vega de Santa María (Ávila)." *Culturas Populares: Revista Electrónica* 4 (January–June 2007). http://www.culturaspopulares.org/textos4/articulos/gomezgarrido.pdf.

Gurza, Agustin. "In a Mexico Groove: Arhoolie Records' Owner Will Share His Vast Collection via a UCLA Project." *Los Angeles Times*, February 1, 2005.

Haney, Peter Clair. "Carpa y Teatro, Sol y Sombra: Show Business and Public Culture in San Antonio's Mexican Colony, 1900–1940." PhD diss., University of Texas, Austin, 2004.

Hernández, Guillermo E. "En busca del autor de el contrabando de El Paso." *Aztlán: A Journal of Chicano Studies* 30, no. 2 (Fall 2005): 139–56.

———. "Las características cómicas del pocho y del pachuco: Sus antecedentes literarios y populares." *Nuevo Texto Crítico* (Stanford University) 2, no. 3 (1989): 171–81.

———. "What Is a Corrido? Thematic Representation and Narrative Discourse." *Studies in Latin American Popular Culture* 18 (1999): 69.

Hietala, Thomas R. *Manifest Design: American Exceptionalism and Empire.* Ithaca, NY: Cornell University Press, 2003.

Jáuregui, Jesús. *El mariachi: Símbolo musical de México.* Mexico City: Santillana Ediciones, 2007.

Limón, José E. *Mexican Ballads, Chicano Poems: History and Influence in Mexican-American*

Social Poetry. Berkeley: University of California Press, 1992.

Maciel, David R., and María Herrera-Sobek, eds. *Culture across Borders: Mexican Immigration and Popular Culture*. Tucson: University of Arizona Press, 1998.

Makley, Michael J. *The Infamous King of the Comstock: William Sharon and the Gilded Age in the West*. Reno: University of Nevada Press, 2006.

Mendoza, Vicente T. "El machismo en México a través de las canciones, corridos y cantares." *Cuadernos del Instituto Nacional de Antropología* (Buenos Aires) 3 (1962): 75.

————. *El romance español y el corrido mexicano: Estudio comparativo*. Mexico City: Universidad Nacional Autónoma de México, 1939.

————. *Lírica narrativa de México: El corrido*. Mexico City: Universidad Nacional Autónoma de México, Instituto de Investigaciones Estéticas, 1964.

Montejano, David. *Anglos and Mexicans in the Making of Texas, 1836–1986*. Austin: University of Texas Press, 1987.

Montemayor, Felipe. "Postemio Antropológico." In *Picardía Mexicana*, ed. A. Jiménez, 229–30. Mexico City: Libro Mex, 1960.

Nicolopulos, James. Liner notes to *The Roots of the Narcocorrido*. Arhoolie CD 7053. El Cerrito, CA: Arhoolie, 2004.

————. "Reversing Polarities: *Corridos, Fronteras*, Technology, and Counterdiscourses." In *Reflexiones 1998: New Directions in Mexican American Studies*, 21–44. Austin: Center for Mexican American Studies, University of Texas, 1999.

Paredes, Américo. "The Ancestry of Mexico's Corridos: A Matter of Definitions." *Journal of American Folklore* 76, no. 301 (July–September 1963): 231–35.

————. *Folklore and Culture on the Texas-Mexican Border*. Edited and with an introduction by Richard Bauman. Austin: Center for Mexican American Studies, University of Texas, 1995.

————. *A Texas-Mexican Cancionero: Folksongs of the Lower Border*. Austin: University of Texas Press, 1995.

————. *"With His Pistol in His Hand": A Border Ballad and Its Hero*. Austin: University of Texas Press, 1958.

Peña, Manuel. "Música fronteriza / Border Music." *Aztlán: A Journal of Chicano Studies* 21, nos. 1–2 (1992–96): 191–225.

Pérez, Emma. *The Decolonial Imaginary: Writing Chicanas into History*. Bloomington: Indiana University Press, 1999.

Rafael, Hermes. *Origen e historia del mariachi*. Mexico City: Editorial Katún, 1982.

Rohter, Larry. "Still the Address of Down-Home Sounds." *New York Times*, November 24, 2010.

Romero, Robert C. *The Chinese in Mexico, 1882–1940*. Tucson: University of Arizona Press, 2010.

Sheehy, Daniel E. *Mariachi Music in America: Experiencing Music, Expressing Culture*. New York: Oxford University Press, 2005.

Strachwitz, Chris. Liner notes to *Arhoolie Records 40th Anniversary Collection: The Journey of Chris Strachwitz, 1960–2000*. CD box set. El Cerrito, CA: Arhoolie, 2000.

Streeby, Shelley. *American Sensations: Class, Empire, and the Production of Popular Culture*. Berkeley: University of California Press, 2002.

Wald, Elijah. Liner notes to *Arhoolie Records 40th Anniversary Collection: The Journey of Chris Strachwitz, 1960–2000*. CD box set. El Cerrito, CA: Arhoolie, 2000.

————. *Narcocorrido: A Journey into the Music of Drugs, Guns, and Guerrillas*. New York, NY: Rayo, 2001.

Sponsoring Organizations

UCLA Chicano Studies Research Center

www.chicano.ucla.edu
The CSRC promotes diverse participation across the campus and the community, providing a vital point of access to the university through its research, press, library, archive, and programming and collaborations with civic leaders, community-based groups, other public institutions, and international programs. The CSRC Library houses over 125 archival and manuscript collections totaling more than 3,000 linear feet of historical material. Generous support for the CSRC's many archival projects comes from the Ford Foundation, the Getty Foundation, the Haynes Foundation, and the Los Tigres del Norte Foundation.

The Strachwitz Frontera Collection of Mexican and Mexican American Recordings

http://frontera.library.ucla.edu/index.html
The project is sponsored by Los Tigres del Norte Fund at UCLA and the UCLA Chicano Studies Research Center (CSRC), in collaboration with the Fund for Folk Culture. Additional funding has been provided by Arhoolie Records, the UCLA Library, the National Endowment for the Humanities, the National Endowment for the Arts, the GRAMMY Foundation, Lucasfilm Foundation, and others.
Director: Chris Strachwitz
Project manager: Tom Diamant

Audio digitizing: Antonio Cuéllar, Alberto Cuéllar, Jim Nicolopulos
Label scanning and database update: Antonio Cuéllar, Alberto Cuéllar, Jim Nicolopulos, Karla Martinez, Tom Diamant, Mauro Garcia
Database entry: Chris Strachwitz, Lyuba Birinbaum, Karla Martínez, Antonio Cuéllar, Alberto Cuéllar, Jim Nicolopulos, Emmanuel Martínez, Juana Garcia, Graciela Blum
Development: John Leopold
Audio digitizing consultant: Advanced Systems Group, Emeryville, California

UCLA Digital Library

http://digital2.library.ucla.edu/
The UCLA Digital Library Program serves as the catalyst for the creation, management, and delivery of digital content in support of the UCLA Library's mission and goals. The program provides for the storage and dissemination of digital objects, including text, images, audio, and video in their various digital manifestations and combinations. The UCLA Library provides a Web presence for digital collections and provides storage, backup, and digital preservation support for all digital content accepted into, or developed by, the library.
Project coordination: Stephen Davison, Lynn DeLacy, Gordon Theil
Programming and website design: Curtis Fornadley, Darrow Cole, Howard Batchelor
Data management and editing: Lynn DeLacy, Samuel Vasquez, Carmen Doane, Hannah Walker, Silvia Mariscal
Audio management: Lynn DeLacy, Timothy Edwards

The Arhoolie Foundation

http://www.arhoolie.org/

The Arhoolie Foundation was established to preserve and promote regional or vernacular music created in the United States. It not only owns an immense collection of records but also assists in producing film documentaries, exhibits, live presentations, and academic research to strengthen America's musical traditions for generations to come. Its Frontera Collection provides access to a rich vernacular music tradition and a window into Mexican American popular culture. Founder and president Chris Strachwitz and a distinguished board of directors from diverse disciplines formed the Arhoolie Foundation in 1995. Once the collection is digitized, the Arhoolie Foundation will develop programs to introduce these recordings into US classrooms.

Los Tigres del Norte Foundation

http://lostigresdelnortefoundation.org/

Los Tigres del Norte decided to institutionalize their charitable efforts with the creation of Los Tigres del Norte Foundation in March 2000. With initial funding provided by the members of the group and the band's record label, Fonovisa, the foundation contributes to worthy nonprofit organizations that further the appreciation and understanding of Hispanic music, culture, and history through education and community outreach programs. The foundation was recognized by *Billboard* magazine for its work and commitment to educational outreach in communities throughout the United States.

Los Tigres del Norte Fund at UCLA

http://frontera.library.ucla.edu/lostigresfund .html

Not content to let their contribution stand in the realm of music alone, Los Tigres del Norte decided to establish a fund at the UCLA Chicano Studies Research Center on April 19, 2000, with a $500,000 donation. The first of its kind, the Los Tigres del Norte Fund at UCLA supports research, acquisition, documentation, dissemination, and presentation of authentic traditional and folk musical traditions in Spanish. Never before has an institution of higher education received such a sizeable gift from a community group to promote the study of cultural traditions. Through the fund's support, students and faculty have the opportunity to conduct important folk music research in such disciplines as ethnomusicology, literature, history, psychology, sociology, folklore, political science, world cultures, and the arts. The generosity of Los Tigres del Norte has enabled the CSRC to begin creating a premier cultural center.

The GRAMMY Foundation

http://www.grammy.org/grammy-foundation

The GRAMMY Foundation was established in 1989 to cultivate the understanding, appreciation, and advancement of the contribution of recorded music to American culture—from the artistic and technical legends of the past to the still unimagined musical breakthroughs of future generations of music professionals. The foundation accomplishes this mission through programs and activities that engage the music industry and cultural community as well as the general public. The foundation works in partnership year-round with its founder, the Recording Academy, to bring national attention to important issues such as the value and impact of music and arts education and the urgency of preserving our rich cultural heritage.

Donating to the Archive

The CSRC Library provides information resources, reference services, and bibliographic instruction for anyone seeking information on Chicano history and culture. It has one of the most important research collections on the Chicano experience in the United States, with over 14,000 books and monographs, 340 periodical titles, and 2,200 microfilms (including some for nineteenth-century publications), plus early dissertations and theses. In addition, the library has more than 1,000 prints and posters and 400 films in various formats. The CSRC houses over 125 archival and manuscript collections totaling more than 3,000 linear feet of historical material. Patrons can also access an increasing number of the CSRC's image and sound collections online that document the Chicano-Latino history of the twentieth century.

The CSRC Library is dedicated to preserving materials that reflect the Chicano and Latino experience in the following areas: immigration, the arts, education, history, language, gender, and sexuality. Like most repositories, the CSRC Library accepts donations as small as a single item and as large as dozens of boxes. Material need not be organized, it need not be "old," and it need not relate to a famous individual, event, or organization in order for it to be historically significant. Generally, however, the CSRC is more interested in a coherent body of material rather than individual items.

Documents that may be archived include personal records (books, diaries, e-mail, financial statements, legal documents, letters, newspaper clippings, photographs, scrapbooks) and organizational records (budgets, business reports, e-mail, legal documents, letters, memoranda, meeting minutes, member rosters, and newsletters, pamphlets, brochures, and flyers).

The CSRC Library provides storage and care for personal collections in a secure, climate-controlled offsite storage facility on the UCLA campus, lowering the risk of damage and subsequent loss of information.

The CSRC Library relies on the goodwill of donors who share the CSRC's interest in preserving Chicano and Latino history and culture through the growth and development of its collections. The archive can best use its limited resources for preserving and cataloging records and making them available to researchers by collecting only materials that will remain permanently in the archive and permanently available to the public for research. For this reason, the CSRC Library does not accept deposits of collections on loan.

The CSRC Library cannot appraise donated materials to determine their fair market value since the archive is considered an interested party in the transaction. Such evaluations do not meet the IRS definition of "qualified appraisal" and are deemed unethical according to the Society of American Archivists' Code of Ethics. To qualify as acceptable for income tax use, the appraisal must be performed by an objective, qualified appraiser who is unconnected with either the donor or the institution and is hired for this purpose by the donor. In addition, the archive cannot provide tax advice or interpretation of the tax laws to answer individual questions. Donors should consult an expert tax advisor for information on the use of gifts or property for charitable contribution deductions.

For more information about donating to the CSRC Library or conducting archival research, contact the CSRC archivist at (310) 825-0648 or, via email, at archivist@chicano.ucla.edu.

Contributors

Agustín Gurza is an award-winning journalist with more than forty years of experience as a writer, reporter, and editor, whose assignments have taken him to major music capitals throughout Latin America and Spain. He started his writing career in the early 1970s as a student journalist at the University of California, Berkeley, where he attended the Graduate School of Journalism. As editor of an independent campus newspaper, *La Voz del Pueblo,* he interviewed major Mexican literary figures, including Octavio Paz and Carlos Fuentes, at their homes in Mexico City. In 1974 the paper won a citation at the national Robert F. Kennedy Journalism Awards, which recognizes outstanding coverage of the disadvantaged. After moving to Los Angeles Gurza worked for *Billboard Magazine,* where he led the launch of the music trade journal's first foreign-language edition, *Billboard En Español.* In 1976, he also started freelancing for the *Los Angeles Times,* pioneering the paper's Latino music coverage.

From 1985 to 1992 Gurza worked as a staff writer for the *Riverside Press-Enterprise,* where he won first place in the Best of the West competition, sponsored by the Society of Professional Journalists, for his probing 1986 series on immigration reform. He then joined the news staff of the *Orange County Register* in Santa Ana, eventually becoming a popular feature columnist. He was recruited by the *Los Angeles Times* in 1999, starting a successful ten-year stint as a full-time columnist and critic, providing an influential voice on film, music, theater, and the arts.

In another life, Gurza owned and managed his own record shops in East Los Angeles and Boyle Heights. He is an avid music collector, an amateur audiophile, and a decent salsa dancer. He is married and has two sons.

Jonathan Clark has devoted the greater part of his life to playing mariachi music and documenting its history. In 1977 he moved to Mexico City, where he began a twelve-year tenure as a guitarrón player in Plaza Garibaldi. Upon meeting mariachi icon Silvestre Vargas in 1979, he embarked on an impassioned study of the history of this music. Returning to his native California in the early 1990s, Clark began giving lectures and writing articles about mariachi music, activities he continues today. To foment the performance of this music, in 1992 he founded the San José State University Mariachi Workshop, a community-based program he directed for eight years. Until recently he directed the Stanford University Department of Music's mariachi program. Clark was one of the founders of the world's first mariachi museum, the Museo Silvestre Vargas, in Tecalitlán, Jalisco, the birthplace of the legendary Mariachi Vargas. He has been collecting and researching mariachi phonograph recordings for over three decades.

Chris Strachwitz has devoted his adult life to recording and documenting the musical traditions of various regional American subcultures. In 1960 he founded Arhoolie Records and later an affiliated publishing firm, Tradition Music Co. He has been a teacher, a record distributor, and the producer of several documentary films with Les Blank, including *Chulas Fronteras, Del Mero Corazón,* and *J'ai Été au Bal.* In 1997 he received a Lifetime Achievement Award from the Folk Alliance, and in 2000 he received a

National Heritage Fellowship from the National Endowment for the Arts. In 2005 he received a second Lifetime Achievement Award, this time from the Association for Recorded Sound Collections.

In 1995 Strachwitz established the Arhoolie Foundation to document, preserve, present, and disseminate authentic traditional and regional vernacular music. The foundation owns the recordings and documents that constitute the Frontera Collection. The Arhoolie Foundation also assists in producing film documentaries, exhibitions, live presentations, and academic research. Strachwitz is the proprietor of the Down Home Music Store in El Cerrito, California. He is always happy to hear from artists, artists' relatives, and collectors who might have records, photographs, posters, or articles to exchange for some of Mr. Strachwitz's large personal cache of duplicate recordings.

Index of Names and Titles